Coproducing Water, Energy and Waste Services

Conventional services, such as water, energy and waste services, have been for a long time physically networked and centrally managed. Today, this delivery model appears increasingly inefficient in two respects. It often fails in guaranteeing its financial viability and equitable service access, and it generally draws heavily on the natural resources conveyed by these services. This book aims thus at exploring how service coproduction, based on public-community collaborations, can represent a valuable alternative to the conventional service provision model. Contributions in this book look into service coproduction and its relationship with the conventional service model both in the Global North (Germany) and Global South (Bolivia, Brazil, Colombia, India, Tanzania). They also address a variety of different perspectives in coproducing conventional services such as the role of service modernisation, the variety of non-networked solutions, and the relationship with the commons, just to cite a few. Eventually, this book provides a first comprehensive exploration of the service coproduction theory in relation to conventional services, such as water, energy and waste.

The chapters in this book were originally published as a special issue of *Urban Research & Practice*.

Luisa Moretto is Professor at the Faculty of Architecture of the Université Libre de Bruxelles (ULB), Belgium. She has a background in architecture and holds a PhD in Analysis and Governance of Sustainable Development from the University of Venice. She is former coordinator of N-AERUS (Network-Association of European Researchers on Urbanization in the South).

Marco Ranzato (PhD) is Researcher at the Faculty of Architecture La Cambre Horta of the Université libre de Bruxelles (ULB), Belgium, coordinator of the LoUiSE research group for the laboratory of territorial engineering Metrolab, and co-director of Latitude Platform for Urban Research and Design.

Coproducing Water, Energy and Waste Services

Edited by
Luisa Moretto and Marco Ranzato

Routledge
Taylor & Francis Group
LONDON AND NEW YORK

First published 2018
by Routledge
2 Park Square, Milton Park, Abingdon, Oxon, OX14 4RN, UK

and by Routledge
711 Third Avenue, New York, NY 10017, USA

Routledge is an imprint of the Taylor & Francis Group, an informa business

British Library Cataloguing in Publication Data
A catalogue record for this book is available from the British Library

ISBN 13: 978-0-8153-7610-1

Typeset in Times New Roman
by RefineCatch Limited, Bungay, Suffolk

Publisher's Note
The publisher accepts responsibility for any inconsistencies that may have arisen during the conversion of this book from journal articles to book chapters, namely the possible inclusion of journal terminology.

Disclaimer
Every effort has been made to contact copyright holders for their permission to reprint material in this book. The publishers would be grateful to hear from any copyright holder who is not here acknowledged and will undertake to rectify any errors or omissions in future editions of this book.

Contents

Citation Information

The chapters in this book were originally published in *Urban Research & Practice*, volume 10, issue 1 (March 2017). When citing this material, please use the original page numbering for each article, as follows:

Chapter 1
A socio-natural standpoint to understand coproduction of water, energy and waste services
Luisa Moretto and Marco Ranzato
Urban Research & Practice, volume 10, issue 1 (March 2017), pp. 1–21

Chapter 2
Water trajectories through non-networked infrastructure: insights from peri-urban Dar es Salaam, Cochabamba and Kolkata
Adriana Allen, Pascale Hofmann, Jenia Mukherjee and Anna Walnycki
Urban Research & Practice, volume 10, issue 1 (March 2017), pp. 22–42

Chapter 3
When urban modernisation entails service delivery co-production: a glance from Medellin
Catalina Duque Gómez and Sylvy Jaglin
Urban Research & Practice, volume 10, issue 1 (March 2017), pp. 43–62

Chapter 4
Between coproduction and commons: understanding initiatives to reclaim urban energy provision in Berlin and Hamburg
S. Becker, M. Naumann and T. Moss
Urban Research & Practice, volume 10, issue 1 (March 2017), pp. 63–85

Chapter 5
'Co-producing affordability' to the electricity service: a market-oriented response to addressing inequality of access in Rio de Janeiro's favelas
Francesca Pilo'
Urban Research & Practice, volume 10, issue 1 (March 2017), pp. 86–101

Chapter 6

The co-production of a constant water supply in Mumbai's middle-class apartments
Cat Button
Urban Research & Practice, volume 10, issue 1 (March 2017), pp. 102–119

Notes on Contributors

Adriana Allen is Professor of Development Planning and Urban Sustainability at the Bartlett Development Planning Unit, UCL,UK. Her work focuses on investigating and promoting transformative links between socio-environmental change and justice and sustainability in urban and peri-urban contexts.

Sören Becker is Researcher at the Department of Geography at Bonn University and at IRI THESys, Humboldt University, Germany. His work relates to bottom-up initiatives and urban development strategies in energy transitions and digital 'smart city' approaches.

Cat Button is Lecturer and Degree Programme Director at the School of Architecture, Planning and Landscape, Newcastle University, UK. Her research focuses on how people and communities cope with having too little (or too much) water, and the domestication of urban responses to climate change.

Catalina Duque Gómez is Secretary General at CITEGO, France.

Pascale Hofmann is Lecturer at the Bartlett Development Planning Unit, UCL, UK. She co-directs the MSc in Environment and Sustainable Development. Her current research focuses on trajectories of water proverty in urban and peri-urban areas of the Global South.

Sylvy Jaglin is Professor at the École d'Urbanisme de Paris (Université Paris-Est) and Researcher at LATTS, France. Her research focuses on basic services in cities of the South, particularly in sub-Saharan Africa, and combines analysis of socio-technical changes and territorial public action in a comparative perspective of urban change.

Luisa Moretto is Professor at the Faculty of Architecture of the Université Libre de Bruxelles (ULB), Belgium. She has a background in architecture and holds a PhD in Analysis and Governance of Sustainable Development from the University of Venice. She is former coordinator of N-AERUS (Network-Association of European Researchers on Urbanization in the South).

Timothy Moss is Senior Researcher at IRI THESys, Humboldt University, Germany. His research revolves around processes of institutional change relating to public goods and their spatiality in general, and urban infrastructure systems in particular.

Jenia Mukherjee is Assistant Professor at the Department of Humanities and Social Sciences, Indian Institute of Technology Kharagpur. Her areas of interest include environmental history, urban water political ecology and development studies.

Matthias Naumann is Interim Professor of Geographical Education at Technical University Dresden, Germany. His research looks at urban and regional development, infrastructure and critical geography.

Francesca Pilo' is Researcher at the Department of Human Geography, Planning and International Development at the University of Amsterdam, The Netherlands. She holds a PhD in Urban Planning (2015) from the University of Paris-Est, France, and the Fluminense Federal University, Brazil (joint-supervision). Her research interests include urban infrastructure, socio-technical urban change and spatial inequalities.

Marco Ranzato (PhD) is Researcher at the Faculty of Architecture La Cambre Horta of the Université libre de Bruxelles (ULB), Belgium, coordinator of the LoUiSE research group for the laboratory of territorial engineering Metrolab, and co-director of Latitude Platform for Urban Research and Design.

Anna Walnycki is Researcher at the International Institute for Environment and Development, UK. Her current work involves research on the role of partnerships in urban poverty reduction, particularly for the delivery of water and sanitation services.

A socio-natural standpoint to understand coproduction of water, energy and waste services

Luisa Moretto and Marco Ranzato

This introductory article of the special issue on 'Geographies of water, energy and waste service coproduction' explores the implications of coproducing these services in terms of both accessibility and environmental sustainability. According to a socio-natural standpoint, provision extent and resources metabolized by the services are equally regarded employing a threefold conceptual framework integrating actor/flow and area fields. A rich variety of service coproduction geographies in terms of actors involved, resources mobilized and urban spaces covered emerges. More importantly, coproduction of water, energy and waste services proves to leverage on both service accessibility and environmental sustainability of the related resources.

1. Introduction

This special issue of *Urban Research and Practice* aims at contributing to the debate on service coproduction by focusing on urban water, energy and waste services. These services belong to the socio-technical '"traditional" variety like water and electricity' (Swyngedouw 2003, 130), as distinguished from those 'of "cybertechnological" kinds like information and communication networks' (Swyngedouw 2003).[1] Urban water, energy and waste services are still mainly conceived and produced through a conventional model, based on a network: 'a set of interconnected structures, centrally planned and managed by a single monopoly-based public utility offering a uniform service in a given area according to an egalitarian access standard' (Jaglin 2014, 434). Nevertheless, networks are no longer the only form for service provision. As pointed out by Coutard et al. (2014, 92), 'the development of "localized", "decentralized", "distributed" or "alternative" technologies' produces a hybrid infrastructure landscape – including connected, disconnected, pre-connected and re-connected configurations – of the so-called post-networked city (Coutard and Rutherford 2012, 2015; Coutard, Ruthgerford, and Florentin 2014).[2] In this article, we refer to *conventional services* to indicate the 'traditional variety' of services historically organized and regulated through this conventional model.

We use the word *coproduction* to refer to 'one way that synergy between what a government does and what citizens do can occur' (Ostrom 1996, 1079). Research on coproduction in this sense has rarely focused on urban services conceived and organized through conventional networks, whether they be water and energy supplies, sanitation and wastewater discharge or solid waste collection, for example. It has, instead, concentrated on social, not networked, services such as education, health facilities and policing (see, for example, Pestoff, Brandsen, and Verschuere 2012; Bovaird et al. 2016; Sicilia et al. 2016). As a consequence, both socio-spatial and environmental implications of public-community synergies in urban services – whether networked and non-networked, bundled and unbundled, and their often complex articulation – remain almost unexplored. The objective of this special issue is to provide a deeper understanding of coproduction in urban water, energy and waste services by empirically exploring accessibility and environmental sustainability in service coproduction. This reveals a rich variety of service coproduction geographies in terms of actors involved, resources mobilized and urban spaces covered.

2. Accessibility and environmental constraints for conventional services

Research on conventional services, which are generally networked (Tarr and Dupuy 1988; Dupuy 1991) is needed since the advent of the 'modernist model of infrastructure provision' (Graham and Marvin 2001), repeatedly showed the limits of conventional approaches. First of all, from a stakeholders' perspective, public utilities have often showed their inability to maintain the infrastructural network and to manage it efficiently, thus generating shortages in services' production and provision. Furthermore, especially in the South, public network programmes developed in the name of the urban poor produced benefits that were captured mainly by middle-income dwellers. In the meantime, land-use planning – including service infrastructure – was barely provided in areas potentially interested by slum formations (McGranahan, Mitlin, and Satterthwaite 2008). Both large private operators' participation in, and market management of, conventional services, on their side, have often produced limited results and drawbacks. These include partial improvements in the quality and efficiency of services, market failures, increased costs and thus tariffs and socio-spatial fragmentation phenomena (Budds and McGranahan 2003; Batley and Larbi 2004; McGranahan, Mitlin, and Satterthwaite 2008).

Second, the networked infrastructure, mediating resource flows for urban water, energy and waste services of the industrialized city, uses ecosystems far beyond the urban bioregion as suppliers of natural resources and sinks for emissions (Monstadt 2009). Through regulation of inputs and outputs characteristic of a 'linear metabolism' model (Girardet 1992), conventional services draw heavily on resources much alike that they are 'key catalysts of environmental problems like air, water, and soil pollution' (Monstadt 2009, 1926). Moreover, these services are based on standardized engineered infrastructure, while making the city dependent from a wider hinterland for resources extraction or waste disposal (Baccini 1997; Brunner 2007; Niza, Rosado and Ferrão 2009), often disregard the local landscape potentials, therefore failing to adjust the city to the carrying capacity of its bioregion. In addition, especially in the Global North, these networks – out of sight and invisible (Kaika and Swyngedouw 2000) – make the service taken for granted (Hommels 2005) or an apparent triviality (Kaika and Swyngedouw 2000), hence fostering shortened care for the resources mobilized and Nimby behaviours with respect to the structures necessary for their delivery.

Finally, the conventional formal model of centralized networked infrastructure has to cope today with 'rapid urbanization or de-urbanization and shrinkage, urban conditions of informality, spatial fragmentation, and low investment in decay infrastructures' (Monstadt and Schramm 2013, 93). Consequently, these systems often fail to deliver and sustain universal, affordable, adapted services.

Thus, general agreement exists on the necessity to overcome the failures of conventional urban water, energy and waste services, both in terms of accessibility and environmental sustainability. This implies moving forward from approaches based either on full public or private sector solutions, and public-private partnerships (Budds and McGranaham 2003; McGranahan, Mitlin, and Satterthwaite 2008; Bakker 2010; McDonald and Ruiters 2012; Becker, Naumann, and Moss 2016), conceived exclusively around centralized large technical infrastructure (e.g. Nelson 2008; Younos 2011; Goldthau 2014), or engineered on the *unlimited* use of resources (e.g. Ludwig, Hilborn, and Walters 1993; Van Bueren 2012). Now, scholars are turning their attention to decentralized (Niemczynowicz 1999; Nelson 2008; Ranzato 2011, 2016; Goldthau 2014), post-networked (Jaglin 2012; Monstadt and Schramm 2013; Coutard and Ruthgerford 2015), or polycentric (Ostrom 1996, 2010) infrastructural systems as alternatives or complements to the traditional centralized ones.

3. Moving towards coproduction of water, energy and waste services

Looking to alternatives to orthodox models in urban service delivery, the option of service coproduction is gaining interest among researchers. According to Ostrom (1996), the concept of coproduction was initially developed in the late 1970s as an alternative response to policy recommendations promoting strong centralization of public service delivery and escalating state expenditures. By coproduction, Ostrom (1996, 1073) means 'the process through which inputs used to produce a good or service are contributed by individuals who are not "in" the same organizations … Coproduction implies that citizens can play an active role in producing public goods and services of consequence to them'.

The roles different stakeholders can play in contributing to service delivery are clarified by Parks et al. (1981), cited in Verschuere, Brandsen and Petsoff (2012, 1085): coproduction is 'the mix of activities that both public service agents and citizens contribute to the provision of public services. The former are involved as professionals, or "regular producers", while "citizen production" is based on voluntary efforts by individuals and groups to enhance the quality and/or the quantity of the services they use'.

Scholars are increasingly investigating the many forms coproduction can assume and the numerous facets it can display. Part of current research on service coproduction concentrates on social, not traditionally networked, services such as education, health facilities and policing. These researchers analyse these services under a variety of service management and public administration perspectives of coproduction (Osborne and Strokosh 2013; Pestoff, Brandsen, and Verschuere 2012) and on the public governance systems favouring this service model (see for example Bovaird 2007; Pestoff 2012; Bovaird and Leoffler 2012; Jakobsen 2013; Pestoff, Brandsen, and Verschuere 2012; Verschuere, Brandsen and Petsoff 2012). According to the literature, coproduction can be the initiative of citizens or governments (Jakobsen 2013); it may include third sector, public organizations, and for-profit organizations (Brandsen, Verchuere, and Pestoff 2012; Verschuere, Brandsen and Petsoff 2012). Coproducers can be qualified as consumers, suppliers, and partners (Alford 2014). Coproduction can be disaggregated into many different service activities such as co-planning, co-design, co-managing, co-delivery, and so on (Bovaird and Loeffler 2012). It can be implemented in multi-level governance settings (Bovaird et al. 2016) and can focus on the operational level – *consumer coproduction* – on the strategic level – *participative coproduction* – or an integration of both of these levels in the form of *enhanced coproduction* (Osborne and Strokosh 2013).

Research has also focused on the ways in which service coproduction often includes inhabitants through their participation in associations, groups and grassroots or community-based organizations. Brudney and England (1983, 63), for example, pointed out that 'both groups and individuals may engage in coproduction, but the more important participants from both practical and equity standpoints are collectivities'. 'Collective coproduction' is defined as 'the *joint* action of citizens to support public services and achieve outcomes' (Bovaird et al. 2016, 51), where either outputs are collectively enjoyed, or inputs collectively supplied or both.

Especially in development studies,[3] the option given by collective coproduction is simply one of the many kinds of service provision alternatives in which citizens play a role. The few existing pieces of research on service coproduction mainly focus on individual cases and present a much narrower and selective approach. They generally emphasize the practices and arrangements that include, for example, a wide range of local actors to universalize service access, make the service affordable, secure political influence for citizens, and create social capital (see, for example, Joshi and Moore 2004; Mitlin 2008; Peters and Muraleedharan 2008; Allen 2012; McGranahan 2013; McMillan, Spronk, and Caswell 2014).

All these researches reveal, on one side, the multiple forms in which service coproduction can take place and, on the other hand, the many approaches and entry points proposed by scholars to understand them. All this is to say coproduction is still an ambiguous term, open to various theoretical interpretations and practised in diverse ways (Jaglin 2005; Pestoff, Brandsen, and Verschuere 2012; McMillan, Spronk, and Caswell 2014; Becker, Naumann, and Moss 2016; Duque Gómez and Jaglin 2016). In spite of recent efforts to understand better the various aspects of service coproduction, it seems that 'conceptual confusion remains a problem' (Brandsen, Verchuere, and Pestoff 2012, 388). In the context of this introductory article, we employ a definition of coproduction that primarily considers the synergies and relationships between professionalized public service providers and users (in line with Ostrom 1996). We also include in our understanding of these relationships both 'collective coproduction' (see also Brudney and England 1983; Ostrom 1996; Joshi and Moore 2004; Bovaird 2007) and 'individual coproduction' (Bovaird et al. 2016). We do not distinguish coproduction from co-management and co-governance (as per Brandsen and Pestoff 2006), but include in the term a wide range of service activities (from co-planning to co-assessment, as presented by Bovaird and Löffler 2012). Unpacking the notion of coproduction helps identify potential coproduction activities in unbundled services. Analysing coproduction in its different phases particularly fits conventional services that experienced heavy unbundling processes in the 1980s.

Despite its conceptual fuzziness, the literature has also shown that collaborations between public actors and citizens, either individually or collectively, may be an alternative form of service provision (Ostrom 1996; Joshi and Moore 2004; McGranahan 2013; Moretto and Allen 2015), not only in terms of increased service quality or quantity (as suggested by Parks et al. 1981), but also of enhanced inclusiveness, empowerment, and citizenship (Batley 2006; Mitlin 2008; Osborne and Strokosch 2013; Moretto 2014; Sicilia et al. 2016).

In this special issue, we discuss the potential contribution of coproduction by examining two sets of case studies with respect to the actors involved. First, we consider explicit cases of collaborations including both individuals and organized communities or groups of citizens, and public service agents, at the municipal, regional and national level. In this category, we encounter the case of water services in Kolkata, Cochabamba and Dar es Salaam (Allen et al. 2016), and that of residential services in Medellin (Duque Gómez and Jaglin 2016).

The second set of case studies reflects service provision experiences that involve other actors (such as private providers), and limited public participation. We question the roles of and contributions by public powers and collectives in service supply, while explaining the reasons for their exclusion. Cases belonging to this category include electricity service delivery in Rio de Janeiro (Pilo' 2016) and water supply for middle-income residents in Mumbai (Button 2016). Energy provision in Germany lies somewhere between these two poles as per the diversity of experiences and practices presented (Becker, Naumann, and Moss 2016).

4. An actor, flow, area approach

The proposed conceptual framework to read these cases rests on the hypothesis that a twofold perspective is necessary to understand whether and how this provision model increases services quality and quantity. Urban conventional services need to be closely examined with respect to the objective of guaranteeing and enhancing their accessibility, based on given social, political, economic and governance structures (e.g. Coutard 2008; Jaglin 2012; Monstadt and Schramm 2013). We must also evaluate them in the light of their aim to improve the use of the environmental resources they convey (e.g. Butler and Maksimovic 1999; Newman 2001; Farrelly and Brown 2011; Robertson 2012; Van Bohemen 2012). Informality, urban fragmentation, rapid urbanization, and de-urbanization, on the one side, and overexploitation of resources on the other, are all urgent issues putting networked services into question. These factors require service provision forms more concerned with the specific resources and spatial conditions of today's city.

The two standpoints here considered draw on Robertson's (2012, 3) search for a comprehensive understanding of urban sustainability, and the mutual influence between the 'access to resources or services' and 'environmental and habitat-related problems'. Robertson (2012) insists on the need for a more encompassing approach in urban sustainable development as alternative to the diverging focus of social sciences (paying attention to social equity and justice) and natural sciences (concentrating on quantifying and mapping resources).

The proposed liaison between accessibility and environmental sustainability in coproduction of conventional services is also inspired by the work of Elionor Ostrom. In the 1990s, she argued that, when considering sustainable management of resource systems 'institutional diversity may be as important as biological diversity for our long-term survival' (Ostrom et al. 1999, 278). Said differently, the involvement and empowerment of end-users are key factors for the long-term, sustainable management of resources (Ostrom et al. 1999), and for increased accessibility, though coproduction options (Ostrom 1996). These outputs can be reached if service provision and the resources they deliver are simultaneously regarded.

To a certain extent, considering both accessibility to and environmental impact on resources management of conventional services is an attempt to bind concerns that fall respectively into the North and the South. As Robertson highlights (2012), the Global North, due to the overconsumption of resources, is especially concerned with the environmental problems whereas, in the Global South, the main concern is inadequate access to resources and services. These are two different but interlinked sustainability challenges that should inform each other. Translated to urban conventional services, if, in industrialized countries, centralized network systems are largely accessible, it is still difficult to meet the environmental standards. By contrast, in the South, the conventional model hinders accessibility for a significant part of the urban population (Coutard, Ruthgerford, and Florentin 2014).

The integration of dwellers' accessibility to services and resources, and resource management related to urban services reminds us of the fundamentals of political ecology emphasizing the oneness of 'man and nature' (Heynen, Kaika, and Swyngedouw 2006; Smith 2006). Accordingly, political and social perspectives grounded in ecology are essential to healing the disjuncture between nature and society that capitalism caused 'in ways more aggressive and complete than any previous social formation' (Smith 2006, XII).

The proposed threefold conceptual framework actor/flow/area owes much to those studies in ecology that assume anthropic and environmental dimensions. In particular, Tjallingii (1996), a Dutch ecologist, has proposed this threefold framework in his ecological conditions strategy to support the planning process. The ecological conditions strategy is not universally known, but is a specific theoretical strategy. Tjallingii considers physical and social conditions of the context as stimulating factors for the planning process. The ecological conditions strategy – a theoretical framework that reaffirms the Spinozian substance monism man–nature – incorporates three strategic aims: 'living areas', or areas considered and treated as living ecosystems; 'responsible flows', or flows regarded as a chain of links; and 'participating actors', or involvement of actors in ecological processes (Tjallingii 1996).

We, therefore, propose this threefold conceptual framework not only as a way of organizing viewpoints to integrated processes in an action–research perspective as is the case of Tjallingii, but also further to understand the impact of coproduction on service accessibility and environmental sustainability of resources.

The actor field is an essential part of the concept of coproduction. Paraphrasing Ostrom (1996), service coproduction implies the contribution of individuals from diverse organizations in producing a service. Stakeholders involved into coproduction vary extremely according to the different service practices analysed. In addition, the relationships between all these agents assume diverse configurations and characteristics. We focus our attention on the diversity of actors involved, the extent of institutionalization of coproduced services, and the diverse phases at which coproduction can take place. With respect to the actors, we pay particular attention to public and citizen coproducers. The institutionalization of coproduced services is reflected in formal/informal, collective/individual, and short/long-term relationships. Co-planning, co-design, co-managing and co-delivery are all aspects of the diverse phases of coproduction systematically analysed.

With respect to the flow field, the coproduction of water, energy and waste services deals with flows of metabolized materials.[4] To produce services, environmental resources, such as water or energy are processed and delivered to the user. Waste products are collected from the user and, if possible, recycled at a later stage. In metabolic terms, distribution and collection are just two of the phases of the overall circulatory processes for the materials involved in service provision. Although coproduction cases of water, energy and waste services often mention the kind of flow that coproduction involves, its metabolic dimension tends to be disregarded. Consequently, coproduction of these services is often 'reduced' to a matter of governance. Ostrom (1996, 1082) states that 'several conditions heighten the probability that coproduction is an improvement over regular government production or citizen production alone' and that '[they] are more likely to be met in a polycentric political system than in a monocentric (or, highly centralized) political system'. The coproduction cases for wastewater services that she proposes describe also more polycentric circulatory processes and infrastructure (e.g. the feeder line of the condominium and the trunk line of the urban street). We want to observe, as far as possible, these complex circulatory processes by first focusing on the variety of environmental resources mobilized by service delivery[5] and then examining the specific relation between coproduction and the processing of both resources and waste products, if any.

The field area concerns the relation between the coproduced service and the space. Water, energy and waste services have a crucial spatial connotation, both in terms of 'spatialization' and 'territorialization' (Dubresson and Jaglin 2005), because of the link with flows of resources, the presence of specific actors and their interactions. The spatial dimension can be more or less complex depending on whether we regard all the circulatory processes concerning the materials delivered and collected by the service. In addition, service coproduction can take place at different spatial scales with consequences for service technical options, the physical characteristics of the territory and the related social forms of organization. From the elementary level (like the household) up to more collective levels (like the block, the district, or the settlement), service coproduction and spatial scales influence each other in a variety of ways. Research on service coproduction, both in industrialized and developing countries, tends to overlook the spatial dimension apart from some isolated and partial exceptions, such as Jaglin (2005), Mitlin (2008) or Albrechts (2013).[6] In our reading of this special issue of coproduction cases, the field area concerns the spatial forms and scales of the service, distinguishing the levels related to the entire circulatory process from the levels of coproduction phases, the form of land occupation by the service recipients, and the spatial integration of its infrastructure.

To understand better the impact of coproduction on service accessibility and environmental sustainability of resources, we draw on the idea of the 'post-networked city'. Coutard, Ruthgerford, and Florentin (2014, 92) used this term 'to describe the forms of organization of urban spaces associated with the hybrid assemblage of a myriad of emerging urban infrastructure configurations' belonging to both conventional and alternative service systems. As previously introduced, *conventional services* here signify a large urban infrastructure that is networked, centralized either through public or private agents and organized through an integrated and uniform service delivery system. *Alternative services* encompass service delivery strategies clearly separated from the conventional formal service. They are mainly decentralized and essentially citizen-driven. We examine the hybrid coproduction space between conventional and alternative solutions through an actor/flow/area approach with the hope of providing a deeper understanding of the 'potential relationship that could exist between "regular" producers … and "clients"' (Ostrom 1996, 1079), and we hope to highlight how citizens may contribute to service universalization and sustainable resources' management.

5. Varied actors and relationships

Coproduction has brought new approaches to the management and organization of services as it shifts the responsibility from a single agent, accountable for a conventional model, to more producers who are not part of the same 'organization' (Ostrom 1996). Papers in this special issue confirm that present models of service delivery include a high diversity of producers, or at least stakeholders, involved in the process. All the following actors are mentioned in this issue's papers: citizens presented as individuals, private providers, households and groups ranging from condominium associations, water committees, user associations, grassroots coalitions, advisory boards and social movements. Public actors at the municipal, regional and national level represent both the general public administration and the public-owned utilities. Finally, there are other non-public and non-community-based actors, often belonging to the private sector, such as big private service providers, small to medium waste collection enterprises, energy cooperatives, non-governmental organizations, etc. Ostrom (1996) suggests that coproduction is the relation and the synergy between government agents, intended as not only regular producers, and citizens, intended as clients but also, in our perspective, as beneficiaries. We thus focus our analysis on these two stakeholder categories, conscious nevertheless that all the previously mentioned actors contribute to different extents to service coproduction.

5.1 Individual or collective participation

Although citizens already contribute to *alternative* service production, management and organizations through, for example, rainwater harvesting, selective waste collection and service bill payments, their collective involvement undoubtedly carries a greater potential to improve access and sustainability in coproduced services. Extended water supply in Dar es Salaam and Cochabamba, for example, benefits from community-managed water supply schemes and community water systems, respectively (Allen et al. 2016). In Medellin, responsibilities for paying bills for water, sewage and electricity for communal areas, together with building maintenance costs, are (temporarily) organized at the condominium level between the public utility and the building leaders or condominium associations (Duque Gómez and Jaglin 2016). Successful referendum for the remunicipalization of energy in Hamburg benefited from the collective mobilization of citizens, through cooperatives and social movement coalitions, which also resulted in 'participatory discussion fora' (Becker, Naumann, and Moss 2016).

Efficient eco-environmental practices in Kolkata in the form of wastewater fisheries, effluence-irrigated paddy cultivation and vegetable farming on garbage substrates are based on regional collaborations with, among others, local cooperatives (Allen et al. 2016). Cooperative society members in Mumbai decide water storage through roof top tanks (Button 2016). In Rio de Janeiro, local associations contend that part of the limitations of the *Light Recicla* programme to make energy more affordable depends on whether 'this type of project prioritizes the idea of individual responsibility' (Pilo' 2016). This confirms that 'collective coproduction' is highly embraced in water, energy and waste services, and that it has the potential to contribute to better practical, financial, environmental, and social outcomes (see Joshi and Moore 2004; Pestoff 2012).

5.2 Re- and de-politicizing public involvement

Let us now move to the other side of service government–citizens service coproduction. Coproduction cases show that generally, when city-dwellers can benefit from collaboration with public agencies in the delivery of a service, quality of and access to services improve and citizens may become further empowered. In the case of water supply schemes in Dar es Salaam, for example, 'examples where there is significant collaboration between poor communities and the authorities have led to the inclusion and representation of low-income dwellers in political processes and decision making' (Allen et al. 2016). In the same time, access to the service is improved, although supply is sometimes uneven in beneficiary settlements. Becker, Naumann, and Moss (2016) conclude that remunicipalization in Hamburg, highly supported by a referendum campaign, 'has paved the way for more stakeholder participation in the governance of the city's energy system and beyond'. The nature of relationships in these cases is predominantly cooperative and collaborative, and both institutions and citizens actively participate in both practical improvements and, to a certain extent, decision making. When synergies occur, coproduction becomes an opportunity to democratize and re-politicise the policy field of these services, previously captured by public monopolies and privatization.

In contrast, in Medellin, despite universal access to residential services in social housing districts being guaranteed by the municipal utility, researchers contend that coproduction is fundamentally a system of regulation and transition towards urban modernization, and empowerment is here downgraded to co-learning (Duque Gómez and Jaglin 2016). This ultimately consolidates the dominant forms of urban operation, living little room for political debate and needs-driven alternative solutions. By contrast again, Pilo' (2016) maintains that the electricity service in Rio de Janeiro has been de-politicized by a scheme 'based on market principles and individual responsibility', and the absence of public powers in the *Light Recicla* programme except for the 'institutional benevolence' from the municipality. Government withdrawal from alternative strategies is a major problem for replicability – and thus equity in access and decision making – of this initiative in the 700 city favelas.

5.3 *Institutionalizing government–citizens relationships*

Besides the diversity and nature of actors, coproduction is also characterized by the extent of institutionalization of service practices and the phase of the coproduction process at which these practices take place. General trends in the degrees and efforts to institutionalize service coproduction can hardly be outlined, as these cases portray a highly heterogeneous scenario in terms of formal/informal and long/short-term relationships. They range from rather latent coordination between public and local actors in wastewater treatment in Kolkata, and ad hoc pragmatic agreements between the public utility and communities to set up water facilities in Dar es Salaam (Allen et al. 2016). Then, they move to a semiformal framework of collaboration between residents, building leaders and municipal service providers in Medellin, which create a multidimensional and multilevel learning process, rather informal, undefined, and continuously negotiated (Duque Gómez and Jaglin 2016). They finally include more institutionalized relationships, as in the case of the continuous and official support from the municipality to formally and legally recognized Water Committees in Cochabamba (Allen et al. 2016), or in the case of cooperative control of the public utility in Berlin and the cooperative Energy Network Hamburg (Becker, Naumann, and Moss 2016).

5.4 *Collaborating at different levels*

This issue's cases also reveal that coproduction of water, energy and waste may happen at very different stages by including a wide range of service activities (Bovaird and Loeffler 2012). In Germany, for example, we face a sort of co-planning and co-design in energy services stemming from political campaigns and referenda on service remunicipalization and the possible resource co-ownership through the cooperative in Berlin. The 10-MW solar project is also presented as a successful case of coproduction at the project scale (Becker, Naumann, and Moss 2016). Co-funding takes place for drinking water in Cochabamba in the form of public financial support for water committees (Allen et al. 2016), for energy services in Rio de Janeiro as energy financial discounts against waste collection (Pilo' 2016), and for the Berlin's energy cooperative (Becker, Naumann, and Moss 2016). Co-management characterizes municipal services in Medellin, where Duque Gómez and Jaglin (2016) define the relationship between agents as 'an example of "consumer coproduction" (Osborne and Strokosch 2013)'. Boreholes for drinking water and simplified sewerage for sanitation are essentially co-planned and co-delivered in Dar es Salaam through an 'interdependent relationship' (Pestoff, Brandsen, and Verschuere 2012), while a larger range of different stages is witnessed in Cochabamba, where improved access to drinking water is co-planned, co-designed, co-funded, co-delivered and co-managed (Allen et al. 2016).

Most authors underline how coproduction is taking place at only some stages. We can describe this as partial coproduction, in contrast to 'full coproduction' (Bovaird and Loeffler 2012) or 'enhanced coproduction' (Osborne and Strokosch 2013). This partial form of coproduction can lead to significant weaknesses in the service delivery process. For example, Allen et al. (2016) stress that coproduction in Dar es Salaam 'is largely limited to the initial stages of setting up public facilities which are then handed over to the communities to operate. Failure to establish stronger forms of co-production partnerships affects the sustainability of many of these interventions and also limits their potential for scaling up'. In the same vein, Becker, Naumann, and Moss (2016) question how far citizen participation in political campaigns or projects can be institutionalized in other coproduction phases, through, for example, genuine involvement in managerial decision making. Coproduction in later phases, such as co-management of residential services in Medellin, or co-delivery for waste collection in Rio de Janeiro, clearly jeopardize an open participatory democracy.

6. Accessible and responsible flows

Looking at flows implies investigating the circulatory processes for the metabolized material distributed or collected by the service. We assume a biophysical emphasis here. According to the biological analogy of urban metabolism, the city cannot exist without inputs of processed materials that, once used, become waste products (Tarr 2002; Smith 2006). Hence, services of water or energy provision and waste collection are vectors of the required inputs/outputs regulation mechanisms. When considering the environmental sustainability of coproduced services, there is a need to unfold the relationship between the consumption of those materials channelized by the service and the properties of the ecosystem where resources are withdrawn and waste discharged. Hence, the cases of conventional service coproduction presented in this special issue are observed according to a 'flow approach' (Van Bohemen 2012) regarding (1) resources and waste products carried by the service and their quality, quantity and distance moved as well as (2) the specific role played by coproduction in the metabolic processing of resources and waste products.[7]

6.1 Using local resources

Coproduced services channel a wide range of resources such as rainwater, groundwater, surface water from lakes and reservoirs, solar radiation and wind power. In most cases, the resources delivered are local: rainwater in Mumbai (Button 2016), groundwater in Cochabamba, and Dar es Salam (Allen et al. 2016), household waste in Rio de Janeiro (Pilo' 2016), waste water of local communities in Kolkata (Allen et al. 2016). The local character of the resources involved often results in short flow circuits instead of long transfers. Therefore, we see low dependence on external ecosystems. However, the cases also show that dependency on local resources can be problematic. For example, Allen et al. (2016) point out the risks related to the local uncontrolled groundwater abstraction both in terms of quality (Cochabamba and Dar es Salam) and quantity (Dar es Salam).

6.2 Regaining the process of metabolic and social transformation of nature

Coproduction of water, energy and waste services tends to expand the relation citizens have with the materials channelized by the service, beyond 'mere' use (in case of service provision) or discharge (in case of service collection and treatment). In most of the cases presented, citizens, through coproduction, directly operate in the flow's circulatory processes by collecting, separating, purifying, reusing or recycling the materials channelized by the service. The case of Kolkata is illustrative. Here, in East Kolkata Wetlands, the wastewater fisheries, the effluence-irrigated paddy cultivation, and the vegetable farming on garbage substrates recycle both wastewater and solid waste generated by the city (Allen et al. 2016). Similarly, in Mumbai, collection and retention of rainwater has potential manifold benefits on the city's metabolism. This diffuse practice reduces the risk of floods in the household basements and downstream, increases groundwater recharge, and reduces the use of drinking water for not potable uses (Button 2016).[8] In Hamburg, the coproduced 10-MW solar project enables the local collection of solar energy, a renewable resource otherwise wasted. Finally, in Rio de Janeiro, the separation of solid waste operated at the household level is key for later recycling of the waste products discharged (Pilo' 2016). On the one side, in all these cases (Kolkata, Mumbai, Hamburg, and Rio de Janeiro), the operations deployed by the citizens within the metabolic processes design more circular trajectories – oriented to recycling/up-cycling the materials delivered – than linear ones (Girardet 1992). On the other side, potentially, the direct participation of citizens in the flow management enhances their knowledge about resource conditions, external boundaries and internal microenvironments. As stressed by Ostrom et al. (1999), these circumstances can increase the benefits users perceive. Citizens can have greater awareness about 'how the resource systems operate and how their actions affect each other and the resource' (Ostrom et al. 1999, 281).

6.3 Implementing environmental programmes and policies

Third, in several of these cases, coproduction explicitly aims at contributing to official environmental programmes for preserving and regulating natural resources. In Mumbai, for example, collection and retention of rainwater is the result of the targets imposed by the municipality to new built projects to decrease storm water discharge and increase groundwater recharge (Button 2016). 'Preserving natural resources and saving energy' (Pilo' 2016) is among the programmatic aims of the *Light Recicla* project promoting discounts on energy bills in exchange for solid waste collection and separation. In Berlin, the cooperatives' initiatives aim to strengthen the energy transition process towards renewable resources thought reinvestments in solar and cogeneration plants (Becker, Naumann, and Moss 2016). Similarly, in Hamburg, the public energy enterprise rose from opposition to a coal-fired plant and instead aimed at promoting 'climate friendly electricity (nuclear and coal-free)' while setting up renewable energy capacities (Becker, Naumann, and Moss 2016).

7. Supportive and creative areas

Conventional services channel metabolized materials – water, energy and waste – through the space to provide services – drinking water supply, energy supply and waste collection. Mobilizing resources from the source to the user, and waste from the user to the sink point, or again to the user, the service describes trajectories on the space. These trajectories materialize in the infrastructure, conveying the materials delivered and thus defining the territory.[9] Therefore, the spatial overtone of coproduced water, energy and waste services is substantial, especially when it comes to understanding the spatial accessibility of the service as well as the spatial distribution of the resources it delivers. In turn, this reveals the service user's proximity to networks, resources and sink points. As the work of geographers has shown, reading how the infrastructure for delivering water, energy and waste intertwines with the space has a double effect. First, it exposes the metabolic circulatory processes related to the service while at the same time revealing sources, trajectories, points of processing, points of use, and sink points for the material distributed or collected (Gandy 2002). Second, it allows the observer to understand how socio-technical services are spatialized and territorialized (Dubresson and Jaglin 2005).

7.1 Expanding the infrastructure portfolio

First, service coproduction seems to make more complex and various the infrastructural portfolio to access the service. Coproduced technical options hybridize the conventional piped networks for distribution and collection in various ways, producing diverse service constellations (see Monstadt and Schramm 2013; Coutard, Ruthgerford, and Florentin 2014) acting in a polycentric physical system. For example, local devices can act as an upgrading of the existing conventional system, either by expanding the same service or by introducing another one. In the first case, community networks interconnected to municipal services provide drinking water to unserved areas in Cochabamba (Allen et al. 2016), as already seen in the literature (see, for example, water supplies in Caracas [Moretto 2014; Moretto and Allen 2015], and energy services in Casablanca [Jaglin 2012]). Roof top tanks and water tankers in middle-class apartments in Mumbai are mostly filled through municipal mains to guarantee a constant supply (Button 2016). In Hamburg, the grid-tied solar panels installed on aircraft construction site, port areas, warehouses, etc., metabolize solar energy that is injected in the existing network (Becker, Naumann, and Moss 2016). In the second case, again in Kolkata (Allen et al. 2016), the *bheris* (aquaculture ponds and irrigated paddies) contribute to treat wastewater delivered through their end-of-line infrastructure into the main networked sewage system.

Coproduced local technical devices can be clearly disconnected from the conventional system, mainly through decentralized systems. This is the case with community-managed boreholes in Dar es Salaam (Allen et al. 2016). In some circumstances, non-networked alternatives – either coproduced or not – produce secondary micro-networks (de Bercegol and Desfeux 2011; Jaglin 2012). In Cochabamba, community-managed local networks develop from local sources like wells (Allen et al. 2016). In Rio de Janeiro (Pilo' 2016), eco-points at the favela entrances serve as solid waste collection points for an alternative private waste collection.

7.2 Appropriating the urban space and multiplying its functionality

Coproduced services highly depend on the spatial conditions of the context, not just in terms of resources such as wind, groundwater or solar radiation, but also in terms of soil conditions and availability of open space. In Rio de Janeiro (Pilo' 2016), for example, the extreme urban density of the favelas – and, therefore, the reduced availability of open space – has been a limiting condition for the location of the eco-points. In Kolkata, the wastewater treatment takes advantage of the low-level terrain conditions of the East Kolkata Wetlands to accommodate wetlands and irrigated paddies. In Hamburg (Becker, Naumann, and Moss 2016), the 10-MW solar project benefited from 'a 3D model of appropriate areas and rooftops for the installation of solar panels', and from suitable available land from local enterprises. Provision of drinking water through tankers in Mumbai has the advantage 'of being called to any area and times of shortage to substitute for another water source' (Button 2016). Adherence to local spatial conditions sometimes allows the infrastructure of service coproduction to show a remarkable multifunctional character, which is often lacking in the mainstream devices of conventional systems. In Kolkata, for example, the aquaculture ponds and irrigated paddies, besides wastewater treatment, also perform as food production and flood control sites, while the vegetable farming patches recycle solid waste and provide nourishment at the same time.

7.3 Relating cities' location to accessibility and environmental drivers

Our analysis shows that service coproduction can develop in informal, illegal and marginalized areas, as in Kolkata, Dar es Salaam and Rio de Janeiro. It can also arise in formal, official urban conditions, such as in Mumbai, Medellin and Hamburg. Furthermore, coproduction seems to be irrespective of geographical latitudes, as it takes place in both the Global South and Global North. However, not surprisingly, the balance between accessibility and environmental sustainability concerns related to service provisions varies according to the specific territory in which the coproduction happens.

The universalization of service access in terms of existence and affordability of the service is clearly a driver to work out alternative coproduced approaches in informal, marginalized areas in the Global South, such as Kolkata, Dar es Salaam, Cochabamba and Rio de Janeiro, and in social housing in Medellin. In contrast, sustainability preoccupations are paramount in official and wealthier urban conditions, where access to the service no longer represents a challenge. This is the case of Hamburg and Berlin, where environmental protection mobilizes citizens in, for example, anti-nuclear protests and renewable energy campaigns. These concerns, in turn, motivate citizens to engage into new coproduction strategies. It is nevertheless particularly interesting to see how, in Berlin, the cooperative 'Citizens Energy Berlin', established to purchase a share of the operating utility, and the social movement coalition 'Berlin Energy Roundtable' promote a broad understanding of sustainability. These organizations promote an ecological objective (based on solar and cogeneration plants), a democratic objective ('in the general design of the cooperative') and a social objective ('cost reduction through energy-saving and efficiency measures') (Becker, Naumann, and Moss 2016).

The Mumbai case represents an exception to this explanation as it describes formal and official ways of dwelling by middle-income groups who, nevertheless, still struggle to obtain a constant and affordable access to the service. The middle-class in Mumbai disregards sustainability preoccupations as its wealth increases, as evidenced by increased water consumption (Button 2016).

7.4 Multiplying the scales of service delivery

Alternative service options presented in this special issue often comprise infrastructural systems of different scales. They range from the household level (with rainwater harvesting, water private vendors, selective waste collection, selective residential services' disconnection), to the condominium level (involving water roof top tankers, building cleaning, and condominium service billing), to the community/settlement level (in the case of boreholes, wells, water interlinked networks, sanitation simplified schemes, and waste collection eco-points), to finally the city or the regional level (in the case of waste water treatment and food production in Kolkata or solar energy installations in Germany).

The household, condominium and community/settlement scales prevail in a decentralized infrastructure, while the city, regional and higher scales often accommodate alternative solutions that include a more centralized infrastructure. The condominium and community/settlement scale are the spaces where most coproduction strategies develop. We would conclude saying that, also for water, energy and waste services, the local level is actually more suitable for exploiting coproduction (as suggested by Bovaird 2007; Verschuere, Brandsen and Petsoff 2012), and that this 'local' is situated at an intermediary scale: that of the condominium, community, settlement levels, rather than the household. According to the articles in this special issue, it is at this scale that citizens more easily gather collectively, in practical and political terms, to secure themselves access to quality services.

8. Understanding service accessibility and environmental sustainability in coproduction

This article – and those included in this special issue – contribute to a better understanding of the ways coproduction of water, energy and waste services generate positive outcomes on service accessibility and environmental sustainability of related resources. Presenting accessibility and environmental drivers for, and effects of, coproduced services separately, in this final concluding section, is hardly feasible. These two aspects are in reality closely interlinked in service coproduction options, as they both aim at contributing to an increased urban sustainability. As a result, besides the research findings previously presented, some additional crosscutting considerations can be drawn by taking into account the actor, flow and area dimensions together. They contribute to further understanding the accessibility and environmental sustainability of coproduction practices, and their relationship.

First, coproduction cases presented in this themed issue show how these approaches hold promise to increase service offer options, while balancing accessibility (affordability, increased service quality, shared service management, constant supply, etc.), and environmental sustainability (environmentally friendly energy resources, the use of more local resources, etc.). This is achieved by expanding conventional service networks, introducing new ones or developing decentralized and disconnected new service systems. Network upgrading, and even more new service systems, were developed through a variety of technical devices using local resources such as rainwater, wastewater, solid waste, solar radiation, and processing these resources at the local level. This aligns with the wide range of environmental studies realized in the past decades extolling self-sufficiency and 'minimizing impact on near and distant hinterlands' (Van Bohemen 2012, 46). Using local resources allows for the implementation of environmentally sustainable short circulatory processes for the materials delivered, often resulting in greater visibility of these processes. The local approach benefits from the integration of less space travelled in the process of collecting, detaining, processing or conveying resources.

Second, another essential aspect emerging in this special issue is the idea of 'collective responsibility'. This notion arises in different ways. In Kolkata, Dar es Salaam and Cochabamba, people are not only forced to rely on multiple strategies, but also to approach access water and sanitation services as a 'collective affair' (Allen et al. 2016). In Medellin, although in the consolidated and formal city individual responsibilities characterize the access to and consumption of residential services, condominium management has requested, and thus entailed, 'forms of collective actions' between residents and the service operator (Duque Gómez and Jaglin 2016). Becker, Naumann, and Moss (2016) underline how the arrival of new actors in energy service in Germany is closely linked to a 'more far-reaching perspective of commoning, embracing alternative visions and contested futures of collective governance'. Again, in Rio de Janeiro, service 'collective responsibility' is defended as a priority by local NGOs (Pilo' 2016). These examples show that both inputs supplied and outputs enjoyed in a collective way are drivers to implementing 'collective coproduction' (Bovaird et al. 2016). Practical positive outputs of coproduced services (either in term of better accessibility or improved environmental sustainability) suggest that, also in these cases, 'political self-efficiency' (i.e. 'people can make a difference') (Bovaird et al. 2016) could be a driver for collective coproduction.

Third, the cases in this special issue confirm that, in service coproduction, the close relation of the citizens/users with the service brings them closer to the resources associated with the service, which is the environmental side of service delivery. They become acquainted with what we can define *Common Pool Resources*. This generates concrete possibilities for them to understand how the resource systems operate and the effects their actions have on the systems (Ostrom et al. 1999). Nevertheless, a greater proximity to resources does not reduce the risk for prevailing short-term interests such as overuse. Consequently, the need for effective rules limiting access and defining rights and duties remains (Ostrom et al. 1999). Further in depth research on this issue is needed.

Finally, water, energy and waste, by their nature, seem to carry a high potential in developing diversified forms of service coproduction. The cases studied confirm that water, energy and waste services allow a great variety of coproduction practices from co-planning and co-design to co-delivery and co-management, although service coproduction is more successful if it activates collaborations from the initial phases of the production process to the delivery. Service coproduction's varied forms seem to confirm Ostrom's suggestions (1996, 1083) that in coproduction, 'potential complementarities may be great, especially when those facilities involve major "trunk" lines and "feeder" lines', as in the case of water and sanitation. This depends on the comparative advantages of government agencies in displaying and managing large monetary resources and planning big scale infrastructure, and on those of 'smaller units' in providing relevant information about local needs and possible local maintenance. This also depends on the priority placed on 'collective goods whose benefits may be enjoyed by the entire community' (Brudeny and England 1983, 64; see also; Bovaird et al. 2016). Research on coproduction of conventional services would benefit from further studies on multi-level governance settings (Sicilia et al. 2016), to understand further the role of accessibility and environmental sustainability drivers for, and effects of, coproducing services.

9. Concluding remarks

To conclude, we propose two final considerations. The first deals with the understanding of the coproduction notion by authors contributing to this special issue. The second relates to the theoretical framework employed. Regarding the understanding of the coproduction notion in the framework of this special issue, the authors adopted different visions and perceptions of service coproduction, thus confirming that this is still a maturing concept (Verschuere, Brandsen and Petsoff 2012), subject to numerous and sometimes conflicting interpretations. As stressed by Sicilia et al. (2016), ambiguity lies both in the 'co-' and 'production' sides. In relation to the 'co-' side, a few authors identify the coproducers as individuals, whether they are users, clients, consumers, or customers (see Pestoff, Osborne, and Brandsen 2006), while most of authors emphasize the collective dimension of coproduction by including other actors such as associations, NGOs, citizens' coalitions, and so on (Bovaird 2007; Alford 2014). Concerning the 'production' side, certain authors adopt an extensive interpretation of coproduction, including the many different phases of the service production process (Bovaird and Loeffler 2012), to specify at which stage and with which characteristics the collaboration between public service agents and citizens take place. In contrast, especially in the case where public participation is actually really limited, other authors embrace a restricted meaning of coproduction (as per Pestoff 2012), identifying it only to the phase of service delivery.

Our second consideration relates to the proposed theoretical framework. Although still in its incipient stages, the proposed actor/flow/area approach internalizes the ecological assumption of the anthropic and environmental dimensions. This unified understanding has afforded insights about both accessibility to the service and resources, as well as environmental sustainability of the resources delivered by the service. However, the distinct reading of actor, flow and area should not mislead us: coproducing water, energy and waste services has implications that go across the observation fields. For example, the analysis here presented reveals that the level of accessibility to a service can be fully understood only by cross-referencing governance settings with its spatial connotations, resources availability and distribution. The same applies for environmental concerns related to the resource delivered by a service.

The criteria and variables attached to the actor/flow/area framework are still generic. Our presentation of the actor/flow/area framework aims at stimulating more studies seeking to grasp the multiform inferences that the coproduction of urban water, energy and waste services has under a true ecological perspective. To do so, we propose three possible paths for future research. First, the systematic integration of spatial and physical factors (here, the area and flow dimensions) into the analysis of coproduced water, energy and waste services is essential to assess the extent to which coproduction contributes to improved service provision, both in terms of better accessibility and increased environmental sustainability. A systematic inclusion of spatiality concerns (see also Moss 2014) can open the way to novel and unconventional research on service coproduction theory. Second, further research is needed on the particularities in coproducing conventional services. This is to understand fully, from one side, to what extent the coproduction literature related to social services can also inform water, energy and waste services organized through a conventional system, and, from the other, to what extent new analytical categories (such as the spatial and flow dimensions) need to be integrated. Third, the actor, flow, area analysis can then be used in more prospective terms and inspire action-oriented research likely to inform policy makers about possible service arrangements that are accessible and environmentally sound at the same time.

Disclosure statement

No potential conflict of interest was reported by the authors.

Funding

Part of this work was supported by the Institut Bruxellois pour la Recherche Scientifique under the grant Prospective Research for Brussels [2012].

Notes

1. Erik Swyngedouw makes this distinction clear while referring to the work of Graham and Marvin (2001) about *Splintering Urbanism*. To support their thesis, Graham and Marvin refer to information and communication technologies as 'cyberspace divides'.
2. Decentralized systems for supplying energy and disposing of rainwater and wastewater, for example, are not a novelty. Traditional, grassroots socio-technological systems are often off-grid (see, for example, Jaglin 2012; Allen et al. 2016). However, since recently, 'the liberalization of network industries, growing concerns for the use of environmental resources and impacts on these resources, new financial arrangements and the increasing individualization of lifestyles are all challenging the supremacy of centralized solutions and promoting the development of alternative technological systems at a more local scale' (Coutard, Ruthgerford, and Florentin 2014, 91).
3. Just to cite some significant examples of how service co-production in the Global South is addressed in literature: Ostrom (1996), Batley (2006), Bovaird (2007), Mitlin (2008), Peters and Muraleedharan (2008), Allen (2010, 2012), Batley and Mcloughlin (2010), Moretto (2010), Booth (2011), McDonald and Ruiters (2012), Albrechts (2013), McGranahan (2013), McMillan, Spronk, and Caswell (2014).
4. Materials is intended here in a wider sense comprising, according to political ecology, both nature and second nature (Smith 1984).
5. For example, in the case of waste delivery, the observation extends to the nature of waste products that the urban service collects and, in turn, discharges. In the service scheme, the waste product collected and the waste product discharged by the service may or not coincide, as the material collected could be further processed/transformed before its final discharge.
6. In the first case, the focus is on the organizational and technical aspects of public service co-production (very often non territorialized nor conventionally networked services) and, partially, on the institutional systems and normative frameworks favouring this service model (see for example Bovaird and Loeffler 2012; Jakobsen 2013; Verschuere, Brandsen and Petsoff 2012; Osborne and Strokosch 2013).The spatial dimension is almost totally absent. In the case of service coproduction in the Global South, the few existing pieces of research seem to present a much narrower and selective approach (see for example Mitlin 2008; Peters and Muraleedharan 2008; McGranahan 2013; Allen 2012; McMillan, Spronk, and Caswell 2014).The socio-spatial dimension is not systematically included in the analysis of their governance architecture or their effectiveness in producing structural service improvements.
7. This analysis of the circulatory processes concerning the flow channelled by the coproduced service is in line with the observation proposed by Girardet (1992) in *The Gaia Atlas of Cities*.
8. However, Button (2016) stresses also that the rainwater collection performed in Mumbai is controversial since the water retained is used for watering the gardens, while the water made infiltrating to recharge groundwater contributes to the operating conditions needed by the water bottling plant.
9. The basic technical services are tangible expression of the relation between a society and a certain space. In Raffestin (1980), space and territory are not synonymous but space becomes territory when concerned with the practices of the actors. Sacks (1986, 19) defines human territoriality as 'spatial strategy to affect, influence, or control resources and people, by controlling area'.

References

Albrechts, L. 2013. "Reframing Strategic Spatial Planning by Using a Coproduction Perspective." *Planning Theory* 12 (1): 46–63.

Alford, J. 2014. "The Multiple Facets of Co-Production: Building on the work of Elinor Ostrom." *Public Management Review* 16 (3): 299–316. doi:10.1080/14719037.2013.806578.

Allen, A. 2010. "Neither Rural nor Urban: Service Delivery Options That Work for the Peri-urban Poor." In *Peri-urban Water and Sanitation Services. Policy, Planning and Methods*, edited by M. Kurian and P. McCarney. London: Springer.

Allen, A. 2012. "Water Provision for and by the Peri-urban Poor. Public-community partnerships or citizens coproduction?" In *Urban sustainability: A global perspective*, edited by J. Vojnovic, 309–340. East Lansing: Michigan State University Press.

Allen, A., P. Hofmann, J. Mukherjee, and A. Walnycki. 2016. "Water trajectories through non-networked infrastructure: Insights from peri-urban Dar es Salaam, Cochabamba and Kolkata." *Urban Research & Practice*. doi:10.1080/17535069.2016.1197306.

Baccini, P. 1997. "A City's Metabolism: Towards the Sustainable Development of Urban Systems." *Journal of Urban Technology* 4 (2): 27–39. doi:10.1080/10630739708724555.

Bakker, K. 2010. *Privatizing Water: Governance Failure and the World's Urban Water Crisis*. New York: Cornell University Press.

Batley, R. 2006. "Engaged or divorced? Cross-service findings on government relations with non-state service-providers." *Public Administration and Development* 26 (3): 241–251. doi:10.1002/(ISSN)1099-162X.

Batley R., and G. Larbi. 2004. *The Changing Role of Government. The Reform of Public Services in Developing Countries*. New York: Palgrave.

Batley, R., and C. Mcloughlin. 2010. "Engagement with Non-State Service Providers in Fragile States: Reconciling State-Building and Service Delivery." *Development Policy Review* 28 (2): 131–154. doi:10.1111/j.1467-7679.2010.00478.x.

Becker, S., N. Naumann, and T. Moss. 2016. "Between coproduction and commons: Understanding initiatives to reclaim urban energy provision in Berlin and Hamburg." *Urban Research & Practice*. doi:10.1080/17535069.2016.1156735.

Booth, D. 2011. "Towards a theory of local governance and public goods provision." *IDS Bulletin* 42 (2): 11–21. doi:10.1111/idsb.2011.42.issue-2.

Bovaird, T. 2007. "Beyond Engagement and Participation: User and Community Coproduction of Public Services." *Public Administration Review* 67 (5): 846–860. doi:10.1111/puar.2007.67. issue-5.

Bovaird, T., and E. Loeffler. 2012. "From Engagement to Co-production: The Contribution of Users and Communities to Outcomes and Public Value." *Voluntas* 23 (4): 1119–1138. doi:10.1007/ s11266-012-9309-6.

Bovaird, T., G. Stoker, T. Jones, E. Loeffler, and M. Roncancio. 2016. "Activating collective co-production of public services: Influencing citizens to participate in complex governance mechanisms in the UK." *International Review of Administrative Sciences* 82 (1): 47–68. doi:10.1177/0020852314566009.

Brandsen, T., B. Verchuere, and V. Pestoff. 2012. "Conclusion: Taking Research on Co-production a Step Further." In *New Public Governance, the Third Sector, and Co-Production*, edited by V. Pestoff, T. Brandsen, and B. Verschuere. London: Routledge.

Brandsen, T., and V. Pestoff. 2006. "Co-production, the Third Sector and the Delivery of Public Services: An Introduction." *Public Management Review* 8 (4): 493–501.

Brudney, J. L., and R. E. England. 1983. "Toward a definition of the coproduction concept." *Public Administration Review* 43 (1): 59–65. doi:10.2307/975300.

Brunner, P. H. 2007. "Reshaping Urban Metabolism." *Journal of Industrial Ecology* 11 (2): 11–13. doi:10.1162/jie.2007.1293.

Budds, J., and G. McGranaham. 2003. "Are the debates on water privatization missing the point? Experiences from Africa, Asia and Latin America." *Environment and Urbanisation* 15 (2): 87–114. doi:10.1177/095624780301500222.

Butler, D., and C. Maksimovic. 1999. "Urban Water Management - Challenges for the Third Millennium." *Progress in Environmental Science* 1: 213–236.

Button, C. 2016. "The co-production of a constant water supply in Mumbai's middle class apartments." *Urban Research & Practice*. doi:10.1080/17535069.2016.1197305.

Coutard, O. 2008. "Placing splintering urbanism: Introduction." *Geoforum* 39 (6): 1815–1820. doi:10.1016/j.geoforum.2008.10.008.

Coutard, O., and J. Ruthgerford. 2012. "From networked to post-networked urbanism: New infrastructure configurations and urban transitions." International roundtable workshop, background paper, Autun, France, July 17–20.

Coutard, O., and J. Ruthgerford. 2015. *Beyond the Networked City: Infrastructure reconfigurations and urban change in the North and South*. London: Routledge.

Coutard, O., J. Ruthgerford, and D. Florentin. 2014. "Towards hybrid socio-technical solutions for water and energy provision." In *Innovations for Sustainable Development*, edited by J. Y. Grosclaude, R. K. Pachauri, and L. Tubiana. Delhi: TERI Press.

de Bercegol, R., and A. Desfeux. 2011. “Alternative au service public d’eau conventionnel: L’exemple des “réseaux de groupes d’usagers” d’un bidonville de Mumbai.’ *Métropoles* 9: 2–22.

Dubresson, A., and S. Jaglin. 2005. “Gouvernance, regulation et territorialisation des espaces urbanises.” In *Le territoire est mort. Vive les territoires!*, edited by B. Antheaume and F. Giraut. 337–352. Paris: Editions IRD.

Duque Gómez, C., and S. Jaglin. 2016. “When urban modernisation entails service delivery co-production: A glance from Medellin.” *Urban Research & Practice.* doi:10.1080/17535069.2016.1156734.

Dupuy, G. 1991. *L’Urbanisme Des Réseaux : Théories et Méthodes*. Paris: Armand Colin.

Farrelly, M., and R. Brown. 2011. “Rethinking Urban Water Management: Experimentation as a Way Forward?” *Global Environmental Change* 21 (2): 721–732. Elsevier Ltd. doi:10.1016/j.gloenvcha.2011.01.007.

Gandy, M. 2002. *Concrete and Clay—Reworking Nature in New York City*. Cambridge: MIT Press.

Girardet, H. 1992. *The Gaia Atlas of Cities*. London: Gaia Books.

Goldthau, A. 2014. “Rethinking the Governance of Energy Infrastructure: Scale, Decentralization and Polycentrism.” *Energy Research and Social Science* 1: 134–140. Elsevier Ltd.

Graham, S., and S. Marvin. 2001. *Splintering Urbanism. Networked Infrastructures, Technological Mobilities and the Urban Condition*. London: Routledge.

Heynen, N., M. Kaika, and E. Swyngedouw. 2006. “Urban Political Ecology: Politicising the Production of Urban Natures.” In *In the Nature of Cities Urban Political Ecology and the Politics of Urban Metabolism*. 1–19. doi:10.4324/9780203027523.

Hommels, A. 2005. “Studying Obduracy in the City: Toward a Productive Fusion between Technology Studies and Urban Studies.” *Science, Technology, & Human Values* 30 (3): 323–351. doi:10.1177/0162243904271759.

Jaglin, S. 2005. *Services d’eau en Afrique Subsaharienne. La fragmentation urbaine en question*. Paris: CNRS Editions.

Jaglin, S. 2012. “Services en réseaux et villes africaines: L’universalité par d’autres voies?” *L’espace Geographique* 41 (1): 51,67.

Jaglin, S. 2014. “Regulating Service Delivery in Southern Cities: Rethinking Urban Heterogeneity.” In *The Routledge Handbook on Cities of the Global South*, edited by S. Parnell and S. Oldfield. London: Routledge.

Jakobsen, M. 2013. “Can Government Initiatives Increase Citizen Coproduction? Results of a Randomized Field Experiment.” *Journal of Public Administration Research and Theory* 23 (1): 27–54. doi:10.1093/jopart/mus036.

Joshi, A., and M. Moore. 2004. “Institutionalised Co-production: Unorthodox Public Service Delivery in Challenging Environments.” *The Journal of Development Studies* 40 (4): 31–49. doi:10.1080/00220380410001673184.

Kaika, M., and E. Swyngedouw. 2000. “Fetishizing the Modern City: The Phantasmagoria of Urban Technological Networks.” *International Journal of Urban and Regional Research* 24 (1): 120–138. doi:10.1111/ijur.2000.24.issue-1.

Ludwig, D., R. Hilborn, and C. Walters. 1993. “Uncertainty, Resource Exploitation, and Conservation: Lessons from History.” *Science (New York, N.Y.)* 260 (5104): 17–36. doi:10.1126/science.260.5104.17.

McDonald, D., and G. Ruiters. 2012. *Alternatives to privatization: Public options for essential services in the global South*. South Africa: Routledge - HSRC - LeftWord Books.

McGranahan, G. 2013. “Community-Driven Sanitation Improvement in Deprived Urban Neighbourhoods. Meeting the Challenges of Local Collective Action, Co-Production, Affordability and a Trans-Sectoral Approach.” Research Report.

McGranahan G., D. Mitlin, and D. Satterthwaite. 2008. “Land and Services for the Urban Poor in Rapidly Urbanising Countries.” In *The New Global Frontiers: Urbanisation, Poverty and Environment in the 21th Century*, edited by G. Martine, G. McGranahan, M. Montgomery, and R. Fernandez-Castilla. London: Earthscan.

McMillan, R., S. Spronk, and C. Caswell. 2014. “Popular participation, equity, and co-production of water and sanitation services in Caracas, Venezuela.” *Water International* 39 (2): 201–215. doi:10.1080/02508060.2014.886844.

Mitlin, D. 2008. "With and beyond the state – co-production as a route to political influence, power and transformation for grassroots organizations." *Environment and Urbanization* 20 (2): 339–360. doi:10.1177/0956247808096117.

Monstadt, J. 2009. "Conceptualizing the Political Ecology of Urban Infrastructures: Insights from Technology and Urban Studies." *Environment and Planning A* 41: 1924–1942. doi:10.1068/a4145.

Monstadt, J., and S. Schramm. 2013. "Beyond the networked city? Suburban constellation in water and sanitation systems." In *Suburban constellation*, edited by R. Keil. Berlin: Jovis.

Moretto, L. 2010. "Coproduction du service d'eau et recomposition de l'espace intra urbain dans la périphérie Sud de Caracas." *Espaces et sociétés* 143 (3): 81–99. doi:10.3917/esp.143.0081.

Moretto, L. 2014. *Assessing Urban Gouvernance: The Case of Water Service Co-production in Venezuela*. Brussels: PIE Peter Lang.

Moretto, L., and A. Allen. 2015. "Co-Producing Water Services in Peri-Urban Caracas: Political Democratisation Without Administrative Decentralisation?" In *Territoires périurbains: Développement, enjeux et perspectives dans les pays du sud*, edited by J. Bogaert and J.-M. Halleux. Gembloux: Presses Agronomiques de Gembloux.

Moss T. 2014. "Spatiality of the Commons." *Urban Studies* 8 (2): 457–471.

Nelson, V. I. 2008. *New Approaches in Decentralized Water Management*. Gloucester. http://sustainablewaterforum.org/new/newappreport.pdf

Newman, P. 2001. "Sustainable Urban Water Systems in Rich and Poor Cities–Steps towards a New Approach." *Water Science and Technology: A Journal of the International Association on Water Pollution Research* 43 (4): 93–99.

Niemczynowicz, J. 1999. "Urban Hydrology and Water Management – Present and Future Challenges." *Urban Water* 1: 1–14. doi:10.1016/S1462-0758(99)00009-6.

Niza, S., L. Rosado, and F. Paulo. 2009. "Urban Metabolism." *Journal of Industrial Ecology* 13 (3): 384–405. doi:10.1111/j.1530-9290.2009.00130.x.

Osborne, S. P., and K. Strokosch. 2013. "It takes Two to Tango? Understanding the Co-production of Public Services by Integrating the Services Management and Public Administration Perspectives." *British Journal of Management* 24: S31–S47. doi:10.1111/bjom.2013.24.issue-s1.

Ostrom, E. 1996. "Crossing the great divide: Coproduction, synergy and development." *World Development* 24 (6): 1073–1087. doi:10.1016/0305-750X(96)00023-X.

Ostrom, E. 2010. "Polycentric Systems for Coping with Collective Action and Global Environmental Change." *Global Environmental Change* 20 (4): 550–557. Elsevier Ltd. doi:10.1016/j.gloenvcha.2010.07.004.

Ostrom, E., J. Burger, C. B. Field, R. B. Norgaard, and D. Policansky. 1999. "Revisiting the Commons: Local Lessons, Global Challenges." *Science (New York, N.Y.)* 284 (5412): 278–282. doi:10.1126/science.284.5412.278.

Parks, R. B., P. C. Baker, L. Kiser, R. Oakerson, E. Ostrom, V. Ostrom, S. L. Percy, M. B. Vandivort, G. P. Whitaker, and R. Wilson. 1981. "Consumers as Coproducers of Public Services: Some Economic and Institutional Considerations." *Policy Studies Journal* 9 (7): 1001–1011.

Pestoff, V. 2012. "Co-Production and Third Sector Social Services in Europe: Some Crucial Conceptual Issues." In *New Public Governance, the Third Sector, and Co-Production*, edited by V. Pestoff, T. Brandsen, and B. Verschuere. London: Routledge.

Pestoff, V., T. Brandsen, and B. Verschuere. (Eds.). 2012. *New Public Governance, the Third Sector, and Co-Production*. London: Routledge.

Pestoff, V., S. P. Osborne, and T. Brandsen, T. 2006. "Patterns of Co-production in Public Services: Some Concluding Thoughts." *Public Management Review* 8 (4): 591–595.

Peters, D. H., and V. R. Muraleedharan. 2008. "Regulating India's health services: To what end? What future?" *Social Science & Medicine* 66: 2133–2144. doi:10.1016/j.socscimed.2008.01.037.

Pilo', F. 2016. "'Co-producing affordability to the electricity service': A market-oriented response to addressing inequality of access in Rio de Janeiro's *favelas*." *Urban Research & Practice*. doi:10.1080/17535069.2016.1154101.

Raffestin, C. 1980. *Pour Une Géographie Du Pouvoir*. Paris: Librairies techniques.

Ranzato, M. 2011. "Integrated water design for a decentralized urban landscape." PhD diss., University of Trento.

Ranzato, M. 2016. "Landscape elements as a basis for Integrated Water Management." PhD thesis, Université libre de Bruxelles.

Robertson, M. 2012. *Sustainable Cities*. Ottawa: Practical Action Publishing.

Sack, R. (Ed.). 1986. "Human Territoriality." In *Human Territoriality: Its Theory and History.* Cambridge: Cambridge university Press.

Sicilia, M., E. Guarini, A. Sancino, M. Andreani, and R. Ruffini. 2016. "Public services management and co-production in multi-level governance settings." *International Review of Administrative Sciences* 82 (1): 8–27. doi:10.1177/0020852314566008.

Smith, N. 1984. *Uneven Development: Nature, Capital and the Production of Space*. Oxford: Blackwell Publishers.

Smith, N. 2006. "Foreword." In *In the Nature of Cities: Urban Political Ecology and the Politics of Urban Metabolism*, edited by N. Heynen, M. Kaika, and E. Swyngedouw, xii–xv. Routledge. doi:10.2747/0272-3638.28.2.206.

Swyngedouw, E. 2003. "Book Review: Splintering urbanism." *Progress in Human Geography* 27 (1): 130–131. doi:10.1177/030913250302700115.

Tarr, J. A. 2002. "The Metabolism of the Industrial City: The Case of Pittsburgh." *Journal of Urban History* 28 (5): 511–545. doi:10.1177/0096144202028005001.

Tarr, J. A., and G. Dupuy. 1988. "Technology and the Rise of the Networked City in Europe and America." In *Technology and Urban Growth*, edited by B. Brownell, D. T. Critchlow, M. S. Foster, M. Rose, and J. A. Tarr. Philadelphia, PA: Temple University Press.

Tjallingii, S. P. 1996. *Ecological Conditions. Strategies and Structures in Environmental Planning.* Wageningen: Institute for Forestry and Nature Research.

Van Bohemen, H. 2012. "(Eco) System Thinking : Ecological Principles for Buildings, Roads and Industrial and Urban Areas." *Sustainable Urban Environments: An Ecosystem Approach* edited by E. Van Bueren and A. Et 2: 15–70. Springer Science+Business Media B.V. doi:10.1007/978-94-007-1294-2.

Van Bueren, E. 2012. "Introduction." In *Sustainable Urban Environments: An Ecosystem Approach*, 1–13. Dordrecht: Springer Science+Business Media B.V.

Verschuere, B., T. Brandsen, and V. Pestoff. 2012. "Co-production: The State of the Art in Research and the Future Agenda." *Voluntas* 23 (4): 1083–1101. doi:10.1007/s11266-012-9307-8.

Younos, T. 2011. "Paradigm Shift: Holistic Approach for Water Management in Urban Environments." *Frontiers of Earth Science* 5 (4): 421–427.

Water trajectories through non-networked infrastructure: insights from peri-urban Dar es Salaam, Cochabamba and Kolkata

Adriana Allen, Pascale Hofmann, Jenia Mukherjee and Anna Walnycki

For many urbanites, infrastructural uncertainty refers to 'predictable shocks' rather than constituting a quotidian experience. By contrast, for the peri-urban poor, the sources of uncertainty underpinning water and sanitation services are endless: uncertainty about cost, about being evicted and indeed about ever becoming connected to networked systems.

Drawing on a number of case studies, we argue that across the urban global south, the future is not one of networked systems but rather one of 'infrastructural archipelagos' that need to be thoroughly understood in order to bridge the growing gap between everyday and large infrastructural planning practices.

Introduction

For many urban dwellers, infrastructural uncertainty refers to 'predictable shocks' (such as increasing water tariffs or lower pressure during certain days of the week), rather than constituting a quotidian experience. The picture is significantly different when it comes to considering the meaning and experience of water uncertainty by the peri-urban poor in the global south. In such context, the sources of uncertainty underpinning access to services are endless: uncertainty about cost, about being evicted, about ever becoming connected (or networked). Indeed, about 60% of the new urbanites expected to live across the global south over the next 25 years, will be exposed to all these uncertainties on a daily basis, without networked infrastructure to access essential basic services such as water and sanitation. In this context, the future is not one of networked systems but rather one of – paraphrasing Karen Bakker (2003) – 'infrastructural archipelagos', shaped by misrecognised practices of everyday planning.

Everyday planning practices are those adopted on the ground by ordinary women and men to access water and sanitation, and they range from 'needs-driven practices', which are based on some form of collective action – whether within communities or between communities and the state – and those that are undertaken individually and might rely either on solidarity among

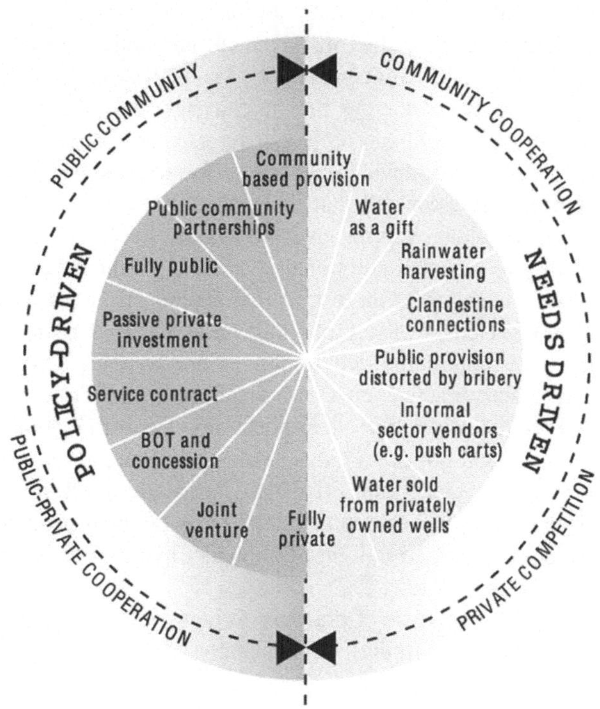

Figure 1. The waterwheel: Mapping the universe of practices governing access to basic services in peri-urban areas. Source: Allen 2005, published in Allen, Davila, and Hofmann (2006a). With permission of Bartlett Development Planning Unit.

households – such as when water to the most vulnerable members of a particular settlement is provided as a ‘gift’ by households who might have a privately owned borehole – or on market-based mechanisms, as in those cases when water is bought from small independent providers, whether these are informal or licensed water vendors. In any given context, everyday practices coexist with what could be termed as ‘policy-driven practices’, undertaken by the state and utilities. The waterwheel (Figure 1) captures the spectrum of practices and the type of relations that are commonly at play in the peri-urban context.

Previous studies revealed that in peri-urban areas developing without or with limited physical networked infrastructure, people tend to rely on a vast diversity of needs-driven practices and are unlikely to get connected to the network in the near future (Allen, Davila, and Hofmann 2006a; Mulenga and McGranahan 2011). There is ample evidence pointing to the fact that policy-driven practices are unable to meet the water needs of the peri-urban poor, failing to support the expansion of centralised network systems to realise the right to water and sanitation in such context (Nganyanyuka et al. 2014; Andreasen and Møller-Jensen 2016; Allen, Davila, and Hofmann 2006b; Mehta et al. 2014; Mehta and Karpouzoglou 2015). Furthermore, conventional formal approaches to urban infrastructural planning and management tend to neglect the potential of urban metabolisms to handle critical resources and material flows in a sustainable way, while treating grassroots incremental responses as substandard practices that are at best tolerated as temporary coping mechanisms or at worst combated as backward and undesirable.

Nevertheless, across the urban global south, infrastructural deficits are being increasingly addressed by active experimentation in new ways to abridge or co-produce community-led efforts with those of the state not just to fill provision gaps but also to do so at scale, while integrating watershed management and activating citizens' rights and entitlements (Allen, Davila, and Hofmann 2006b; Marshall et al. 2009; Allen 2014). As many countries appear to be endorsing the human right to water and in some cases shifting into distinctive 'post-neoliberal projects', diverse configurations of public, private and community providers are fast developing to meet the water and sanitation needs of the unserved. For instance, it is estimated that there are over 80,000 community-led water systems in Latin America alone, serving over 40 million people in rural and peri-urban areas and with capacity to serve an additional 18 million (Ochoa, Soto, and Burt 2011). While the redistributive capacity of these systems in rural areas has been the subject of various investigations (Boelens, Getches, and Guevara-Gil 2010), there has been little in-depth research into how community-led initiatives are working with the state to co-produce water management practices in the urban fringe. Furthermore, while a number of studies have explored the more strategic implications of co-production partnerships and their scope to redress unequal power relations (Joshi and Moore 2004; Mitlin 2008; Allen 2012; Bustamante, Crespo, and Walnycki 2011), the wide spectrum of alliances and relationships emerging through these partnerships have rarely been considered in great depth and even less been examined in light of the wider hydro-political trajectories of the urban regions in which they operate.

This article explores the universe of practices to be found in the peri-urban context of three urban regions: Kolkata (India), Cochabamba (Bolivia) and Dar es Salaam (Tanzania), where unmet needs are growing fastest and where conventional centralised networks are unlikely to become the norm now or in the future. The concept of 'infrastructural archipelagos' allows us to move beyond a focus on networked provision to consider the growing gap between everyday and large infrastructural planning practices. In doing so, we pay particular attention to those practices that rely on some form of collective action, whether this involves cooperation among grounded organisations of the poor, or with state-led agencies. Furthermore, our focus is not just on the extent to which these practices are improving access to water and sanitation services but also on their capacity to disrupt unjust trajectories through governance approaches that abridge community-led and state-led efforts. As revealed through the contrasting trajectories found in each of the three aforementioned urban regions, what emerges is a spectrum of co-production partnerships with varying potential towards more just peri-urban water futures.

The analysis draws on primary and secondary research undertaken by the authors and consolidated through a seed-grant awarded by the International Social Science Council (ISSC). The ISSC project[1] entitled 'Translocal Learning for Water Justice' focused specifically on exploring the transformative potential of alternative water supply arrangements (small-scale, low-cost management practices and new configurations of water governance) that are undertaken for and by the peri-urban poor in the three aforementioned urban regions. Applying the same analytical framework to reflect on fieldwork that was undertaken independently in each urban region provided the authors and project partners with an opportunity to examine how and with what consequences basic services are being co-produced between ordinary citizens and the state in three contrasting scenarios. Individual fieldwork was carried out periodically between 2008 and 2015 and involved ethnographic and participatory research through qualitative interviews, focus group discussions, transect walks and observations. Where possible, the researchers linked their activities in each region to existing processes of community knowledge production.

Kolkata: water poverty in a water-flush city

The city of Kolkata is often described as 'triple-blessed': possessing a river for drinking water, another to dispose of waste and the wetlands in between to treat its sewage and produce its food (Banerjee and Chaudhuri 2012). Yet, despite these rich advantages, significant disparities exist across the growing population of 14.38 million of Kolkata Metropolitan Area (KMA) – and particularly in relation to the access to and control over water and sanitation services (Census 2011). Two agencies are jointly responsible for water supply and sanitation of Kolkata: Kolkata Municipal Corporation (KMC) and Kolkata Municipal Water and Sanitation Agency (KMWSA). While KMC is in charge of water supply to all the wards within KMC, KMWSA covers the rest of the metropolitan area. KMC officials claim to cover 85% of the population by piped supply and 50–55% by sewerage network.[2] A recently published Technical Assistance Consultant's Report of the Asian Development Bank (ADB) entitled *India: Preparing for Kolkata Environmental Improvement Project Phase II* claims that the municipal piped water supply system covers almost 92% of the KMC population, the current coverage being higher than the national average of 81% but 8% short of the 100% national target benchmark. However, the water supply service level is distinctly different for the various water supply zones – respectively supplied from Palta, Garden Reach, Jorabagan and Watgaunge Water Treatment Plants or by groundwater supply (Map 1). Similarly, the sewerage and drainage service level in the central city area is distinctly different to that enjoyed in the outer areas of KMC (Asian Development Bank 2012). Though water is provided free of charge by the municipality, this piped coverage is disproportionately lower (and almost non-existent) in the peri-urban areas of Kolkata Metropolitan Area. Here, lower-income communities residing in informal neighbourhoods rely upon groundwater extraction of poor quality, or the use of water vendors, at a cost of 5–20 Indian Rupees for a jar of 20 litres (0.08–0.4 USD approximately).

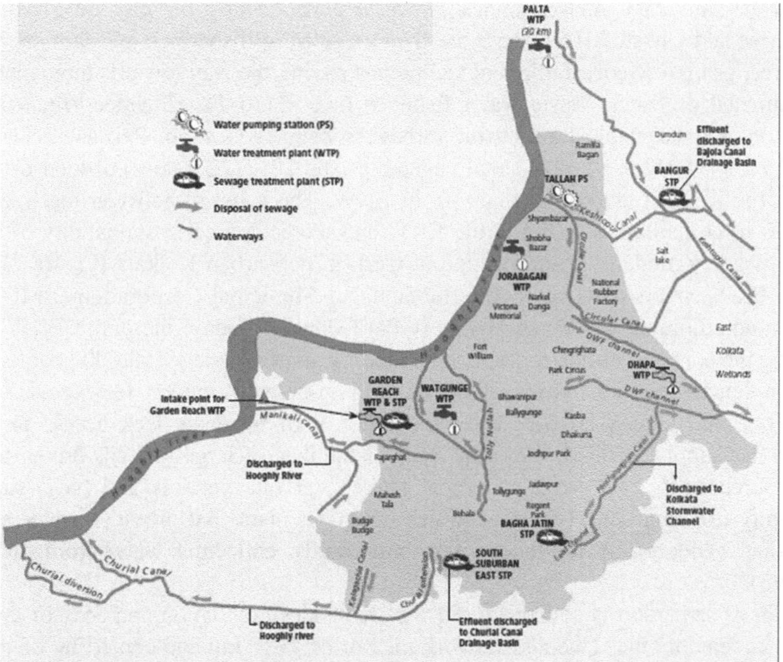

Map 1. Major water treatment plants and sewage treatment plants in Kolkata. Source: adapted from Banerjee and Chaudhuri (2012).

Photo 1. Fishermen in the East Kolkata Wetlands. Source: Pascale Hofmann (January 2015). Image reproduced with permission of the rights holder.

This unequal distribution of services is perhaps nowhere more evident than in the south-eastern peri-urban interface of the city, known as the East Kolkata Wetlands (EKW). Here, lack of policy-driven municipal water and sanitation services has prompted residents to develop a range of co-produced water and waste management (CWWM) practices to meet their quotidian needs.

The peri-urban wetlands play a critical role in the socio-ecological functioning of the city. The EKW and the adjacent Dhapa landfill area absorb currently 750 million litres of waste water and 2500 metric tonnes of waste generated by the city on a daily basis (Mukherjee and Ghosh 2015). These are then recycled by fishermen and farmers residing in the area, using low-cost traditional techniques paving the way towards three major eco-environmental practices: waste water fisheries (see Photo 1), effluence-irrigated paddy cultivation, and vegetable farming on garbage substrates (Kundu, Pal, and Saha 2008). Around 25% (150 tonnes) of the total vegetables and 20% (22 tonnes) of total fish traded daily in the Kolkata market originate from EKW. The synergy between the livelihoods strategies of communities living in the EKW and the ecological sustainability of the city represents a key mode of co-production at work in peri-urban Kolkata (Figure 2).

The EKW covers parts of KMC, Bidhannagar Municipal Corporation (BMC) (ward no. 17) and adjoining gram panchayats (GPs) (Map 1). Today, the entire EKW region, including the core and buffer zones, is inhabited by approximately 150,000 people, mostly living in houses on the narrow strips of land in-between *bheris* (sewage-fed ponds) (Mukherjee and Ghosh 2015).[3] The vast majority of residents lack access to filtered piped water supply. Instead, they rely upon a number of largely needs-driven arrangements: purchasing water from municipal tankers, private vendors and NGO-supported community drinking water projects (water treatment plant that provides water at lower prices than vendors), or for the poorest households, collecting water from the *bheris* (Figure 3).[4]

As far as sanitation is concerned, 50% of Kolkata's population and 55% of the KMC area are covered by the sewerage network measuring 1610 km and consisting of 1430 km of piped sewers and 180 km of brick sewer lines (Anon 2011). KMC and Kolkata Metropolitan Development Agency (KMDA) are in charge of these sewerage networks.

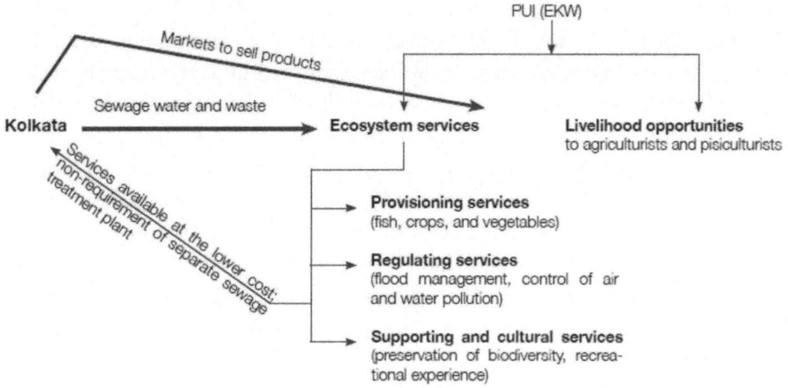

Figure 2. Sustainable flows between Kolkata and its peri-urban interface. Mukherjee, J. 2015b. Sustainable flows between Kolkata and its peri-urban interface: Challenges and opportunities. Figure 2.1: Sustainable Flows between Kolkata and its PUI, 36. In Untamed Urbanisms, edited by A. Allen, A. Lampis and M. Swilling. New York: Routledge. Reproduced with permission from Palgrave McMillan.

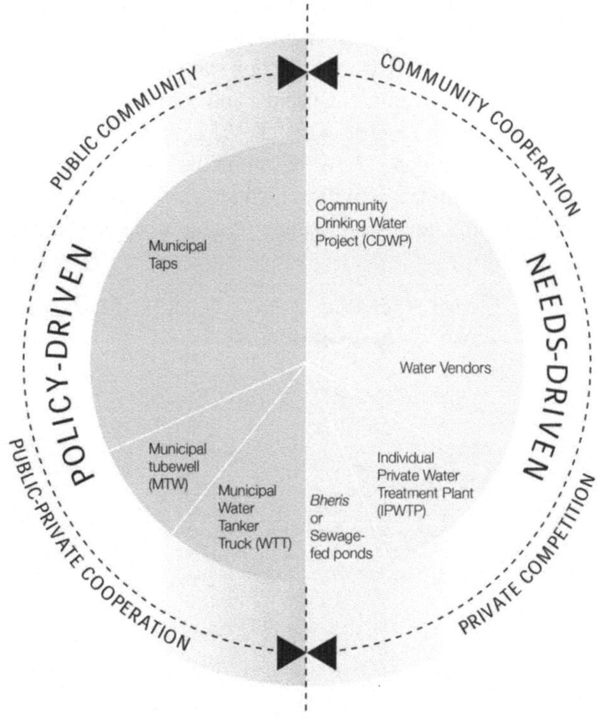

Figure 3. Water practices in peri-urban Kolkata (EKW). Source: Mukherjee and Ghosh (2015). With permission of Bartlett Development Planning Unit.

The city has no sewage treatment plants (STPs) within municipal boundaries. There are three small KMC treatment plants located outside the municipal limits at Bangur, Garden Reach and Bagha Jatin (Map 1) but with low capacities of 45 million litres per day (mld),

48 mld and 2 mld, respectively. The KMC intends to upgrade the Garden Reach STP from 48 to 52 mld. Therefore, the EKW serves as the only and major natural recycling infrastructure, relying upon low-cost techniques adopted and practiced by poor farmers and fishermen following a complex mechanism (Ghosh 1991, 1997; Kundu, Pal, and Saha 2008; Carlisle 2013; Mukherjee 2015a). It has an interesting history of evolution and emergence since the colonial times when canals were excavated (known as the 'eastern canal system') with a dual purpose of trade–transportation and drainage–sewerage–sanitation of the rapidly expanding city (Mukherjee 2015b).The city drains the bulk, over 75% of its rainwater and sewage, through channels into the Kulti River, which acts as the major outfall channel, through the EKW. However, despite this significant contribution to the overall 'environmental sanitation' of the city, at the household level, residents of EKW lack adequate access to sanitation options. Here, individual sanitation practices vary from the use of single and double pit latrines connected to septic tanks, to makeshift community sanitation systems interconnected to municipal canals (CSIMC), to open defecation. While these options remain limited, cooperative fisheries operating in the area are now highly discouraging open defecation and CSIMC practices, as these ultimately degrade the *bheris*. Though fish in the *bheris* consume faecal matter, cooperative members have recently become aware that this may reduce the price of fish in the Kolkata market. Some cooperative fisheries like the *Baro Chaynavi* (with 67 members) in Bidhannagar ward no. 17 have begun to allocate funds and/or loans to their own members with zero interest rates to enable households to construct their own pit latrines. 60 out of 67 members have now pit latrines constructed with support from the cooperative.

In the three types of *bheris*: government, private and cooperatives, distinguished primarily through their ownership patterns (Figure 4),[5] CWWM practices involve multilevel stakeholders. Fishermen and farmers depend on the municipal supply of waste water and solid waste for pisicultural and agricultural activities. Fish production in the *bheris* is determined by a number of factors including the coordination among various stakeholders. Within the

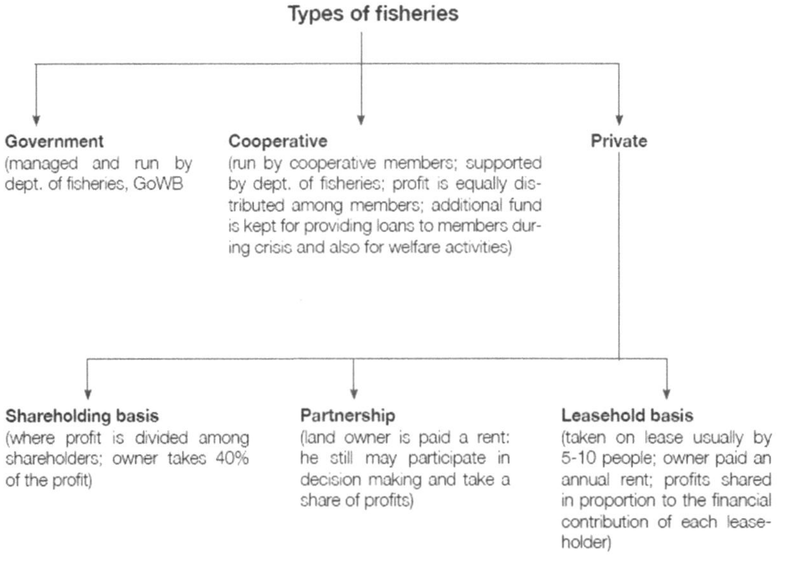

Figure 4. Types of fisheries based on ownership pattern. Source: Own elaboration based on Edwards (2002) and fieldwork data.

government, this includes the KMDA, KMC, the Department of Irrigation and Waterways (DoIW), the Department of Environment (DoE), the Department of Fisheries (DoF) and the West Bengal Pollution Control Board (WBPCB). It also involves external supporting agencies and programmes such as the ADB that funded the Kolkata Environmental Improvement Investment Programme (KEIIP). Finally, this also includes fish producer associations and fishermen and women.

However, in recent years, a number of threats have been experienced to the detriment of the ecological and socio-economic fabric of the EKW. Cooperative fisheries are increasingly becoming privatised, selling *bheris* to commercial companies operating in the region. This has been particularly problematic for the fishermen making a living in the EKW, who generally receive lower wages from private companies, ranging between 100 and 150 Indian rupees per day (1.5–2.3 USD), and suffer from a greater level of job insecurity. Unlike fish farms managed under the cooperative model, private farms focus primarily on the generation of profits and do not engage in the distributive activities of the cooperatives, including the allocation of funds to members for welfare measures, such as the construction of pit latrines, or other community and household goods. Moreover, in recent times, there has been an escalating conflict among the KMC, KMDA, DoIW and Fish Producer Associations over the operation of lock-gates on the main sewage canal at Bantala, which controls the flow and supply of waste water into the *bheris*. A recent report published in *The Times of India* commented: 'The flow of sewage into the fish farms or bheris has been deliberately reduced in an attempt to snuff out fishery and farming and make way for conversion of the land into real estate' (Niyogi 2015). To clarify this point, the waste is directly flowing into the Kulti River without diversion and treatment through EWK. Instead of allowing accumulation of the water to a certain height so that it can smoothly flow to EKW via linked channels and cuts constructed by fishermen, the irrigation department is diverting water to the outfall channel at reduced height. This is harming the lives and livelihoods of fishermen and also affects the river that is receiving untreated waste (Niyogi 2015). This mirrors wider trends of urban development within the city, impinging upon hard-fought rights for the ecological protection of the wetlands.

CWWM practices in Kolkata's fringe, while holding a critical impact at the city scale, also offer hints for alternate modes of cooperation which have the potential to address some of the everyday challenges of water and sanitation for residents of the EKW. These can contribute to both the ecological sustainability and empowerment of local communities, and show potential to be scaled up across different sites but would require support from the government, for example, the irrigation department to start with. More detailed examination and exploration on how these operate, would facilitate the recognition of the value of these networks, building upon the strength of these practices, and generating the conditions and opportunities to foster greater dialogue and interdependence among multilevel stakeholders operating in Kolkata and its peri-urban interface and embedded, integrated and complex land(water)scape.

Dar es Salaam: a pragmatic approach to bridging service gaps

Critically, Dar es Salaam is facing growing challenges with the equitable provision of adequate quality water services. Over the past 25 years, rapid population growth exacerbated by accelerated urban sprawl (Andreasen and Møller-Jensen 2016) has generated new requirements for residents of the city (see Map 2). Demands for water have intensified with the increase in population and concurrent growth of economic activities requiring water as an input, including hydropower generation, large-scale irrigated agriculture, industries, tourism, mining, raising livestock, domestic uses, fisheries and wildlife and forestry

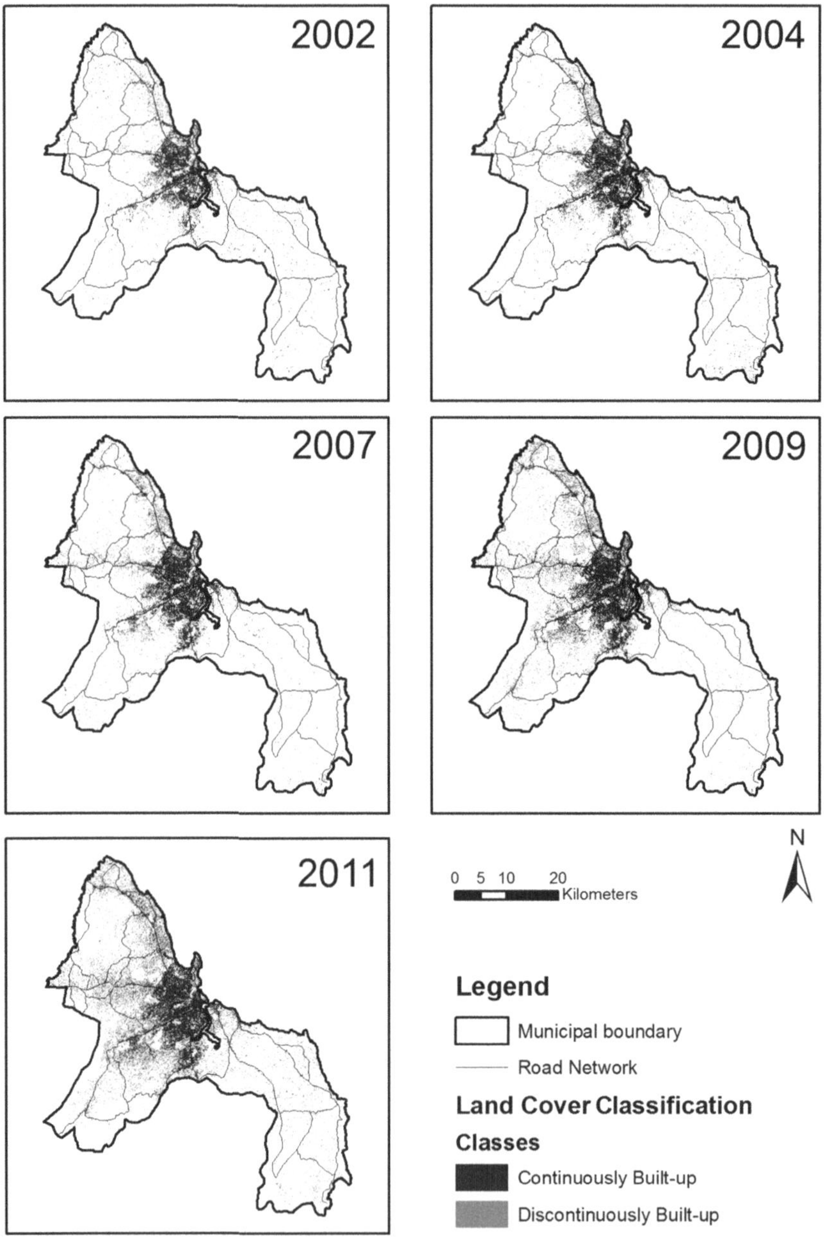

Map 2. Urban growth of Dar es Salaam between 2002 and 2011. Source: Congedo and Munafò (2014) Urban Sprawl as a Factor of Vulnerability to Climate Change: Monitoring Land Cover Change in Dar es Salaam. Figure 5.4: Land Cover Classifications of Dar es Salaam, 84. In Macchi, S. & Tiepolo, M. (Eds.) Climate Change Vulnerability in Southern African Cities. Cham, Switzerland: Springer International Publishing. With permission of Springer.

activities. Further factors contributing to stress on local water resources include degradation due to pollution, over-extraction, poor land use practices and the encroachment of land for agriculture, urbanisation and industrial development (URT 2012).

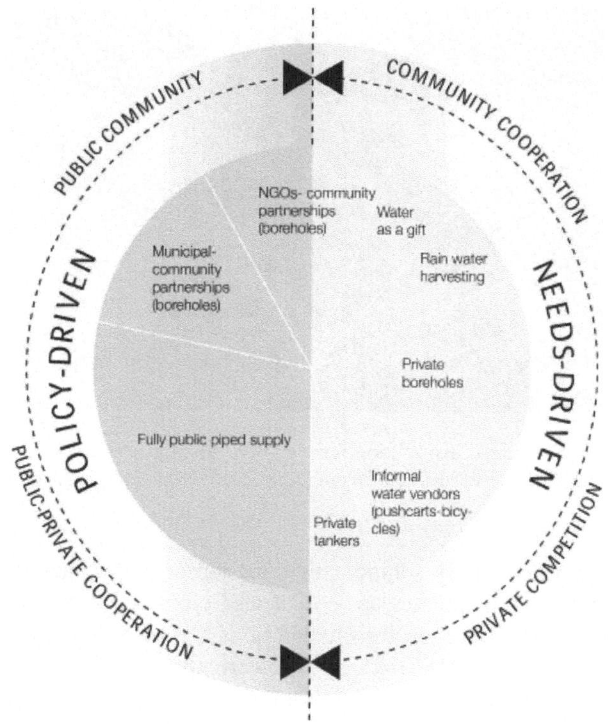

Figure 5. Policy-driven and needs-driven water practices in peri-urban Dar es Salaam. Source: Kombe, Ndezi, and Hofmann (2015). With permission of Bartlett Development Planning Unit.

After recent local government policy reforms, public service provision, including water, falls under the responsibility of Dar es Salaam's three municipalities (MoW 2011). Following a short period of private sector participation in the early to mid-2000s, the city's water supply and sanitation system (WSS) is currently managed by two public entities. The Dar es Salaam Water and Sanitation Authority (DAWASA) is the asset holder, while the Dar es Salaam Water and Sanitation Corporation (DAWASCO) is in charge of operation and maintenance through a lease contract with DAWASA. According to recent official statistics, the formal system reaches approximately 50% of the city population, largely benefiting higher-income citizens, as 44% of domestic connections supposedly serving 17% of households in low-income areas of the city are dysfunctional (EWURA 2014; Pauschert, Gronemeier, and Jebens 2012). The remaining inhabitants, first and foremost almost 90% of those living in informal low-income areas, rely on alternative practices to meet their water needs at a cost that is often considerably higher compared to the official rates charged by the utility (Kombe, Ndezi, and Hofmann 2015; Pauschert, Gronemeier, and Jebens 2012). Most of these practices are needs-driven (see Figure 5) and heavily dependent on the unregulated use of groundwater sources, as a result of diminishing surface water supplies and the limited coverage of the network infrastructure. More than 40% of low-income residents in Dar es Salaam rely on water from private boreholes (Pauschert, Gronemeier, and Jebens 2012).

Roles and responsibilities of local government in WSS are ambiguous as they are not well defined but there are examples in Dar es Salaam, particularly in more peripheral settlements lacking provision by the utility, where the municipality has taken an active

Photo 2. Community-managed distribution point in peri-urban Dar es Salaam supplied with water from a local borehole. Source: Pascale Hofmann (June 2015). Image reproduced with permission of the rights holder.

role in developing water supply solutions that are subsequently managed by local communities. Each of the municipalities has a dedicated cross-departmental team that works with local communities under their jurisdiction on issues of **wa**ter, **h**ealth, **e**ducation and **co**mmunity development (WAHECO). The state currently considers community-managed water supply systems as the most feasible option to provide low-income settlements with water, particularly in peri-urban areas far away from the mains. In 2003, DAWASA established a small Community Liaison Unit (CLU) with the purpose of supporting community-managed non-networked WSS schemes, initially adopted as part of a World Bank project to improve WSS in Dar es Salaam.

Only recently, in 2014, DAWASCO followed suit with a dedicated pro-poor unit to extend services to lower-income households. It is unknown how many community-managed schemes exist across the city but estimates are high, as approximately 75–80% of the city population live in informal settlements where formal utility supply is extremely limited. The majority of these schemes tend to be community-managed boreholes where water is pumped to overhead storage tanks and subsequently supplied through a number of distribution points installed across the settlement (see Photo 2) and an increasing number of household connections.[6] Costs to run these systems include electricity bills, stipends for water vendors and security personnel and repair and maintenance expenses. While the technical arrangements are largely the same, the city portrays a range of community-managed systems with regards to how they emerge and concerning their management. WAHECO teams and CLU have been involved in establishing a number of these water supply schemes. In other areas, NGOs have worked with communities to set up local systems. They are managed by water committees or water user associations (WUAs), with the former granting local government most of the decision-making power while the latter represents a more institutionalised and autonomous form of collective management whereby WUA members, that is, the users of the system, take the decisions. Preliminary findings reveal potential of some of these schemes to address water injustices in the city at scale, particularly those where residents and public authorities are jointly involved in the delivery of services. However, contributions by the state (be it the utility and/or municipal government), both in terms of financial and human resources, tend to concentrate on putting the system in place with limited support during operation and maintenance. As these community-managed schemes are expected to be financially and managerially self-sufficient government involvement is largely limited to occasional technical support and the approval of spending requests (Hofmann, fieldwork notes 2015).

Dar es Salaam further demonstrates several innovations in co-produced sanitation. These range from decentralised waste water treatment solutions (DEWATS) where the role of the state is latent, to more active collaborations with the utility to develop affordable sanitation solutions through simplified sewerage.[7] DEWATS are schemes run by small-scale businesses or community-based organisations (often with support from NGOs) that provide natural faecal sludge treatment through low maintenance, decentralised plants that do not require energy inputs. The treated water can be used for agricultural irrigation and some of the plants also produce biogas that can be used for cooking (see http://www.borda-sea.org for more information). Not all of these schemes are functioning well and challenges remain to bring them to work at scale (Banana et al. 2015). Dedicated units in DAWASA and DAWASCO for WSS provision in lower-income communities offer a good basis towards pro-poor service delivery but unless their approach is mainstreamed across the institutions, the capacity for scaling up is limited, particularly since both units are extremely small (5–6 staff members) compared to overall members of staff in the utility (Peal and Drabble 2015). Furthermore, water committees and WUAs often face problems in relation to management and monitoring with limited capacity to expand the system and increase the number of beneficiaries.[8] Performance varies across the city and is largely dependent on the individual management capacity of each committee or WUA. Where they do work, access to WSS has improved considerably for their users, though not all of the schemes have succeeded in enhancing poor people's citizen status.

Those schemes where collaboration with and support from government authorities is minimal and the community largely steps in to compensate for the limited capacity of the state show no evidence of increased recognition of those hitherto neglected by the formal WSS system (Allen 2012). Conversely, examples where there is significant collaboration between poor communities and the authorities have led to the inclusion and representation of low-income dwellers in political processes and decision-making (Banana et al. 2015). Nevertheless, most schemes are not fully inclusive. Limited availability of funding and scarcity of available land to install the necessary infrastructure, such as boreholes and water distribution points, is one of the factors that influences the location of WSS schemes and has led to an uneven supply of facilities in beneficiary settlements. In the case of co-produced sanitation provision like the simplified sewerage project, beneficiaries tend to be homeowners and landlords with a slightly better income or access to microcredit and tenants are likely to be disadvantaged unless they have developed a good relationship with their landlord (Hofmann forthcoming). What is more, the fact that most of the community-managed water supply systems rely on unregulated groundwater abstraction puts a strain on the water source and jeopardises the long-term use and replicability of such schemes.

Cochabamba: grades of state-community service co-production

Cochabamba is a city of just under a million people, but it gained its international notoriety when irrigator communities, communal urban drinking water providers and local citizens organised to overturn the concession awarded to the Bechtel-led Aguas Tunari concession in 2001 (see Aguilar 2008; Perreault 2005; Olivera and Lewis 2004). The uprising served to further legitimise the role of 'informal' community water providers in the eyes of the state, and also attracted financial support from national and international NGOs. The public utility has been plagued by institutional challenges, lack of investment

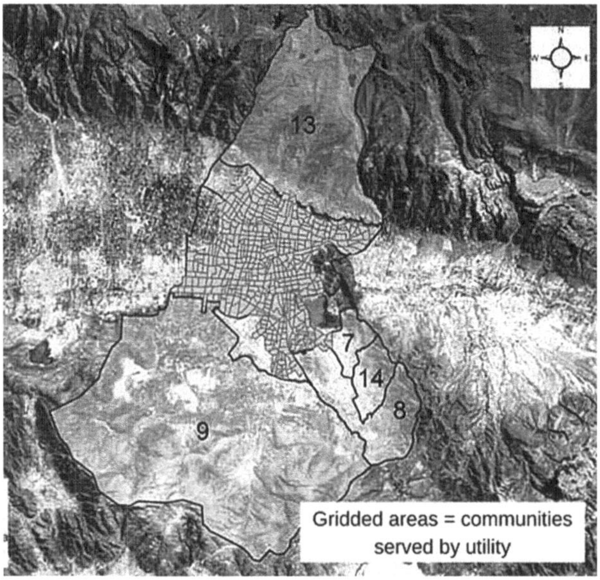

Map 3. Limits of Cochabamba city, surrounded by the Metropolitan area (east and west), and highlights its outskirts (districts 7, 8, 9, 13 and 14), which are not covered by the public network (gridded area). Adapted from Ledo, C. (2005), Pobreza, Vulnerabilidad y Exclusión social en Bolivia, CEPLAG-UMSS, Cochabamba, Bolivia.

and water shortages. The utility relies on a few local water sources, and the system is subject to significant losses through leaks and clandestine connections (Shultz and Draper 2008). The long-awaited Misicuni dam, due to be completed in 2015, but which has been plagued by significant financial and institutional setbacks, promises to bring a more reliable water source, although this continues to be contested. The utility does not extend to the peri-urban southern Zone or *Zona Sur* of the city (districts 7, 8, 9 and 14) (Map 3). This is the poorest part of the city, which urbanised largely without formal infrastructure, and so the formal and informal communities here rely exclusively on community-led drinking water providers and water vendors (Walnycki, fieldwork notes 2011).

The state has engaged with and supported drinking water committees (DWCs) indirectly through decentralisation and reforms linked to popular participation during the 1990s (see Torrico and Walnycki 2015). More recently, support has been given through national reforms that were ushered in following the Water War, and following the election of Evo Morales which led to a constitutional commitment to universalise access under the banner of the right to water. Since 2006, there have been a range of national and local processes that have sought to consult, capacity build, fund or develop infrastructures for DWCs, as a means of improving access to water in low-income communities. This seemingly progressive approach sought to develop and incorporate informal providers in low-income settlements (see Walnycki 2013).

However, the processes by which the state has engaged with different community providers has been inconsistent. Cochabamba is often referred to as a dual city, because of the patterns of socio-economic segregation that exist, and are particularly pronounced between the centre and the southern fringes of the city. By taking a closer look at the informal water service providers that have emerged in the *Zona Sur* and the partnerships that they have

Photo 3. Carolinas – informal settlement of less than 5 years – without communal drinking water provider. Source: M.E. Torrico. Image reproduced with permission of the rights holder.

developed with the state over time, it is clear that the diverse coping mechanisms that have developed reflect high degrees of socio-economic inequality within the Zona Sur.

Levels of formality clearly relate to different coping mechanisms to access water across Cochabamba's outskirts. Formally recognised settlements can access municipal resources through the local district council (e.g. by using the *Ley* de *Participación Popular*[9]) and many use these resources to develop water services. Meanwhile, informal settlements have to manage with their own resources and/or depend on NGOs support. The path towards formalisation in some cases can be difficult, costly and slow. The poorest communities, which tend to be newly established informal communities, tend to rely on water tankers, which provide the most expensive and least reliable water source (Photo 3). It takes time to develop the communal structures to invest and build a water system, particularly in the newest barrios in the hills on the edge of the city. There are also specific resource challenges, as it is difficult to access good water sources in the area, which means that communities have to raise enough money not only to build their water networks, but to buy water in bulk.

Community water systems are prevalent in the more established communities, but they take diverse forms. A recent study from Ledo (2013) has been able to georeference around 200 independent systems in districts 7, 8, 9 and 14 of Cochabamba city. The predominant form of managing these systems is through water Committees (46%), followed by water Associations (20%), the Territorial Base Organizations (OTBs, 15%) and the Cooperatives (11%). Meanwhile, the Metropolitan Master Plan MMAYA (2013) has identified 189 small local systems managed by OTBs (23 cases), self-management (122), small cooperatives (11), private urbanisations (26) and agrarian *sindicatos*[10] (7). These diverse forms reveal a little about the sort of engagement that they may have had with the state. Community water providers linked to OTBs will have developed using decentralised development funds that are made available to communities on a per capita basis as part of the Popular Participation Law that was introduced in 1994. These funds are only accessible to formal or legal communities. Water Committees are informal community water providers, while water associations are community water providers that have applied for a license, and are thus formally recognised by the state. In principle, these organisations can receive technical and capacity building support from the state to address infrastructural deficits, capacity deficits and institutional challenges, in order to build the sustainability of these water providers. There have also been a series of programmes and projects that the

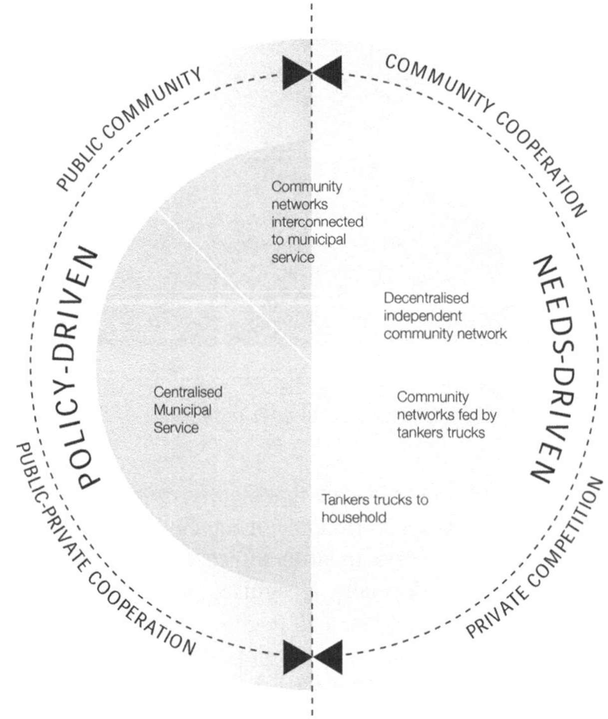

Figure 6. Policy-driven and needs-driven water practices in peri-urban Cochabamba. Source: Zegada et al. (2015). With permission of Bartlett Development Planning Unit.

state has developed since 2006 to extend infrastructure or provide funding for infrastructural development at the community level, however, they have been undermined by water shortages. Infrastructure is in place but there is no water flowing through the pipes, as communities in the Zona Sur await the completion of the controversial Misicuni project.

Figure 6 sets out the wide variety of needs-driven and policy-driven practices that can be found in this context. The only policy-driven practice in the city of Cochabamba for both drinking water and basic sanitation is the municipal service provided by Semapa, which has a coverage level of approximately 50% (a little bit more in sanitation than water).

Citizens engage in the four needs-driven practices that we have identified and sometimes more than one is practiced simultaneously. These include community systems with and without own water sources, and the provision of water through the domiciliary purchase of water from tanker trucks. In the latter case, households buy water directly from tanker truckers (private water vendors), paying an average of up to 20 USD for the first 5 cubic meters, and store the water in barrels or home storage tanks.

Meanwhile community systems can be divided in three types: those with their own water source (usually wells), those without (virtual networks) and those interconnected to the municipal system. Systems with water source are more independent, but quality of water may be low because of underground water contamination. Systems without a water source are called virtual networks: they buy water from private vendors such as tanker truckers, fill their storage tanks, and then distribute the water to households through their piped network. Management is independent, but the sourcing of water depends on private vendors (quality and prices). Another kind of systems are those interconnected to the municipal system: instead of buying from tanker trucks, the system buys water from Semapa, who delivers an amount of water to the community system that is then distributed to the beneficiaries (household connections). In Cochabamba's southern outskirts it is most common to find the first three needs-driven practices, namely: households directly buy from private water vendors, community systems with water source and systems with virtual networks. Interconnections to Semapa are not yet very widespread, although some virtual network systems are considering this option for the future, once the Misicuni project is a reality.

Navigating through non-networked trajectories

The three case studies examined reveal the multiple paths through which ordinary women and men access water in contexts where non-networked water supply is the norm, and how these trajectories might develop in the future. In all three cases, people are not only forced to rely on multiple strategies – in which access is stratified through their ability to pay – but also to approach access to basic services as a collective affair.

In the case of Kolkata, this is underpinned by a long history of cooperativism eroded in recent decades through the gradual privatisation of the bheris. This process in turn has broken previous links between common livelihoods and common settlements, as the bheris are a source of livelihoods for some, of water to others and the only treatment facility available to digest millions of gallons of waste water produced daily by the much larger population of metropolitan Kolkata. Although the latter enjoy the graceful gift of the ecological services provided by the wetlands at scale and without any cost, the understanding of this system as a common patrimony only features in the mind of a few. With the state obstructing the continuation of waste water reuse the future of EKW is in jeopardy.

In the case of Dar es Salaam collaboration between the government and low-income communities materialises in different ways, with most current schemes focusing on water supply and a few initiatives on sanitation. Existing arrangements demonstrate different ways by which communities can fill gaps where the government has limited capacity to provide a service. In Dar es Salaam, support from the utility and local government in the operation and management of water services in low-income settlements is generally in short supply. However, units like CLU have been actively engaged in establishing and testing different community-managed models and are exploring ways to replicate and scale up such initiatives using savings from the revenue collected. However, service co-production appears to be approached here as a relatively ad hoc route, with insufficient resources devoted to support community-led initiatives. The priorities of the utility are unlikely to disrupt the infrastructural archipelagos that characterise the development of Dar es Salaam, thus offering little potential for more progressive and pro-poor service governance arrangements.

In Cochabamba, efforts to institutionalise service co-production on the basis of regular cooperation between citizens and the state have been stronger than in the other two cases. There is a grey area between needs-driven and policy-driven practices. There have been specific policies and projects that have indirectly or directly provided support to community water providers over time. This has included decentralisation, which provided funds for communities to develop their water sources since 1994, and fuzzy legislative and regulatory frameworks that tolerated and sometimes sustained informal community water providers. Since 2006, the state has developed institutions and implemented projects to build capacity and regulate community water providers. This has been part of a process that gained some ground as part of reforms to realise the right to water, but which has lost steam in recent years.

While co-production mechanisms exhibit potential to bridge concerted action between the state and grassroots groups in all three cases, such arrangements are characterised by diverse water struggles and institutional trajectories. In Kolkata, co-production is rather latent in the management of waste water flows at the metropolitan scale, while at a more local scale, those settled in areas without networked infrastructure rely on precarious forms of free public provision complemented by unstable and expensive forms of informal water provision. The longstanding notion that the state should provide for basic services such as water is not enough to meet in practice the needs of peri-urban dwellers but this is not openly recognised, therefore preventing more proactive experimentation with abridged forms of state–citizen provision. In Dar es Salaam by contrast, the state and utility seem to be taking a pragmatic approach, engaging in some form of cooperation with poor communities outside the network on an ad hoc basis. Public sector involvement is largely limited to the initial stages of setting up public facilities, which are then handed over to local communities to operate. Failure to establish stronger forms of co-production partnerships affects the sustainability of many of these interventions and also limits their potential for scaling up. In Cochabamba, we witness a process towards the institutionalisation of state–citizen service co-production. However, this is not without tensions or shortcomings, as many peri-urban dwellers continue to fall through the net of ongoing initiatives.

Building meaningful and transformative alliances between low-income and politically marginalised groups and the state presents a number of challenges. As demonstrated in the Bolivian case, the process is often iterative and by no means linear. Communities might move two steps forward, only for local or national political shifts to take the relationship a step back, while nevertheless offering opportunities for low-income groups to influence service provision and policy. Meanwhile tolerance of and tokenistic support for informal service provision, reveals that often co-production operates in a latent form, whether intermittently (as seen in Dar es Salaam) or over an extended period (as in Kolkata). Latent co-production might improve people's access to services but without offering strategic scope for low-income groups to influence planning and development.

A key lesson offered from a cross-reading of these three case studies is that efforts to bridge the growing gap between everyday and large infrastructural planning that underpins peri-urbanising processes need to be fully grounded on the local and wider social, spatial and environmental relations that regulate the politics of service provision and the management of nature outside networked urban futures. Otherwise, these processes are unlikely to promote and sustain new forms of governance that can disrupt the production and reproduction of infrastructural archipelagos and the unjust trajectories that many of the peri-urban poor are subjected to.

Acknowledgements

This article draws from a collaborative research project supported by a seed-grant from the ISSC Transformations to Sustainability Programme entitled '*Translocal Learning for Water Justice*' T2S_PP_292 http://j.mp/watjust. Information about the case of Dar es Salaam also draws on the doctoral research conducted by Pascale Hofmann with support from the Engineering and Physical Sciences Research Council (EPSRC): [Grant Number EP/G037698/1.]

Disclosure statement

No potential conflict of interest was reported by the authors.

Funding

This work was supported by the International Social Science Council [T2S_PP_292] and Physical Sciences Research Council (EPSRC): [Grant Number EP/G037698/1].

Notes

1. The project is part of International Social Science Council's (ISSCs) Transformations to Sustainability Programme, which is funded by the Swedish International Development Cooperation Agency (Sida) and serves as a contribution to Future Earth. Supplementary support for seed grants is provided by the Swedish Secretariat for Environmental Earth System Sciences (SSEESS), the Netherlands Organisation for Scientific Research (NWO), the Economic and Social Research Council (ESRC) UK through the Newton Fund and the National Research Foundation of South Africa.
2. A series of interviews were conducted with officials of Kolkata Municipal Corporation (KMC) and Kolkata Municipal Water and Sanitation Agency (KMWSA) between December 2014 and February 2015 as a part of the ISSC project.
3. The core area of 12, 500 hectares was declared a Ramsar site in 2002, that is, a wetland of international importance under the Ramsar Convention, which is an international treaty to conserve and sustain the utilisation of wetlands. This happened in response to environmental activism of leading NGOs of the city and other grassroots action groups (Dembowski 2001).
4. The findings are based on fieldwork conducted in the three selected areas of East Kolkata Wetlands (EKW): Bidhannagar (ward no. 17), Bantala and Dhapa, as a part of the ISSC-funded project mentioned above.
5. In 1995, when the *Land Reforms Amendment* was passed in West Bengal, many private *bheris* were vested from their owners by the state and transferred to fishery groups and cooperatives. This led to the decline of large privately owned fisheries; though some smaller, household-managed ponds continued to exist. Some of the large fisheries also became directly acquired by the government through the State Fisheries Development Corporation.
6. The city also has over 200 DAWASCO water kiosks that are connected to the utility network, however, only a fraction of them actually provide water (EWURA 2014; Hofmann, fieldwork notes 2014).
7. The simplified sewerage scheme connects household toilets to a nearby sewerage stabilisation pond using simplified technology. The utility has been a collaborator in the setup of the system and its main responsibility now focuses on operation and maintenance of the manhole and the ponds while the community, with local NGO support, is in charge of the system until it reaches the manhole.
8. With lack of reliable data, it is difficult to quantify the number of beneficiaries for such schemes across the city. Based on estimates arrived through data collected during fieldwork for some of these schemes, a borehole system with 10–15 distribution points can serve between 200 and 400 households in addition to household connections, which can range between 60 and more than 300 per scheme (Hofmann, fieldwork notes 2014 and 2015). It is not uncommon to find more than one community-managed borehole system per settlement.
9. The Ley de Participacion Popular (Popular Participation Law) was introduced as part of a series of political and administrative decentralising reforms across Bolivia. The reforms decentralised development processes and decision-making to the local level, and provided formally recognised communities with per capita resources for upgrading (see Torrico and Walnycki 2015).
10. Agrarian Sindicatos (peasant unions) are organisational structures created after the Agrarian Reform of 1953, and constitute the maximum authority at rural community level. They are both formally recognised as a legal organisation and it usually legitimately represents the inhabitants in each community. Every person owning land in a community must affiliate to the Sindicato. Many local issues, which in many cases include local water management for irrigation and domestic purposes, are governed through the Sindicato, and it is through this organisation

that each community establishes contact with state and non-state organisations. Although Cochabamba city is a majoritarily urban space, there are still agricultural lands particularly in districts 8 and 9, where sindicatos may still persist as a communal organisational structure.

References

Aguilar, R. G. 2008. *Los ritmos del Pachakuti: Movilización y levantamiento indígena-popular en Bolivia*. Vol. 6. Buenos Aires: Tinta Limón Ed.

Allen, A. 2005. *Governance and Service Delivery in the Peri-urban Context: Towards an Analytical Framework*. London: Development Planning Unit. Unpublished paper prepared for the Research Project Service Provision Governance in the Peri-urban Interface of Metropolitan Areas.

Allen, A. 2012. "Water Provision for and by the Peri-Urban Poor: Public-Community Partnerships or Citizens Co-Production?" In *Sustainability: A Global Urban Context*, edited by I. Vojnovic, 309–340. East Lansing, MI: Michigan State University Press. http://discovery.ucl.ac.uk/1329266/

Allen, A. 2014. "Peri-Urbanization and the Political Ecology of Differential Sustainability." In *A Routledge Handbook on Cities of the Global South*, edited by S. Parnell and S. Oldfield, 522–538. London: Routledge.

Allen, A., J. D. Davila, and P. Hofmann. 2006a. *Governance of Water and Sanitation Services for the Peri-urban Poor: A Framework for Understanding and Action in Metropolitan Regions*. London: Development Planning Unit.

Allen, A., J. D. Davila, and P. Hofmann. 2006b. "The Peri-Urban Water Poor: Citizens or Consumers?" *Environment and Urbanization* 18 (2): 333–351. doi:10.1177/0956247806069608. Accessed 10 June 2013.

Andreasen, M. H., and L. Møller-Jensen. 2016. "Beyond the Networks: Self-Help Services and Post-Settlement Network Extensions in the Periphery of Dar es Salaam." *Habitat International* 53: 39–47. doi:10.1016/j.habitatint.2015.11.003.

Anon. 2011. *71- City Water-Excreta Survey 2005-06*. New Delhi: Centre for Science and Environment.

Asian Development Bank. 2012. "India: Preparing for Kolkata Environmental Improvement Project Phase II." Technical Assistance Consultant's Report. Accessed 12 November 2015. http://www.adb.org/sites/default/files/project-document/78767/42266-012-ind-tacr-01.pdf

Bakker, K. 2003. "Archipelagos and Networks: Urbanization and Water Privatization in the South." *The Geographical Journal* 169 (4): 328–341. doi:10.1111/j.0016-7398.2003.00097.x.

Banana, E., P. Chikoti, C. Harawa, G. McGranahan, D. Mitlin, S. Stephen, N. Schermbrucker, F. Shumba, and A. Walnycki. 2015. "Sharing Reflections on Inclusive Sanitation." *Environment and Urbanization* 27 (1): 19–34. doi:10.1177/0956247815569702.

Banerjee, S., and J. Chaudhuri. 2012. *Excreta Matters: 71 Cities – A Survey*. New Delhi: Centre for Science and Environment.

Boelens, R., D. Getches, and A. Guevara-Gil. 2010. *Out of the Mainstream: Water Rights, Politics and Identity*. London: Earthscan.

Bustamante, R., C. Crespo, and A. Walnycki. 2011. "Seeing Through the Concept of Water as a Human Right in Bolivia." In *The Right to Water: Politics, Governance and Social Struggles*, edited by F. Sultana and A. Loftus. London: Earthscan.

Carlisle, S. 2013. "Productive Filtration: Living System infrastructure in Calcutta." Landscape Urbanism. Accessed 15 September 2013. http://landscapeurbanism.com/article/productive-filtration-living-system-infrastructure-in-calcutta/

Congedo, L., and M. Munafò. 2014. "Urban Sprawl as a Factor of Vulnerability to Climate Change: Monitoring Land Cover Change in Dar es Salaam." In *Climate Change Vulnerability in Southern African Cities*, edited by S. Macchi and M. Tiepolo. Cham: Springer International Publishing.

Dembowski, H. 2001. *Taking the State to Court: Public Interest Litigation and the Public Sphere in Metropolitan India*. New Delhi: Asia House. Accessed 17 November 2014. https://www.asienhaus.de/public/archiv/taking_the_state_to_court.pdf

Edwards, P. 2002. "Institutional Assessment: Reviewing Policies, Processes and Stakeholder Positions at the Kolkata Peri-urban Interface." Working Paper 3. Bangkok, Thailand: Asian Institute of Technology.

EWURA. 2014. *Water Utilities Performance Review Report 2013 /2014*. Dar es Salaam: EWURA.

Ghosh, D. 1991. "Ecosystem Approach to Low-cost Sanitation in India, Where the People Know Better." Proceedings of the International Conference on Ecological Engineering for Wastewater Treatment, Sweden, March 24–28.

Ghosh, D. 1997. *Environmental Agenda for Calcutta: Conserving the Water Regime for an Ecologically Subsidized City*. Banabithi: Department of Environment and Forests, Government of West Bengal.

Government of India. 2011. "Census 2011." Ministry of Home Affairs. Accessed 12 November 2015. http://censusindia.gov.in/

Hofmann, P. forthcoming. "Multilayered Trajectories of Water and Sanitation Poverty in Dar es Salaam." In *Urban Water Trajectories*, edited by A. Allen, S. Bell, P. Hofmann, and T.-H. Teh. Cham: Springer International Publishing.

Joshi, A., and M. Moore. 2004. "Institutionalized co-production: Unorthodox public service delivery in challenging environments." *Journal of Development Studies* 40 (4): 31–49. doi:10.1080/00220380410001673184.

Kombe, W. J., T. Ndezi, and P. Hofmann. 2015. *Water Justice City Profile: Dar es Salaam, Tanzania, Translocal Learning for Water Justice: Peri-Urban Pathways in India, Tanzania and Bolivia*. London: UCL Bartlett Development Planning Unit.

Kundu, N., M. Pal, and S. Saha. 2008. "East Kolkata Wetlands: A Resource Recovery System through Productive Activities." Proceedings of Taal 2007: the 12th World Lake Conference, Jaipur, October 29–November 02, 868–881.

Ledo, C. 2005. *Pobreza, Vulnerabilidad y Exclusión social en Bolivia*. Cochabamba: CEPLAG-UMSS.

Ledo, C. 2013. *El auga nuestra de cada dia, Retos e iniciativas de una Cochabamba incluyente y solidaria*. Cochabamba, Bolivia: Universidad Mayor de San Simón.

Marshall, F., L. Waldman, H. MacGregor, L. Mehta, and P. Randhawa. 2009. "On the Edge of Sustainability: New Approaches to Peri-Urban Dynamics." STEPS Centre Working Paper 35. Accessed 26 February 2015. http://sro.sussex.ac.uk/24849/

Mehta, L., J. Allouche, A. Nicol, and A. Walnycki. 2014. "Global Environmental Justice and the Right to Water: The Case of Peri-Urban Cochabamba and Delhi." *Geoforum* 54: 158–166. doi:10.1016/j.geoforum.2013.05.014.

Mehta, L., and T. Karpouzoglou. 2015. "Limits of Policy and Planning in Peri-Urban Waterscapes: The Case of Ghaziabad, Delhi, India." *Habitat International* 48: 159–168. doi:10.1016/j.habitatint.2015.03.008.

Mitlin, D. 2008. "With and Beyond the State-co-production as a Route to Political Influence, Power and Transformation for Grassroots Organizations." *Environment and Urbanization* 20 (2): 339–360. doi:10.1177/0956247808096117.

MMAYA. 2013. *Plan Maestro Metropolitano de Agua Potable y Saneamiento del Area Metropolitano de Cochabamba*. La Paz: Ministerio de Medio Ambiente y Agua (MMAYA).

MoW. 2011. *Water Sector Development Programme 2006-2025 Programme Implementation Manual*. Dar es Salaam: The United Republic of Tanzania Ministry of Water.

Mukherjee, J. 2015a. "Beyond the Urban: Rethinking Urban Ecology Using Kolkata as a Case Study." *International Journal of Urban Sustainable Development* 7 (1): 1–16. doi:10.1080/19463138.2015.1011160.

Mukherjee, J. 2015b. "Sustainable Flows between Kolkata and its Peri-Urban Interface: Challenges and Opportunities." In *Untamed Urbanisms*, edited by A. Allen, A. Lampis, and M. Swilling. New York: Routledge.

Mukherjee, J., and A. Ghosh. 2015. *Water Justice City Profile: Kolkata, India. Translocal Learning for Water Justice: Peri-Urban Pathways in India, Tanzania and Bolivia*. London: UCL Bartlett Development Planning Unit.

Mulenga, M., and G. McGranahan. 2011. "Groundwater Self-Supply in Peri-Urban Settlements in Zambia." Paper presented at 6th Rural Water Supply Network Forum 2011, Rural Water Supply in the 21st Century: Myths of the Past, Visions for the Future, Uganda, November 29–December 01.

Nganyanyuka, K., J. Martinez, A. Wesselink, J. H. Lungo, and Y. Georgiadou. 2014. "Accessing Water Services in Dar es Salaam: Are we Counting What Counts?" *Habitat International* 44 (2014): 358–366. doi:10.1016/j.habitatint.2014.07.003.

Niyogi, S. 2015. "Man-Made Sewage Crisis Spells Doom for Kolkata Wetlands." *The Times of India*. Accessed 6 February 2015. http://timesofindia.indiatimes.com/city/kolkata/Man-made-sewage-crisis-spells-doom-for-Kolkata-wetlands/articleshow/46137442.cms

Ochoa, E., L. Soto, and P. Burt. 2011. "Organizaciones comunitarias de servicios de agua y saneamiento." In Modelos de Gobernabilidad Democrática para el Acceso al Agua en América Latina, Fundación AVINA. Accessed 23 January 2015. http://avina.net/esp/wp-con tent/uploads/2011/11/agua.pdf

Olivera, O., and T. Lewis. 2004. *Cochabamba!: Water War in Bolivia*. Boston, MA: South End Press.

Pauschert, D., K. Gronemeier, and D. Jebens. 2012. *Informal Service Providers in Tanzania: A Differentiated Perspective on Managing the Unwanted Side of Water Service Provision*. Eschborn: GIZ.

Peal, A., and S. Drabble. 2015. *Stand-Alone Unit or Mainstreamed Responsibility: How can Water Utilities Serve Low-Income Communities?* London: Water & Sanitation for the Urban Poor (WSUP).

Perreault, T. 2005. "State Restructuring and the Scale Politics of Rural Water Governance in Bolivia." *Environment and Planning A* 37 (2): 263–284. doi:10.1068/a36188.

Shultz, J., and M. Draper. 2008. *Dignity and Defiance: Stories from Bolivia's Challenge to Globalization*. Berkeley: University of California Press.

Torrico, M. E., and A. Walnycki. 2015. "¿Las Chompas en el poder? El mito de la participación en los barrios pobres de Cochabamba." *Bolivia Medio Ambiente y Urbanización* 82 (1): 81–116 (36).

URT (United Republic of Tanzania). 2012. "WSDP 8th JSM Aide Memoire." May 2012. http://www.maji.go.tz/?q=sw/filebrowser/download/93

Walnycki, A. M. 2013. "Rights on the Edge: The Right to Water and the Peri-Urban Drinking Water Committees of Cochabamba." Doctoral dissertation, University of Sussex.

Zegada, A., G. Heredia, R. Bustamante, and A. Walnycki. 2015. *Water Justice City Profile: Cochabamba, Bolivia, Translocal Learning for Water Justice: Peri-Urban Pathways in India, Tanzania and Bolivia*. London: UCL Bartlett Development Planning Unit.

When urban modernisation entails service delivery co-production: a glance from Medellin

Catalina Duque Gómez and Sylvy Jaglin

Through the example of Ciudadela Nuevo Occidente, a large social housing district in Medellín, this article describes a process that primarily involves co-learning and micro-negotiations that help produce the cognitive alignment necessary to the management of services. The hypothesis put forward in this article is that the frictions caused by the residents' difficulties in adapting to the socio-economic, cultural and cognitive frameworks of their new environment, imposed by urban modernisation running processes, engender forms of service co-production that ultimately strengthen the utility's capacity to extend and adapt its delivery model while enhancing the quality of services.

1. Introduction

The processes of urban transformation underway in the city of Medellín since the early 2000s are driving changes in ways of life and necessary adjustments to urban management. Here, we examine the rehousing of populations – often from informal districts – in apartment buildings, exploring how it puts pressure on the provision of residential services, on the nature of the relations between providers and users, and the distribution of responsibilities in the day-to-day management of the service.

Whereas the literature on networked services in cities of the South, especially in South America, has emphasised the challenges of supplying services in poor and informal – not to say illegal – neighbourhoods (Moretto 2010; Pilo' 2015; Pírez 2013) and discussed at length the effects of privatisation and liberalisation reforms (Botton 2004, 2007; De Gouvello and Fournier 2002; López Rivera 2013; Pírez 2000), this paper has a different point of view. It examines the role of residential services (water, sewerage, electricity and gas) in urban modernisation, highlighting their contribution to three processes of change: the formalisation of relations between residents and urban institutions; the extension of individual social benefits associated with homeownership in apartment buildings; and the integration of new groups of dwellers in the provision of residential services, thereby producing adjustments in their management.

The notion of co-production of urban networked services in cities of the South is often associated with different forms of partnership between state and non-state actors like CBOs and NGOs in contexts of fiscal constraints and/or weak public authorities (Allen 2013; Allen, Dávila, and Hofman 2006; Batley and Mcloughlin 2010; Jaglin 2005; Joshi and Moore 2004; Moretto 2014). Recently, it has also been associated with delivery of services by informal private providers (Ahlers et al. 2014). We argue that Medellin offers another configuration of the 'multiple facets of co-producing' (Alford 2014) under the 'classical interpretation of co-production as the involvement of individual citizens and groups in public service delivery' (Verschuere, Brandsen, and Pestoff 2012, 1086). In the case of Ciudadela Nuevo Occidente (subsequently referred to as 'Ciudadela'), a new social housing district for first-time buyers, the provision of residential services brings together residents, as direct consumers; their representatives in the condominiums (the building leaders); the municipal service operator, Empresas Públicas de Medellín (EPM); as well as the municipality (mainly through its social housing institute, ISVIMED). We use the concept of co-production to define this configuration, in which interactions between heterogeneous actors involved in the provision of service (Ostrom 1996) entail forms of coordination and processes of co-learning and micro-negotiations that help produce the cognitive alignment necessary to the management of services in social housing estates where EPM meets heterogenous public.

The focus is on those processes of interactions that produce particular service modalities: we look at the 'small' arrangements that make the service work, including for those who, otherwise, would be excluded by formal rules. This is based on the premise that 'the production of a service, as contrasted to a good, [is] difficult without the active participation of those supposedly receiving the service' (Ostrom 1996, 1079). Therefore, we understand co-production as 'an essential and inalienable core component of service delivery' (Osborne and Strokosch 2013, S32), and we analyse how it manifests in operational terms as a 'consumer co-production' according to Osborne and Strokosh's typology (2013, S37). Our approach combines three levels of analysis.

The first one focuses on the household and its living space, where residential services are a vehicle for the routinisation of 'proper' consumer's practices associated with homeownership and official connection to the municipal networks. The relationship with EPM (through individual subscription, metering and billing) is thus part of a 'regularisation' process (Pilo' 2015) through which residents and the utility jointly contribute to the advent of a 'modern' city. Co-production appears here in the way households juggle with service delivery conditions, shifting exceptional commercial measures into daily and recurrent solutions in order to cope with formal service.

The second level is the condominium. Co-production is in this case related to the distribution of responsibilities regarding fraud and payment of communal bills, leading to the gradual construction of a semiformal framework of collaboration between agents – residents, building leaders and service providers – who need to find shared collective rules, mechanisms of social control and methods of conflict settlement in the management of condominiums.

At the third level, we examine how service delivery in Ciudadela is an outcome negotiated between EPM, local institutions and the new dwellers rather than one dominated by the utility alone. This shows that, although inhabitants of social housing do not take part directly in the delivery of residential services, they contribute to it: their input is decisive to build trust and facilitate the process of cognitive alignment required for more efficient and affordable services. Even though inhabitants bear the greater part of the effort to adapt their behaviour and consumer practices, the service arrangements that really work result from a co-construction with EPM and other institutional actors, whose compromises are also necessary. More than 'technologies of government' enacted through disciplinary and regulatory devices by EPM, the co-production of services then becomes an experimental method for stabilising and regulating the techno-commercial relationship established between the utility, local housing actors and residents both as individuals (households) and collectives (condominiums).

The paper is divided into four parts. The first situates the Ciudadela district in relation to urban modernisation policies, the residential pathways of the households surveyed and the methods and theoretical framework of the argument. Each of the next three considers the arrangements for the co-production of services at a different level: the household level, the apartment building level and the social housing district. The study's main findings about the co-production of services in southern cities are summarised in the conclusion.

2. Systems of co-production and urban modernisation

Medellín attracts international attention because of the 'urban transformation' underway since the early 2000s. The municipal programmes of recent years[1] have applied a vision of the modern city based on planning urban development (control of urban sprawl, densification, regularisation of land ownership and economic activities, construction of amenities and public spaces...), restoring institutional presence in working-class neighbourhoods, involving the private sector in the making of the city and producing 'decent' living conditions for the whole population (education, health, housing, employment, transports, etc.). 'Sharing the benefits of development' and correcting a 'historical debt' to the inhabitants of working-class districts abandoned by the State are at the heart of political discourses explaining urban policies. Since the term of office of Sergio Fajardo (2004–2007) and the implementation of a communication and urban marketing strategy around the 'social urbanism model', transformations combining competitive modernisation and inclusion have become more visible and have acquired significant international recognition.[2] Physical transformation – through Proyectos Urbanos Integrales (PUI), the modernisation of transport infrastructures (Metrocables and Metroplus) and the construction of educational facilities – is to 'achieve the urban integration of neighbourhoods and increase opportunities for those who live and work there' (Dávila 2012, 12) and is recognised as a lever of social transformation (Brand 2013, 6).

2.1. Co-production: collaborative learning for urban integration

Strategic as it is, however, the material transformation of the built fabric alone is not enough to accomplish all the changes involved in the urban modernisation plan. Changes in urban ways of life, in the use of public space and in consumption practices of services are equally important, and require the support of the city's inhabitants. We focus here on inhabitants rehoused in an area of social housing condominiums. Since many come from precarious neighbourhoods where they had access to services (water, electricity) on a collective and informal basis, they face a steep learning curve on issues such as apartment life, formal homeownership and its consequences (in particular taxes and meters), the individualisation of commercial relations with the operator and the collective management of condominiums. But, even when the principle of payment and the disciplining mechanisms associated with a 'modern' urban life are not contested, a meter, a water tap or an electrical connection do not guarantee that users are able to manage the socio-technical chain that constitutes a properly operating service (Akrich 1998, 2010). In Medellin, as in many other southern cities, urban policies of modernisation targeting low- and middle-income neighbourhoods combine two components: the commodification of many urban goods and services that were previously free in informal settlements and the formalisation of citizenship. The implementation of this 'social compact' through urban networked services has been well documented (Jaglin 2005, 2014; Luque-Ayala 2016; Pilo, 2015), and studies on Colombian utilities also emphasise how they combine reforms associated with neo-liberalisation, extension of (water) supply and the modernisation pursued by urban policies (Acevedo Guerrero, Furlong, and Arias 2015; Furlong 2013; López Rivera 2013). Against this backdrop, we question how strategic policies are developed into workable actions by utilities in a social housing district in Medellin: we examine the material effects, places and modalities of EPM–dweller interactions, the content of their everyday negotiations to domesticate the conditions of service delivery, their results and limitations.

We consider the activities of both dwellers, supported by political actors, and EPM's and ISVIMED's (municipal social housing institute) staff contributing to the provision of services in social condominiums to be a form of co-production that is an unstable and pragmatic process of collaboration between heterogeneous actors. At first sight, it follows the general definition provided by Ostrom: 'By co-production, I mean the process through which inputs used to produce a good or service are contributed by individuals who are not 'in' the same organization' (1996, 1073). Under this definition, the notion covers the processes observed in Medellín but fails to describe them accurately and distinguish them from those found in other urban situations.

In the South, the concept has multiple meanings and has been associated with different policies and objectives. In the 1970s and 1980s, the co-production of services was mainly associated with a substitutive principle in which government inputs were replaced by contributions in money and in kind from communities in poor neighbourhoods. From the 1990s onwards, in the wake of the so-called privatisation reforms, co-production was conceived more as a form of cost sharing between utilities and consumers, the last being considered as active asset-holders in the service relationship. More recently, it has been suggested 'that informality in the water sector is best understood as a process of co-production' (Ahlers et al. 2014, 5), while the formalisation of hybrid delivery configurations through micro-partnerships is the route taken by many African urban authorities to 'regularise' the informal economy of services (Jaglin 2016). This background explains why the co-production of services is mainly documented in the context of urban regularisation of poor and insecure neighbourhoods (Baron and Bonnassieux 2013; Moretto 2010; Naulet, Gilquin, and Leyronas 2014). As a form of participatory engineering, it arises from a more general interest in the management of common-pool resources and services as well as in the conditions of emergence and consolidation of norms of cooperation between public operators and citizen organisations at a community scale (Ostrom 1996; Tendler 1997). Some studies highlight the political dimension of co-production (Mitlin 2008), or the spatial and political integration brought about by institutionalised co-production when it goes together with the recognition and regularisation of illegal neighbourhoods (Jaglin 2005; Moretto 2010, 2014), while others emphasise the 'subversive' power of co-production when it requires interactions which, far from being collaborative, are instead 'tense and riddled with power asymmetries and political aspirations, thereby producing uneven and highly contested water service provisioning' (Ahlers et al. 2014, 2).

The processes we describe as co-production in Medellín are taking place in a significantly different context, since service supply is almost universal and provided by a conventional operator; social condominiums surveyed are formal, and the people live there with a legal status. Co-production is therefore neither about extending incomplete and failing public provision, nor developing a participatory way of jointly producing services, let alone sharing strategic decisions with users. Nevertheless, consumers receiving services from EPM need to incorporate new rules while the utility also needs to adapt to these new consumers: in that sense, co-production refers to a process having similarities with what, for instance, Jeannot defines as a co-produced service in France, in which users are involved in the definition of the 'actual' rules that govern the service daily (Jeannot 1998). It also bears similarities with what Vershuere et al. call co-management, 'meaning that non-governmental actors have a say in the design of the service, or put time or other resources (e.g. money, skills, expertise) in the delivery of public services' (2012, 1086). In Medellin, it refers to a non-formalised (and non-institutionalised) cooperation between the residents and EPM, focusing on routine management operations (connection/disconnection, metering of consumption, billing, aftersales service) relating to the provision of individual services (at household scale) and collective services (at the scale of social condominiums). It is therefore an example of 'consumer co-production' (Osborne and Strokosch 2013), with a character that is 'undefined, informal, and renegotiated almost continuously' (Joshi and Moore 2004, 40), of which we scrutinise the retroactive learning effects both on household consumption practices and on EPM's operations, thereby adapting the service delivery scheme through modest adjustments.

The hypothesis put forward in this article is that the frictions caused by the residents' difficulty in adapting to the socio-economic, cultural and cognitive frameworks that constitute the urban modernisation project engender forms of service co-production that ultimately strengthen the utility's capacity to extend and adapt its delivery model while enhancing the quality of services, which is one outcome identified in the literature (Duque Gómez 2015; Verschuere, Brandsen, and Pestoff 2012). However, our surveys do not show other expected outcomes often outlined in literatures situating 'co-production as a normative alternative to prevailing funding or structural models used to deliver public service' (Osborne and Strokosch 2013, S33). In the social condominiums surveyed, co-production is neither something claimed by the residents nor sought by the operator; it is rather a pragmatic outcome of learning to negotiate the sharp edges of a mutual adaptation. Transforming the model of supply and placing the inhabitants at the heart of a more democratic decision-making process are not expressed in explicit requests. As in other cities of the South (Criqui 2015; Pilo' 2015), households' consent to EPM model is primarily an expression of their will to participate in a threefold movement: of formalisation (of residential statuses and modes of access to services), of extension of individual social benefits associated with homeownership and of urban integration through the regularisation of service delivery (Jaglin 2016). Co-production is thus driven by a mutual desire for the gradual establishment of rules that maintain long-term service delivery in a context where the users and the provider do not, in principle, share the same technical culture or the same representations of urban 'modernity'.

Under this definition, the co-production of services fits within a particular temporal scheme: associated with regularisation processes, it tends to not only regress to 'lighter' forms as inhabitants get used to the urban norm of modernity, but also re-emerge in the event of sudden changes in services (new technical systems, change of operator, institutional reforms. . .) or in the conditions of residents (rehousing, impoverishment. . .). The formal and norm-based framework of service supply in Ciudadela requires a two-way domestication process that is neither smooth nor instantaneous, and co-production supports this transition: it is neither an end in itself nor an idealised issue of participation or 'empowerment'. Its purpose is collaborative learning and the marginal adjustment of shared and acceptable rules for the day-to-day management of services in social condominiums. Coupled with and subordinate to the urban modernisation project, the purpose of co-production is less to promote participatory democracy than to boost the effectiveness of public services and facilitate the urban integration of a heterogeneous citizenry.

2.2. Ciudadela Nuevo Occidente: our fieldwork location

The construction of Ciudadela Nuevo Occidente goes back to the early 2000s, with the Plan Parcial Pajarito project (2002, reviewed in 2012), which plans the development of one of the last remaining areas of unbuilt land on the north-western side of Medellín. This former rural area was earmarked for social housing in order to remedy a significant housing shortage[3] going back several decades and exacerbated by the need to rehouse some of the inhabitants of districts where urban and infrastructure projects had been carried out as part of the 'transformation' of the city. This sector, built on the model of big apartment building estates for first-time buyers, is ultimately intended to house between 110,000 and 150,000 people[4] (Plan Parcial Pajarito, 2012). It accounts for a significant proportion of local housing policy implementations and of the national policy for '100,000 free homes'.[5] The first dwellings were delivered in 2006, and construction work is still in progress.[6] This sector is divided into 18 sets of tower blocks (*urbanizaciones*), each containing between 42 and 86 apartments, generally seven floors in height.

The residential services in these buildings are provided by the EPM, the municipal multi-utility firm (water, sewerage, electricity, gas and telecoms (through its subsidiary company UNE)) and the main service provider in the metropolitan region. It transfers to the municipality (its sole owner) at least 30% of its annual benefits, allocated to social investment programmes (public amenities, educational and health programmes, etc.). Medellin's mayor presides the company's board and chooses the board's members and the company's CEO.

The apartments, measuring 42–45 m^2, are delivered with the necessary installations for all residential services: water, sewerage, gas, telephone and Internet. However, only water, sewerage and electricity connections are active when the apartment is delivered, with the connection costs being included in total construction costs. The gas installation is in place, but households have to pay the connection costs directly to the supplier (financed over 36 or 48 months) if they wish to activate the service. The same is true for telecommunications. In addition, the social housing blocks also receive bills for drinking water, sewerage and electricity services for consumption in the communal areas.[7]

While the construction of this district represents a pragmatic response to housing shortage, it has multiple consequences for the households and institutions involved in its day-to-day management. For the former, the sense of security linked with homeownership is quickly counterbalanced by a sense of geographical exclusion and isolation, reinforced by the lack of amenities, shops and job opportunities. In response, many households have converted part of their apartments into moneymaking premises (workshop, mini market, hairdresser, bar, recycling material storage, etc.). This 'informality' is one of a series of learning processes through which households adjust income to expenditure in this new environment, their consumption practices and billing in 'modern' dwellings, interactions with neighbours, in the quest for temporary or more lasting solutions. For the later, we could at least name two main consequences. The first one is having to manage an ex-centred[8] and highly dense area, with important needs in terms of urban amenities (education, health, transports, economic activities, etc.) that were insufficiently taken into consideration by the urban project and its building schedule (not enough classrooms were ready on time, health facilities were constructed 8 years after the first apartments were delivered). The second one is having to face conflicts related to the transposition of the co-ownership legal frame to an inexperienced and not always consenting community. This has a direct impact on service delivery, as it will be developed further.

There are two mechanisms by which households move to Ciudadela[9]: one is by rehousing after expropriation associated with an urban development operation (22% of the households interviewed) or a de-urbanisation of high-risk areas[10] (15% of the households interviewed); the other by allocation to housing benefit recipients who have signed up with family service funds (19% of the households interviewed) or as beneficiaries of local and national social programmes (44% of the households interviewed) for low-income households[11] or households classified as displaced by armed conflict. These different residential pathways have implications for the way households appropriate their homes and their new living environment: among the relocated populations, some have to face paying bills for residential services for the first time; almost all the inhabitants 'discover' the constraints of apartment life (limited space, proximity of neighbours, impossibility of changing accommodation conditions) and the obligations associated with the status of owner and co-owner, which include paying the bills for the communal areas of the building.

2.3. Study methodology

In a city where access to services is almost universal according to local statistics (Encuesta de Calidad de Vida 2013), and where service delivery is based on a highly stabilised commercial and legal model, the case of Ciudadela allows us to analyse how substantial changes on living conditions affect this apparent stability. The field study[12] sought to identify and analyse the processes contributing to the different levels of adjustment needed to reconcile individual situations (material, financial, cognitive and cultural) with the objectives of the political modernisation project, for which service delivery plays an important role. To do this, we chose to observe the difficulties, tensions and conflicts encountered by households in their use of residential services after settlement in a social housing apartment, with attention to three levels: the domestic residential unit, the condominium, the service operator EPM.

The household surveys required a particular approach.[13] Contact was first established with activist community leaders working to draw the authorities' attention to the situation in Ciudadela. They enabled us to attend internal meetings among building leaders, meetings with institutional representatives and a variety of meetings between inhabitants. These meetings were essential to understanding the problems facing the inhabitants and institutions, and to observing some of the processes adopted to try to develop appropriate solutions. Semi-directive interviews with building leaders (12) and households (27) were then employed to explore the individual and collective experiences of these adaptation processes. Institutional interviews with town hall officials and employees of the service provider (EPM) rounded off these approaches, by soliciting the views of the institutional actors.

3. Residential services: learning about 'regular' urban life while juggling with commercial measures

> The services are very important, because no one can live without water, and in any case if you let the bills accumulate, you have to pay interest and penalties! It's only now that I realise that it is very important to pay for the services. It was starting to be counter-productive, because since we didn't have individual bills I almost wasn't given an apartment. [...] [At the time of

> rehousing] they [the municipality] stopped paying the rent for people who had never paid for their services and had had their services cut off, and they were not allocated a home. In any case, we have to pay, because if no one pays the company won't be able to operate anymore and we'll find ourselves without a service provider! [...] there are a lot of people who have left here, who have abandoned their apartment and put it up for rent, because they didn't have the means to pay. EPM sent somebody to educate people, because they have a lot of problems paying. (Female resident of El Tirol, rehoused from Sinaï, interviewed in May 2013)

Service delivery in Ciudadela entails three relative novelties for households: connection, along with metered payment; new, less subsidised prices; and a bigger range of services included in the residential package. In this part, we examine how households adapt their practices to their new living conditions through a learning process that supposes their capacity to understand and make their service delivery rules. This results in a first type of co-production that relates to the bypass of commercial rules, and results in the perpetuation and normalisation of 'specific' or 'exceptional' measures.

3.1. *Facing conventional multiservice delivery: a learning process*

Households have experienced different kinds of access to services before coming to Ciudadela: from self-built networks to conventional connections, including along the way nonconventional systems such as *pilas públicas*[14] or 'community aqueducts' (Table 1). The move to Ciudadela represented for some of them a 'forced' shift from informal to conventional access, leading to new types of relations with service consumption and with the provider. One former inhabitant of the informal district of Vallejuelos, who lives on the Las Flores estate (interviewed in April 2013), gave us her account of the change: 'I wasn't used to paying! It was at an [information] meeting that they told us that here we have to respond responsibly, it's not like where we used to live.' This means learning to manage money differently:

> We knew that for the services, we would have to pay, that it's not like at Oasis. [...] I have paid the bills with the money I won playing 'chance' [lottery] and by selling a piece of jewellery. I pay for the services even if I have to go hungry. I keep my money for the services, my daughter gives me some to pay for groceries. (Residents of La Cascada, a household relocated from El Oasis, Moravia. Interviewed in April 2013)

Furthermore, being billed for actual consumption is also a novelty for half the households interviewed (52%).

Table 1. Ciudadela: regularisation and uniformisation of residential connections.

	Type of connection in previous dwelling					Connection in Ciudadela
	Informal	*Pila pública*	Conventional	Shared conventional	None	Conventional
Electricity	5	6	12	4	0	27
Water	9	3	11	4	0	27
Gas	0	0	6	0	21	27
Telephone	0	0	16	0	11	26
Internet	0	0	2	0	25	15

> In Moravia, EPM made us pay a flat fee and not for actual consumption. What we were interested in was the average and the flat fee, not our consumption. EPM would come and count how many people lived in the house, and charged us on that basis. That way, we had no disconnection problems [service suspended for non-payment]. But here we know that we have to find the money to pay for the services. We have to do everything we can, but it's more difficult because it's more expensive. (Residents of La Huerta, former inhabitants of El Morro, Moravia, Interviewed in May 2013)

In addition to this, households have to manage a broadening of the range of residential services (provided by a single company and generally combined in a single bill, except for telecommunications) and cope with the reduction in subsidies, which are based on the socio-economic strata system. This system classifies housing into six categories (strata), according to the physical characteristics of the building (materials, communal spaces) and the neighbourhood (infrastructures and urban amenities). Roughly, as shown in Table 2, households living in strata 1 to 3 housing beneficiate from subsidies, applied in the form of discounts on the basic prices below the 'subsistence consumption' threshold defined by the government. In contrast, households living in strata 5 and 6 pay a surcharge on the real price for their whole consumption that goes into the equalisation funds.

Because the physical conditions of the accommodation and facilities in Ciudadela are better than those in their previous location, 52% of the households interviewed undergo a 'level increase'. While most of the households interviewed expressed a wish to keep up-to-date with their bill payments, they also described the problems: according to the accounts given, 63% of the households had encountered payment difficulties since settling in Ciudadela and had been obliged to pay late, to put off other spending or to borrow money, whereas only a third had experienced similar difficulties in their previous accommodation.

This broad spectrum of services and 'regrading' contribute to households' greater expenditure, at a time when they have to assume higher costs on housing (home loans[15] and property taxes), and household revenues and benefits are falling (lack of local economic tissue, the need to use transportation to find an economic activity). If households claim their willingness to respect these new service delivery conditions, this doesn't happen submissively. As we will see it on the following sections, households go through a process of individual appropriation of commercial conditions.

Table 2. Subsidies for residential services based on socio-economic strata.

	Electricity*	Water and sewerage**	Gas**
Strata 1	−60%	−60%	−50% *
Strata 2	−50%	−40%	−37% *
Strata 3	−15%	−15%	Real price
Strata 4	Real price	Real price	Real price
Strata 5	+20%	+50%	+20%
Strata 6	+20%	+60%	+20%

Note: Subsidy in the form of a discount on the real price up to a basic consumption threshold of 130 kWh for electricity and 20 m^3 for water and gas. Consumption above this threshold is billed at the real price.
+ Contribution, a surcharge on the real price that goes into the equalisation funds that finance the subsidies.
* No fixed charge.
** Subsidy set by the municipal councils, can vary from year to year. Water and gas price rates applied by EPM for the city of Medellín in February 2015.

3.2. From exceptional measures to day-to-day commercial arrangements: a first level of co-production

In order to face these changes and to meet their obligations as clients (i.e. paying their bills), households have to understand the rules imposed by the EPM. A learning process takes place through experimentation and experience transfer between neighbours. This process allows households to balance service delivery rules with their own needs and constraints, making some exceptional measures become routine, which we claim is a way of co-production. Our investigations identified two main categories.

In the first, households aim to regain their capacity to make their own choices and designate their spending priorities, as they (do their best to) continue to meet their paying obligations. In a context where connection to all services is imposed, households introduce priorities and selective connection/disconnection practices. Some choose to cancel service supply contracts or to let the service they consider less essential be ‘cut off’, sometimes letting the arrears build up until they are disconnected (after two consecutive unpaid bills). This is mainly true for telecommunications services and gas, which are seen as low priority.

In the second, households seek to manage their budget, adopting their own paying rhythm, coping with deadlines and other commercial measures. In order to meet their needs (groceries, housing, transport, education,...) and ensure their capacity to pay their bills, households learn to juggle with payment deadlines. This allows them to report expenditures from one month to the other, according to their priorities. So we find that 41% of the households interviewed build up two months of arrears,[16] during which they focus on other spending, even if it means having to make an additional effort to pay off their debt. Similarly, 41% pay a few days late, often when they receive the second monthly wage, with the penalty of paying interest on the arrears.[17] Some households, however, use non-payment to apply for a prepay electricity meter.[18] Households see prepay meters as a way to control their spending and make their money go further. These attempts are not always successful but, even when they end in a return to informal connection, they reflect an underlying wish to become part of the norm, at least in the first instance.

These juggling acts show that household budgets are under pressure and that paying for services gives rise to various tactics for bypassing the commercial rules, depending on how they are understood by households. The households in Ciudadela therefore demonstrate a gradual and pragmatic adaptation to their new living environment, and to the new rules that regulate it. One main conclusion can be made so far: co-production is related to a reciprocal learning process, by which households acquire knowledge to control and prioritise EPM’s service delivery rules. In doing so, they are not directly involved in the delivery of the services, but they contribute to creating the conditions for it.

4. Learning about co-ownership and communal services in condominiums

The second level we have analysed is the condominium, where co-production leads to collective arrangements about the distribution of responsibilities related to service delivery in communal areas. When they become owners of their apartments, households also become co-owners of a building, something none of the households in the sample had previously experienced. Despite the information given by the Medellín Housing Institute (ISVIMED) and the family welfare funds during the housing allocation procedure, many households were not given sufficient information and did not understand their collective obligations as co-owners.[19] For them, the urban regularisation embodied in the move to Ciudadela very quickly led to inflated new obligations and expenditure, which included paying the bills for water, sewerage and electricity for the communal areas, as well as the building maintenance costs.

The new residents are therefore required to assume collective responsibilities that demand a preliminary understanding of the collective issues and a minimum of consensus around shared rules of occupancy and management for communal areas and assets. Co-owners are supposed to build an administrative structure to cope with these new responsibilities. Certain residents, the so-called 'building leaders',[20] have become dominant in condominium management, while in a few buildings, 'manager teams' have formed and shared out the roles: budget management and payments, resolution of conflicts between neighbours and monitoring of compliance with the building rules (*convivencia* committee) and building maintenance (cleaning, repairs, improvements). In some cases, the building leaders are compensated, but most work free of charge, except for certain activities such as cleaning. With very limited management skills, they are the main agents in the construction of collective norms and the primary interlocutors with the institutions. Some of them have approached the *Comités de Desarrollo y de Control Social de los Servicios Públicos Domiciliarios* (utility service users' associations), which insure a legal and political support to their demands. These associations are directly or more discreetly linked to political parties, and are main bodies for democratic control over EPM. Service billing for communal areas (corridors, stairwells, technical equipment) exposes the building leaders and co-owners to complex situations: refusal to pay collective service charges, wire-tapping of the electrical connections in the communal areas and meter fiddling. These situations play an essential role in the collective learning of condominium management and co-production of service under specific conditions of sharing responsibilities between co-owners, EPM and local authorities. Below, we describe two situations that illustrate how these tensions and the negotiations and adjustments to which they give rise contribute to the co-production of a more suitable supply of services in collective areas. We will focus on two types of situations regularly handled by the utility in traditional (non-collective housing) districts: tapping and unpaid bills.

4.1. Facing disconnection: social outsourcing or co-responsibility?

As we saw earlier, households have to assume higher charges once they arrive in Ciudadela, leading for some to unpaid bills and service disconnection. Whereas informal reconnection is common in the traditional neighbourhoods (townhouses; small, self-build apartment buildings) and is considered as part of the utility's 'commercial losses', it becomes a sensitive matter in Ciudadela since in social housing buildings these fiddles have an impact on collective costs.

Urban planning standards and the architecture of collective housing provide less opportunity for fiddling. For example, the power poles are not near the apartments, the water pipes are buried and it would be a considerable feat to route a wire or a pipe to the fourth floor illegally without being noticed. The solutions are of two types: fiddling the meters (reopening the valve, 'turning back' the water meter) and direct connection to installations in the communal areas of the building. These two solutions have a direct impact on the collective billing, since a 'general meter' calculates the total amount of services supplied to the building, and the consumption from the communal areas is calculated by deducting the consumption of individual apartments. When a household 'turns back' the water meter, for example, their consumption is not measured by their individual meter, and is therefore reported as part of the communal areas' consumption. Co-owners have to deal with these temporary or semi-temporary fixes put up by households that have been disconnected for non-payment or that try to reduce the amount they pay by tapping on communal areas' connections.

While there are moralistic responses to reconnections or connections to the communal areas, there is also a general awareness of the social difficulties of many families. One woman resident of Chagualón explains that 'there are people who previously paid 5000 pesos for a fraud, but now have to pay bills of 80,000 pesos per month and communal charges. Some of them cannot afford all those expenses' (inhabitant of Chagualón, former resident of Las Margaritas, interviewed in March 2013). In the same way that, according to the accounts given, EPM shows (temporary) tolerance regarding informal connections in certain parts of the city, there are cases where connection to the communal areas is tolerated by the co-owners for households in particularly difficult circumstances, after a death or in the case of single-parent families. This tolerance, always temporary, depends on the building leader's capacity to arouse solidarity between neighbours. It can also be allowed in return for services such as cleaning the building.

These situations can be understood as a form of social outsourcing, where co-owners face a collective action problem to deal locally with disconnections and illegal connections while, in other housing contexts, they would be considered to be part of EPM's commercial responsibilities. Co-owners become an 'external manager' for EPM, controlling and informing on tapping, and assuming the financial consequences.

4.2. Negotiating a 'payment culture' with or without legal condominium associations

According to a former official at Gerencia de Ciudadela (interviewed in January 2012), 80% of conflicts between neighbours are associated with the payment of electricity, water and sewage bills for the communal areas. In some buildings, unpaid communal bills summed up quite high, as is the case with one building in La Cascada where the debt for water bills reached 13 million pesos (leaders' meeting, January 2013). Co-owners' resistance to pay collective bills is based on a mix of mistrust and misunderstanding, as is illustrated by this leader comment: There are people who say that they are not going to pay the communal service charge, because in any case if they lose [the apartment] it doesn't matter, since in any case it didn't belong to them before, and they can move back into a shack. (Building leader, La Cascada, interviewed in April 2013)

In response, the building leaders develop different strategies aiming to promote what they call a 'payment culture': displaying the name of the non-paying household and the amount owed at the entrance to the building, cutting off the electricity or water service to the whole building to put collective pressure on bad payers, exclusion of households from activities such as Christmas parties or building improvements, etc. These social control tactics are partly inspired by the spread of examples from middle-class and wealthy buildings, which the building leaders have access to not only via their personal or professional networks, but also by EPM's commercial practices.

While co-owners struggle to recover unpaid contributions for collective bills, contributions for collective bills, leaders, EPM and ISVIMED agreed after long discussions to "individualise" them, meaning that EPM includes into the individual bill for an apartment a part of the collective bill corresponding to the consumption in the communal areas.[21] There are, however, two prerequisites for the adoption of this system: the negotiation of the debt with EPM and the creation of a legal condominium association. Such an association is needed for legal pathways to be employed in the event of disputes among co-owners as well as between co-owners and other entities, such as builders or service providers, but not all co-owners agree to create the legal figure.

Individualisation provides a certain degree of 'comfort' for the building leaders and offers a guarantee of collection for EPM, since the households cannot separate the two bills. Nonetheless, not all the building leaders and residents agree on this. Some express a certain mistrust of the billing mechanisms and believe that individualisation limits their collective capacity to monitor consumption and the amounts billed. They explain that it is only when they receive bills for the communal areas that they can identify any variation in consumption, which may be explained by an informal connection in the corridors or other problems. When the amount billed is divided by 80 apartments, this usually represents slightly under 1000 pesos, an amount that is usually invisible to households, particularly because of fluctuations in service tariffs.

It is therefore largely through informal exchanges between the building leaders that learning takes place, that 'good practices' circulate, that problems and their solutions are discussed and management skills gradually developed. During discussions between the building leaders, sometimes very heated debates take shape around subjects such as the payment of utility bills or the assignment of responsibility for maintenance work. One of the issues that came up several times in the interviews is the following: 'given that they are the ones [the municipality, ISVIMED] who put us here and in this situation, why should it be up to us to deal with all this?' By 'all this', the leaders mean the maintenance of the buildings, the work needed to tackle their rapid deterioration, informal connections by households who cannot or will not pay for services, etc. Through these discussions, the residents question the assignment of responsibilities in urban management, challenge the legitimacy of each stakeholder role and assess their own share of work, calling on the local institutions when the task is beyond their control. The latter, in their turn, try to promote the autonomy of the inhabitants, which begins with the legal establishment of condominium associations. For example, in response to the deterioration of the stairways and corridor railings in a building that had been occupied for a little over six months at the time of our interview, one leader exclaimed: 'as long as we have no legal status [for the condominium] they won't do anything!' (leader of El Tirol, interviewed in April 2013). In March 2013, ISVIMED organised a one-day meeting to promote the creation of condominium associations in all the social housing buildings. The results were mixed: some buildings reached agreements with ISVIMED about repairs and agreed on the payment of their debts with EPM but others expressed 'resistance'.

5. Service delivery in social condominiums: an emerging framework resulting from collective learning

While households and co-owners gradually adapt to their new environment, the utility also adapts its professional routines and practices to the conditions of its activities in the social housing districts. At this level, however, service delivery is also affected by technical and political choices made by actors beyond EPM and households, and who include constructors, local authorities, the housing institute and civic movements. All of them play an essential role in stabilising the emergent arrangements and therefore contribute to the co-production of services by strengthening the utility's capacity to extend and adapt its delivery model while enhancing the quality of services. We will review how these other actors contribute to service co-production at the household and condominium levels.

5.1. *Towards transitional arrangements?*

In their efforts to adapt, households interact in different ways with the utility as well as other institutional players: both dialogue and conflict promote a mutual recognition, and in certain cases lead to shared innovations and reciprocal adaptations. As said earlier, households arriving in Ciudadela then face a reduction in the tariff subsidies, which are calculated according to the socio-economic strata system. This system is based on a national methodology and set of criteria that determine the buildings' classification and directly impact the bills that households have to pay for their service consumptions. This issue was a subject of discussion and negotiation at the time of the rehousing of the former residents of two informal settlements: Moravia and La Iguaná. In order to reach an agreement on the rehousing, the municipality agreed on an exceptional measure on the socio-economic strata methodology. According to this agreement, Moravia and La Iguaná former dwellers beneficiate of a level 1 strata for 10 years (Decreto n°2586 of 2013), although they live in buildings that are classified as strata 2 or 3. In this case, negotiations between local leaders and the municipality bypassed service delivery regulations, granting a special status to a group of households because of their residential past. This temporary measure smoothens the cost of households' adaptation to their new living conditions while at the same time reducing the risk of non-payment. We suggest that this example emphasises a case of co-production where users were able, through resistance and negotiations, to involve the local political authorities alongside the utility in order to deliver affordable services.

5.2. *From treating to preventing problems in condominiums' collective services*

What both co-owners and EPM have learnt in co-producing services, particularly in the communal areas of social condominiums, and the resulting arrangements have had real impacts on new housing projects. Increased coordination between the constructors, the housing institute or the family service funds (that are legally responsible for the buildings until the co-owners' association is created) and EPM has also been institutionalised.

Rising debts, residents' refusals to pay and also the involvement of political actors and consumer rights organisations have led to the opening of a dialogue between ISVIMED, EPM and the Municipality. The inhabitants' difficulties in adopting the legal framework for condominium management (Act 765 of 2001) made legal avenues difficult: in the absence of official condominium associations, many buildings have remained under the responsibility of ISVIMED, the legal holder of utility bills and unpaid bills, which in the case of water amounted to around €100,000 in 2013 (265 million pesos). In response, in 2012, ISVIMED launched the *Vecinos y amigos* programme to encourage the creation of condominium associations and provide them educational material on their rights and duties. Moreover, to convince the residents, ISVIMED also agreed that, once a condominium association was set up, the building's water bills would be definitively settled and the maintenance and repair works completed. According to the accounts of the building leaders and the *vocales* de *control*,[22] it was the pressure from EPM, in response to the unsustainable increase in debt, that led to the opening of a stable and serious dialogue between all the stakeholders.

This has resulted in concrete arrangements. Thus, apartment buildings constructed after 2013 are delivered with an 'individualised' billing system, which includes consumption for the communal areas in the individual household bills. In order to reduce the part of collective consumptions, electricity installations in communal areas have also been redesigned in some of the new buildings. For example, those in El Tirol were designed so that the corridor lighting is controlled from inside the apartments: a bulb is located opposite the entrance door of each apartment with a switch inside the home. Each household chooses to illuminate or not the corridor, reducing part of the collective billing but reinforcing individuality in the buildings' day-to-day management. Arrangements have also been made in order to protect meters from tapping.

None of these new arrangements is perfect and most have side effects, but the difficulties encountered in the years following the delivery of the first social housing buildings have served as a learning experience for adapting the conditions of service supply to the socio-economic realities of their occupants. They also highlight the long-standing ability of EPM to successfully meet and accompany urban change: with the *Habilitación Viviendas* programme in the early 1960s, the *Pilas Públicas* system in the 1980s and the prepay meters from 2007. What seems to be new in Ciudadela, compared to the company's responsiveness and capacity for innovation demonstrated in earlier experiences, is the co-production of services in which both the users and the utility agree to get involved in the name of a common vision or at least one shared 'desire' of urban modernity.

6. Conclusion

The process of urban modernisation in Medellín has given rise to numerous analyses of the physical transformations to the city (Blanco and Kobayashi 2009; Brand 2013; Dávila 2012; Echeverri Restrepo and Orsini 2012; Martin and Corrales 2009; Quinchía-Roldán 2013), but the living conditions of inhabitants rehoused into the new social housing districts and their interactions with the municipal utility are less well known. Our case study of Ciudadela Nuevo Occidente highlights both the challenges of a reciprocal 'domestication' and the extent of informal cooperation between the residents and EPM. We suggest that the resulting arrangements are a form of co-production of services supported by a dynamic of formalisation of citizenship and of regularisation of access to networks.

As stressed by Verschuere, Brandsen, and Pestoff (2012), there is still 'conceptual confusion' in studies that refer to co-production and more empirical evidence is needed. By focusing on everyday practice and experience of service delivery, we highlight and discuss in this case study three important aspects of collective action which, in our opinion, contribute to add texture to our understanding of co-producing services.

First, we find that residential services involve constant negotiations and contestation (about payment of the bill, delays, temporary informal connections, arrears, etc.) that contribute to shaping the service delivery configuration in social housing. Second, we emphasise that enforcing collective binding decisions on condominium inhabitants is not the exclusive capacity of a formal body like EPM but also rests in the hand of neighbours and building leaders who, together with the utilities' professionals and other local actors, help lay the foundation for ownership of services by residents. Third, the ordinary experience of service delivery in Ciudadela shows that cooperative arrangements between the inhabitants and the utility are temporary and that their aim is less the transformation than the regulation of service delivery configurations in social condominiums. Co-production is thus a key process through which ordinary citizens encounter the utility and progressively learn to negotiate their role and responsibilities in the service relationship.

As a process accompanying urban modernisation, co-production of services is therefore a framework to master and negotiate the pace of change and to share adaptation efforts. As such, it is more important for what it makes possible (formalisation of citizenship and regularisation of access to networks) than for what it is in itself (a mechanism of co-management, not intended to be lasting). However, since co-production is still often resisted by regular providers, public and private, the ability to interact with users in alternative ways has in itself a significant potential of institutional innovation. Finally, as shown by the detailed arrangements negotiated in Ciudadela, co-producing services also has an operational efficacity, the political implications of which should not be underestimated, since the incorporation of populations from informal neighbourhoods into the formal city is key to municipal projects of urban modernisation.

Disclosure statement

No potential conflict of interest was reported by the authors.

Funding

This work was supported by Université Paris-Est under a PhD grant (2011-2014) and the ANR project Trajectoires Energétiques dans les Régions MétrOpolitaines des Suds (TERMOS).

Notes

1. The names given to the municipal programmes since the end of the 1990s illustrate this vision: « Por una ciudad más humana » [For a more humane city] (Juan Gómez Martínez, 1998-2000), « Medellín Competitiva » (Luís Pérez, 2001-2003), « Medellín: Compromiso de toda la ciudadanía » [Medellin: The involvement of all citizens] (Sergio Fajardo, 2004-2007), « Medellín es Solidaria y Competitiva » [Medellín is community minded and competitive] (Alonso Salazar, 2008-2011), « Medellín un hogar para la vida » [Medellín, a home for life] (Anibal Gaviria, 2012-2015).
2. The city's transformation has been celebrated through different international events since 2005. It has hosted events such as the World Urban Forum (2014), the South American Olympic Games (2010) and the OAS 38th General Assembly (2008). The city has also earned various international awards such as the Innovative City of the Year (2013), the International Sustainable Transport Award (2012), UN-Habitat Scroll of Honour Award (2010), Dubai International Award for Best Practices (2008), etc.
3. The Strategic Housing Plan assessment (PEHMED 2020) estimates the shortage of dwellings at 19% and equality deficit at 10%. This plan provided for the building of 1 million new dwellings between 2005 and 2009, to offset the rise in the shortage. (Alcaldía de Medellín, Instituto Social de Vivienda y Hábitat de Medellín -ISVIMED, Universidad Nacional – Escuela del Hábitat -CEHAP, & Corporación Viva la Ciudadanía, 2011, p. 113).
4. According to Medellín municipality, there were around 46,000 inhabitants in 2014. (http://www.metrosalud.gov.co/inter/joomla/index.php/noticias/675-alcaldia-de-medellin-entrego-la-primera-fase-de-la-unidad-hospitalaria-nuevo-occidente, accessed 27 March 2015).
5. The city's housing policy, which has a target of building 15,000 dwellings per year, has been reinforced since 2012 by the national '100,000 free homes' policy, which has resulted in the building of 8489 new homes in Medellín, 30% of them in Ciudadela Nuevo Occidente (http://www.minvivienda.gov.co/sala-de-prensa/noticias/2014/junio/el-ministerio-de-vivienda-ya-termin%C3%B3-el-81-de-las-viviendas-gratis-a-entregar-en-cundinamarca, accessed 27 March 2015).
6. According to public data from the Housing Institute (ISVIMED), 2010 apartments divided into five blocks were under construction in October 2014. (http://www.isvimed.gov.co/evolucion-de-proyectos-en-construccion, accessed 27 March 2015)
7. The communal areas of the buildings consist of the entrance halls, stairways, shared corridors and service premises, which contain the water tanks and pumps for pumping water to the top floors.

8. In order to face this, the municipality created a structure called *Gerencia* de *Pajarito* (Pajarito's management unit), whose main roles are to coordinate institutional action within this area and to offer a local assistance to Ciudadela's dwellers on administrative procedures, in order to reduce their need to travel to downtown. However, this structure has not worked on a continuous way, since it is highly dependent on an unstable political will: it has been closed for long periods and the team's turnover is high.
9. There is a lack of statistical data on Ciudadela Nuevo Occidente. The 'quality of life' surveys conducted every year by Medellín Municipality include Ciudadela in the San Cristobal *corregimiento* (rural locality), making it difficult to isolate specific data for the district. In addition, since housing construction is still in progress, it is difficult to make estimates based on data for the San Cristobal sector.
10. High-risk zones are those vulnerable to geophysical threats because of their proximity to watercourses (flood risk) or unstable soil (risk of landslides). There exist different levels of risk, defined in terms of the technical and economic possibility of carrying out mitigation and prevention work. (For more information, see the thesis written by López Peláez 2008.)
11. Not exceeding the two minimum salaries, i.e. 1,232,000 pesos, around €450.
12. Fieldwork was carried out by C. Duque-Gómez as part of a thesis on urban planning. It took place in the course of two stays between December 2011 and June 2013. Thirty-nine interviews were conducted with the inhabitants of Ciudadela Nuevo Occidente and 11 with institutional, local associations and economic actors.
13. The months that preceded the first fieldwork in Ciudadela (fin 2011) were marked by the resurgence of violence between armed groups competing for the control of this territory. For reasons of safety, 'building leaders' were approached to facilitate interviews with the households. While the public order situation grew calmer in 2012, this approach based on intermediaries was maintained, in particular because of people's mistrust of outsiders. This has methodological implications and limits the representativeness of the sample. In addition, the absence of official data on the populations of Ciudadela meant that the individual situations of households were assessed on a more empirical than statistical basis.
14. Pilas públicas are group connections whereby the supplier bills households a flat fee, based on the average consumed by the same category of users. This technical system was adopted by EPM in the 1980s to provide electricity supply in areas where urban development was impossible (informal settlements, unstable ground) and where *Habilitación Viviendas* – the main service expansion policy – could not be applied.
15. The monthly amount paid by households for their apartment varies depending on the household's profile and the reasons of their arrival in Ciudadela: rehousing, beneficiaries of social national and local programmes or family service funds. We encountered difficulties to gather reliable information on households' revenues through our interviews, making it difficult to develop a thorough analysis on their financial situation and the impact of housing expenses. However, according to the interviews, we can see that, for those who go through family service funds and some beneficiaries of social housing programmes (not rehoused or displaced by armed conflict), the expenses represent in average 30% of their revenues, which vary from 80,000 pesos to 3,000,000 pesos per month (the legal minimum wage in 2013 was 589,500 pesos (306 US$). The exact amount of their monthly contribution depends on their start-up capital contribution.
16. There is a deadline for paying bills without incurring a charge, but the supply is only cut off after the second month without payment.
17. In Colombia, monthly wages are paid in two goes, 'per fortnight'. Households often spread out their main spending by, for example, allocating one 'fortnight' to rent and major shopping, and the other to bills and school fees. The households point out that one big difficulty in paying bills is that the deadline often falls between the 26th and 28th of the month, whereas wages are paid on the 1st or 15th of each month.
18. Prepay meters have been adopted by EPM in 2007 as a method of reconnecting households in default. One of the conditions required to apply for the meter is to have arrears on four consecutive bills.
19. According to the law (Act 675 of 2001), co-owners are legally responsible of condominium management. Local authorities (ISVIMED) and housing project developers withdraw from daily management once 51% of the apartments are assigned.

20. Their profiles vary from historically engaged persons that used to be active in their former neighbourhoods (through political parties, religious groups or other types of associations) to 'newcomers' that become active because they are concerned for their patrimony as owners or those who see on their engagement an opportunity to have a future income linked to the management activities. Until 2013, leaders were auto-proclaimed or designated by co-owners on an informal basis, but since March 2013 co-owners have to create a legal syndicate, whose members are elected on the annual assemblies.
21. Broadly speaking, in a building with 40 apartments where the communal areas consume 120 kWh of electricity, households are billed 3 kWh at the rate applicable to the communal areas (full price, unsubsidised), in addition to their monthly consumption. The amount equivalent to these 3 kWh is included into the sum to pay and may under no circumstances be paid separately.
22. Representatives of the Comités de Desarrollo y de Control Social de los Servicios Públicos Domiciliarios, the main bodies for democratic control over the operation and quality of service of service supply companies.

References

Acevedo Guerrero, T., K. Furlong, and J. Arias. 2015. "Complicating Neoliberalization and Decentralization: The Non-Linear Experience of Colombian Water Supply, 1909–2012." *International Journal of Water Resources Development 32* (2): 172–188. doi:10.1080/07900627.2015.1026434.

Ahlers, R., F. Cleaver, M. Rusca, and K. Schwartz. 2014. "Informal Space in the Urban Waterscape: Disaggregation and Co-Production of Water Service." *Water Alternatives* 7 (1): 1–14.

Akrich, M. 1998. "Les Utilisateurs, Acteurs De L'innovation." *Education Permanente* 1 (134): 79–90.

Akrich, M. 2010. "Comment Décrire Les Objets Techniques ?" *Techniques & Culture* (54–55): 205–219. doi:10.4000/tc.4999.

Alford, J. 2014. "The Multiple Facets of Co-Production : Building on the Work of Elinor Ostrom". *Public Management Review* 16 (3): 299–316. doi:10.1080/14719037.2013.806578.

Allen, A. 2013. "Water Provision for and by the Peri-Urban Poor. Public-Community Partnerships or Citizens Coproduction?" In *Urban Sustainability: A Global Perspective*, edited by J. Vojnovic, 309–340. East Lansing: Michigan State University Press.

Allen, A., J. Dávila, and P. Hofman. 2006. "The Peri-Urban Water Poor: Citizens or Consumers?" *Environment and Urbanization* 18 (2): 333–351. doi:10.1177/0956247806069608.

Baron, C., and A. Bonnassieux. 2013. "Gouvernance Hybride, Participation Et Accès À L'eau Potable Le Cas Des Associations D'usagers De L'eau (AUE) Au Burkina Faso." *Annales De Géographie* 693 (5): 525–548. doi:10.3917/ag.693.0525.

Batley, R., and C. Mcloughlin. 2010. "Engagement with Non-State Service Providers in Fragile States: Reconciling State-Building and Service Delivery." *Development Policy Review* 28 (2): 131–154. doi:10.1111/j.1467-7679.2010.00478.x.

Blanco, C., and H. Kobayashi. 2009. "Urban Transformation in Slum Districts through Public Space Generation and Cable Transportation at Northeastern Area: Medellin, Colombia." *Journal of International Social Research* 2 (8): 75–90.

Botton, S. 2004. "Les 'Débranchés' Des Réseaux Urbains D'eau Et D'électricité À Buenos Aires: Opportunité Commerciale Ou Risque Pour Les Opérateurs?" *Flux* 2–3 (56–57): 27–43.

Botton, S. 2007. *La Multinationale Et Le Bidonville: Privatisations Et Pauvreté À Buenos Aires*. Paris: Karthala Editions.

Brand, P. 2013. "Governing Inequality in the South through the Barcelona Model: 'Social Urbanism' in Medellín, Colombia." Presented at the "Interrogating Urban Crisis Governance Contestation and Critique" conference, De Montfort University, Leicester, September 9. http://www.dmu.ac.uk/about-dmu/schools-and-departments/leicester-business-school/politics-and-public-policy/finalconferencepapers.aspx

Criqui, L. 2015. "Infrastructure Urbanism: Roadmaps for Servicing Unplanned Urbanisation in Emerging Cities." *Habitat International* 47 (93): 93–102. doi:10.1016/j.habitatint.2015.01.015.

Dávila, J., ed. 2012. *Movilidad Urbana Y Pobreza: Aprendizajes De Medellín Y Soacha, Colombia*. London: Development Planning Unit, UCL and Universidad Nacional de Colombia.

De Gouvello, B., and J.-M. Fournier. 2002. "Résistances Locales Aux 'Privatisations' Des Services De L'eau : Les Cas De Tucuman (Argentine) Et Cochabamba (Bolivie)." *Autrepart* 21 (1): 69. doi:10.3917/autr.021.0069.

Duque Gómez, C. 2015. "L'accès Pérenne À L'électricité À Nairobi. Diversité D'expériences Et Tensions Sur Le Réseau." In *Sociologie De L'énergie – Gouvernance Et Pratiques Sociales*, edited by M.-C. Zélem et C. Beslay, 73–81. Paris: CNRS Editions.

Echeverri Restrepo, A., and F. M. Orsini. 2012. "Informality and Social Urbanism in Medellín." In *Medellín Environment Urbanism Society*, edited by M. Hermelin, A. E. Restrepo, and J. G. Ramírez, 132–156. Medellín: Universidad EAFIT, Centro de Estudios Urbanos y Ambientales - URBAM.

Furlong, K. 2013. "The Dialectics of Equity: Consumer Citizenship and the Extension of Water Supply in Medellín, Colombia." *Annals of the Association of American Geographers* 103 (5): 1176–1192. doi:10.1080/00045608.2013.782599.

Jaglin, S. 2005. *Services D'eau En Afrique Subsaharienne : La Fragmentation Urbaine En Question*. Paris: CNRS Éditions.

Jaglin, S. 2014. "Regulating Service Delivery in Southern Cities: Rethinking Urban Heterogeneity." In *A Routledge Handbook on Cities of the Global South*, edited by S. Parnell and S. Oldfield, 434–447. London: Routledge.

Jaglin, S. 2016. "Is the Network Challenged by the Pragmatic Turn in African Cities? Urban Transition and Hybrid Delivery Configurations." In *Beyond the Networked City. Infrastructure Reconfigurations and Urban Change in the North and South*, edited by O. Coutard and J. Rutherford, 182–203. London: Routledge.

Jeannot, G. 1998. "Les Usagers Du Service Public." Puf, QSJ? n° 3359, Paris.

Joshi, A., and M. Moore. 2004. "Institutionalised Co-production: Unorthodox Public Service Delivery in Challenging Environments." *The Journal of Development Studies* 40 (4): 31–49. doi:10.1080/0022038042000213184.

López Peláez, J. 2008. La *construction sociale* du *risque* à *Medellin (Colombie): gouvernance locale et representations*. PhD diss., École des Hautes Études en Sciences Sociales, Paris.

López Rivera, D. M. 2013. "Flows of Water, Flows of Capital: Neoliberalization and Inequalities in Medellin's Urban Waterscape." *desiguALdades.net Working Pa*per *Series*, 38. http://www.desigualdades.net/Resources/Working_Paper/38_WP_Lopez_Online.pdf

Luque-Ayala, A. 2016. "From Consumers to Customers: Regularizing Electricity Networks in São Paulo's Favelas." In *Retrofitting Cities: Priorities, Governance and Experimentation*, edited by M. Hodson and S. Marvin, 171–192. Abingdon: Routledge.

Martin, G., and D. Corrales. 2009. *Medellín Transformación De Una Ciudad. Modelo De Bueno Gobierno Y Desarrollo Social Integral*. Medellín: Alcaldia de Medellin, Banco Interamericano de Desarrollo. http://fr.scribd.com/doc/31891665/Libro-Transformacion-Ciudad-de-Medellin

Mitlin, D. 2008. "With and beyond the State – Co-Production as a Route to Political Influence, Power and Transformation for Grassroots Organizations." *Environment and Urbanization* 20 (2): 339–360. doi:10.1177/0956247808096117.

Moretto, L. 2010. "Co-Production Du Service D'eau Et Recomposition De L'espace Intra-Urbain Dans La Périphérie Sud De Caracas." *Espaces Et Sociétés* 143 (3): 81–99. doi:10.3917/esp.143.0081.

Moretto, L. 2014. *Assessing Urban Governance: The Case of Water Service Co-production in Venezuela*. Brussels: P.I.E. Peter Lang.

Naulet, F., C. Gilquin, and S. Leyronas. 2014. "Eau Potable Et Assainissement Dans Les Villes Du Sud : La Difficile Intégration Des Quartiers Défavorisés Aux Politiques Urbaines." In *Débats Et Controverses*. Vol. 8. Paris: GRET and AFD. http://www.gret.org/publication/eau-potable-et-assainissement-dans-les-villes-du-sud-la-difficile-integration-des-quartiers-defavorises-aux-politiques-urbaines/

Osborne, S. P., and K. Strokosch. 2013. "It takes Two to Tango? Understanding the Co-production of Public Services by Integrating the Services Management and Public Administration Perspectives." *British Journal of Management* 24: S31–47. doi:10.1111/bjom.2013.24.issue-s1.

Ostrom, E. 1996. "Crossing the Great Divide: Co-Production, Synergy, and Development." *World Development* 24 (6): 1073–1087. doi:10.1016/0305-750X(96)00023-X.

Pilo', F. 2015. La *régularisation* des *favelas par l'électricité. Un service entre Etat, marché et citoyenneté*. PhD diss., Université Paris -Est, ENPC, Marne la Vallée.

Pírez, P. 2000. "Servicios Urbanos Y Equidad En América Latina: Un Panorama Con Base En Algunos Casos." In *Serie Medio Ambiente y Desarrollo*. Vol. 26. Santiago de Chile: CEPAL. http://archivo.cepal.org/pdfs/2000/S00090784.pdf

Pírez, P. 2013. "Los Servicios Urbanos En América Latina." In *Vol. 2 of Teorías Sobre La Ciudad En América Latina*, edited by B. Rebeca and E. Pradilla, 455–504. Mexico: Universidad Autónoma Metropolitana. http://www.ungs.edu.ar/catedrasur/?page_id=30

Quinchía-Roldán, S. M. 2013. "Discurso Y Producción De Ciudad: Un Acercamiento Al Modelo De Urbanismo Social En Medellín, Colombia." *Cuadernos De Vivienda Y Urbanismo* 6 (11): 122–139.

Tendler, J. 1997. *Good Government in the Tropics*. Baltimore: Johns Hopkins University Press.

Verschuere, B., T. Brandsen, and V. Pestoff. 2012. "Co-production: The State of the Art in Research and the Future Agenda." *Voluntas* 23 (4): 1083–1101. doi:10.1007/s11266-012-9307-8.

Between coproduction and commons: understanding initiatives to reclaim urban energy provision in Berlin and Hamburg

Sören Becker, Matthias Naumann and Timothy Moss

This article explores new geographies of coproduction emerging in urban energy politics. It analyses processes of remunicipalisation of urban utilities, involving the re-establishment of public ownership with a strong democratic and ecological agenda for governing energy infrastructures, with case studies of the German cities of Berlin and Hamburg. Seeking ways of understanding these developments which transcend conventional binaries, such as public vs. private ownership or consumer vs. producer, we interpret them in relation to debates first about coproduction and then about urban commons. This latter concept, we argue, provides deeper analytical purchase on new grassroots energy initiatives and the politics that unfold in remunicipalisation conflicts, offering a new avenue for enriching research on the coproduction of energy.

1. Introduction

The rise of renewable energies not only represents a technological shift to smaller-scale generation facilities, but also involves new actors beyond energy corporations that engage in electricity or heat generation and thus become coproducers of energy services. In many European countries, among them Denmark, Germany and the Netherlands, the energy transition has resulted in a reshuffling of market shares, bringing to the fore a more dispersed actor constellation of municipal, cooperative or citizen-led initiatives involved in energy production (Hisschemöller and Sioziou 2013; Nielsen and Jørgensen 2015; Yildiz et al. 2015). Although energy corporations still retain their importance, and citizen-owned wind turbines, 'prosumer' photovoltaics and community-owned energy grids (Bruns and Ohlhorst 2011; Burger and Weinmann 2012; Jenssen, König, and Eltrop 2014) only paint part of the picture, these developments highlight the increasing involvement of new actors and new forms of governance emerging alongside new energy technologies.

This article focusses on the role of social movements in processes of remunicipalisation in the two German cities of Berlin and Hamburg. Remunicipalisation generally refers to the (re-)establishment of utilities owned, at least partly, by the local state. This involves either creating a new utility, purchasing shares of an existing one or giving concessions to existing municipal utilities (Bauer 2012, 337). Such transitions in the ownership of organisations often result in shifts in the ownership of physical infrastructure, such as plants, grids and other distribution technologies. Cases of remunicipalisation are significant as they often reverse previous privatisations in the public sector, involve new actors in public service provision and open up new governance pathways in the respective cities.

Recent studies cite some 200 such cases remunicipalisation since 2005 in the German energy sector alone (Berlo and Wagner 2013). Beyond that there are instances of remunicipalisation in the French water sector (Hall, Lobina, and Terhorst 2013), relating to electricity in the United States (Hess 2011), and in a number of countries of the Global South (McDonald and Ruiters 2012). While recently some literature has emerged on the multiple reasons and motivations for remunicipalisation and state activity as part of urban climate and energy policies (Matecki and Schulten 2013; Bulkeley, Broto, and Edwards 2014), this article develops a somewhat different perspective by focussing on the involvement of social movements, their ideas and impact on urban governance in the course of remunicipalisation processes.

The ambition of this article is not merely to describe this novel phenomenon of social activism for a new, more participatory kind of energy utility, but to interpret it as a contribution to scholarly debate on coproduction as a mode of collective resource management and service provision. In line with this special issue we, first, draw on the concept of coproduction, which has been discussed as a way to increase the quality of public services through the inclusion of 'clients' and 'consumers' in planning, managing and physically providing services, such as water, education and security (Evans 1996; Ostrom 1972, 1996). We, secondly, seek to supplement this body of scholarship by relating it to recent research on urban commons and processes of 'commoning'. Associated primarily with the remarkable body of work on the governance of common goods and common pool resources by Ostrom and her colleagues (Ostrom 1990, 2008), a new strand of commons research is using the concept to analyse alternative forms of collective (re-)production (Angelis 2003; Bakker 2007; Linebaugh 2008; Radywyl and Biggs 2013).

We explore the analytical power of these two concepts with a discussion of two case study cities – Berlin and Hamburg – recently experiencing new approaches to public and citizen ownership of energy grids and services. Both cities have witnessed attempts to remunicipalise energy systems in new ways involving a number of participatory elements. In both cities social movements have organised referenda for re-installing public ownership of the cities' energy grids and cooperatives have emerged to buy shares in the grid operator.

Referring to these two cases and considering ways of interpreting them in terms of coproduction and commoning, this article seeks to answer the following research questions: (1) How can the concept of coproduction raise our understanding of the propositions and governance visions expressed by these initiatives? (2) What added value can the notions of urban commons – in their more recent, critical sense – bring to the analysis of new forms of remunicipalisation?

In answering these questions, we will first introduce the different initiatives and forms of organisation that are enrolling citizens in energy provision or grid operation in Berlin and Hamburg, revealing how they transcend simplistic notions of public or private ownership. In Section 3, we discuss the classical and critical approaches to coproduction and commons as a prelude to exploring their analytical capacity to interpret the remunicipalisation initiatives in Berlin and Hamburg afresh in Section 4. We summarise the main findings and their implications for research on coproduction in Section 5. Methodologically, our research is based on the analysis of available official documents, an intensive study of the newspaper coverage in both cities and expert interviews that were conducted in 2013 (Berlin, 3 interviews and participant observations) and 2014–2015 (Hamburg, 16 interviews).

2. New energy for Berlin and Hamburg: remunicipalisation and new actors

2.1. The German energy transition and development trajectories in Berlin and Hamburg

In Germany, the energy transition (*Energiewende*) has not only yielded a huge build-up of renewable energy generation capacities from wind, solar and biomass plants. Most significantly, the feed-in tariffs guaranteed by the Renewable Energy Law (EEG) have spawned massive investment in local, decentralised energy systems (Couture and Gagnon 2010). As a consequence, citizens, farmers and municipalities have been motivated to invest in renewable energy facilities. In total, the generation of energy from renewable sources amounted to 12.4% of the gross final energy consumption in 2013 (Eurostat 2015). Out of the overall installed capacity of renewable electricity in 2012, only 5% was operated by the four biggest energy corporations, while almost half of the entire capacity was held by private citizens and farmers (Trend:Research, and Leuphana University Lüneburg 2013). Additionally, energy grids have become an issue, as concession contracts, previously concluded with the major 'Big Four' electricity providers in Germany (*Vattenfall*, E.ON, *RWE* and *EnBW*), have come up for renegotiation. This has opened up a field of political negotiation, and even conflict, in some cities as the options of remunicipalising energy grids and forming local utilities represent a reversal of privatisation processes that were characteristic of the liberalisation of European energy markets in the late 1990s.

Turning to the two case studies Berlin and Hamburg, their point of departure is very similar. Both cities look back on a long tradition of a local energy supplier: the *Berliner Städtische Electricitätswerke Aktiengesellschaft* (BEWAG) and *Hamburgische Electricitätswerke* (HEW) date back to the late nineteenth century, although they were not publicly owned throughout the entire period. In the case of Berlin, the local enterprise even survived the period of the city's division and was reunited after the fall of the Berlin Wall (Moss 2014). Both utilities had their main field of interest in the electricity sector; both were among the largest German energy utilities in the 1990s. However, both were sold step-by-step to the Swedish state company *Vattenfall* around the year 2000. The main reasons were threefold: first, there was a fear that local energy utilities would not be able to withstand the rising competitive pressure after the liberalisation of the European energy market (for this 'dying local utility' thesis, see Bontrup and Marquardt 2010, 354f.); second, the sell-off of public utilities and property was seen as a means to reduce public debt; and, third, the prevalent neoliberal assessment of public ownership as unaccountable, inflexible and prone to corruption legitimised privatisation in the general public (Rügemer 2006).

While the history of the cities' energy utilities is comparable, the overall development of the two cities since the 1990s differs. While Berlin's aspirations to become a growing capital and global city have taken shape only slowly (Krätke 2001), Hamburg has managed to retain its role as one of the most important industrial centres in Northern Germany and a major European port as well as developing into a post-fordist service agglomeration (Bauriedl and Wissen 2002). Against these wider urban development trajectories, both Berlin and Hamburg have become important sites of a local 'Right to the City' movement (Mayer 2012; Beveridge and Naumann 2016). This movement found expression in a number of protests and collective actions around issues of housing and urban development. A link to infrastructure was made in Berlin in the shape of a successful referendum to publish the contracts underlying the privatisation of the Berlin water utility in 2011, played out as an important strategic experience in challenging the local authorities (Beveridge, Hüesker, and Naumann 2014). For Hamburg, a long history of controversy and conflict over its nuclear and coal-based power plants dating back to the height of anti-nuclear protests in the 1980s proved an important backdrop to today's developments (Interview Zukunftsrat). Explicating this context is important to understanding that recent energy initiatives are embedded in a broader context of urban social movements in both cities. In the subsequent two sub-sections we introduce the different initiatives, their proposed or practised models for the involvement of citizens and the impact they have had on urban energy governance.

2.2. Cooperative vs. participatory public ownership: different organisational models in Berlin

Debates about the future of Berlin's energy supply has attracted widespread attention since two initiatives, the social movement coalition *Berliner Energietisch* (Berlin Energy Roundtable) and the cooperative *BürgerEnergie Berlin* (Citizen Energy Berlin), proposed different organisational models as an alternative to the existing private sector dominated model of energy provision. On the one hand, Berlin is an illuminating case for comparing different organisational and ownership models for the operation of the city's energy networks. On the other hand, it allows for a deeper analysis of how collective and grassroots initiatives come to play a role and challenge urban energy policy (Blanchet 2015; Kunze and Becker 2015), as well as neoliberal urban governance in general.

2.2.1. Berlin Energy Roundtable – for a participatory, ecological and socially just energy utility

The Berlin Energy Roundtable is a grassroots social movement that campaigned for a new participatory form of energy utility in Berlin (Becker, Beveridge, and Naumann 2015; Blanchet 2015). In 2010, even before the onset of a public debate over awarding the concession for the city's electricity grid, a small group of activists had published a concept paper on the formation of a possible new municipal utility, outlining that it should both produce electricity from renewable energy sources and provide participatory structures (attac Berlin, BürgerBegehren Klimaschutz, and PowerShift 2011). This concept laid the foundation stone for a movement that was coordinated by the Berlin Energy Roundtable, a grassroots coalition to campaign for the remunicipalisation of the electricity grid. It involved around 40 different actors, such as large environmental organisations, small NGOs, leftist activist groups and anti-gentrification initiatives, as well as some professionals from the field of renewable energy (Interview Roundtable Activist).

As it became clear that the city government – first run by the Social Democrats and the Left Party in coalition and from 2011 by the Social Democrats and the Christian Democrats – would not support specific steps towards remunicipalisation, it was decided to organise a referendum to pressurise local politics (Interview Roundtable Professional). An elaborate law was drafted in a consensus-oriented discussion process within the Roundtable. The draft law laid out different stipulations for a so-called 'Citizens Utility' (*Bürgerstadtwerk*) that should be democratic, ecologically oriented and socially just. The draft foresaw public meetings, an Advisory Board with directly elected citizen representatives and an obligation to make core documents accessible to the public (Berliner Energietisch 2012). Additionally, the entity should serve as a means for increasing the share of renewable energy used in the city and take measures against energy poverty. In its final step, however, the referendum failed on 3 November 2013, as only 24.1% of the required 25% of the city's electorate approved the draft law, with the vast majority of these voting in favour of the referendum (Landeswahlleiterin Berlin 2013). It was, nevertheless, an impressive display of opposition to an incumbent utility that only narrowly failed. In the aftermath of the failed referendum, the Energy Roundtable continues to put pressure on the city's energy policy.

2.2.2. Citizen Energy Berlin – a cooperative with aspirations as an ecological shareholder

Parallel to the calls for a participatory public utility as articulated by the Energy Roundtable, the cooperative Citizen Energy Berlin (*BürgerEnergie Berlin*) proposed a different organisational model for citizen involvement that is based on direct collective ownership. While the Roundtable chose the path of political pressure, the approach of the cooperative Citizen Energy Berlin is to purchase a share of the grid operating utility as a citizen collective. Their central strategic goal is to gather enough capital to become a partner in a cooperation model in which a municipal (or private) utility holds a majority share of the grid operator and the cooperative controls up to 49% (Interview BürgerEnergie). Cooperating with a local utility from Southern Germany, Citizen Energy Berlin was one of the bidders in the concession process. Launched in 2011, it had 2300 members and a capital shareholding of about €11 million by September 2015 (according to their website accessed on 20 October 2015). Members are mainly recruited from people genuinely interested in energy issues, spanning various social groups from students to pensioners (Interview BürgerEnergie). To become a member, you have to buy five shares at €100 each. It is, however, not a condition to be a citizen of the city of Berlin to become a member. As with the Roundtable's plans, the objectives of the cooperative cover ecological, democratic and social issues. Ecologically they aim to strengthen Berlin's potential to achieve an energy transition by earmarking 10% of profits for reinvestment in solar and cogeneration plants. Their attempts to advance democracy are embodied in the general design of the cooperative, which grants each member one vote and revenue according to the member's shares. In social terms, the cooperative argues in favour of cost reduction through energy-saving and efficiency measures. The core strategy of the cooperative to attract new members is to appeal to people both as an ecological project and as an opportunity to invest (Becker, Beveridge, and Naumann 2015, 81). Currently the cooperative is active in lobbying the local government to be incorporated into a future local utility as a minority shareholder.

2.2.3. Impact and outlook

The existence and the divergent aspirations of the two initiatives have generated a highly polarised debate on the future of Berlin's energy grid, involving arguments about both the initiatives' goals and financial means to achieve them (Moss, Becker, and Naumann 2014, 2015; Becker, Beveridge, and Naumann 2015). The incumbent concessionaire *Vattenfall* mobilised a campaign focussed on the quality of service provision in the past; other private suitors have also expressed an interest in gaining the concession. Above all, the Roundtable's campaign succeeded in altering the public discourse and pressurising the government into forming a public utility, albeit without a strong participatory organisational structure (Becker, Beveridge, and Naumann 2015, 82). This new utility, *Berlin Energie*, was later granted the concession for the gas network in the city – a decision that, however, resulted in a split within the administration as the Senator of Justice took legal steps against the move (Zawatka-Gerlach, Törne, and Keilani 2014). Additionally, no decision on the future of the concession for the electricity grid was taken; the concession with *Vattenfall* is still in place. In May 2015, the Senate devised an internal compromise concerning the electricity and gas network, not aiming for a full remunicipalisation of ownership, but for 'the best possible influence' on the utilities and long-term cooperation with an industrial partner (Zawatka-Gerlach 2015). While the prospects for remunicipalisation in Berlin are still contested, the city of Hamburg has already undertaken steps towards publicly owned energy facilities.

2.3 From Hamburg Energie to 'Our Hamburg – Our Network': increasing citizen involvement in Hamburg

Though attracting less scholarly attention, Hamburg is also an interesting case for new forms of citizen involvement in local energy politics. As with Berlin, the city of Hamburg has witnessed a referendum on the remunicipalisation of its energy grids. In contrast to Berlin, the referendum succeeded by a narrow majority of 50.9%. Additionally, the referendum was preceded by the foundation of the public energy enterprise *Hamburg Energie* in 2009. So while both cities are informative in terms of different models of organisation, in Hamburg one can observe the first effects of remunicipalisation and the implementation of a referendum decision on the future of energy networks.

2.3.1. A green public utility – the formation of Hamburg Energie in 2009

Hamburg Energie is a public utility that was founded with a clear ecological orientation and later complemented with participatory provisions to include the voices of citizens and business clients. Against the background of a history of energy-related conflicts in the city, it was the plan to erect a new coal-fired plant of 1.6 GW that proved the most divisive issue in the early 2000s (Interview Zukunftsrat). In the course of this debate, the Green Party – previously a strong opponent – came to form a coalition government with the Christian Democrats. While the new administration approved the plant, the Green Party was now given free rein to establish a public utility with a clear ecological mission statement (Norddeutscher Rundfunk 2014). *Hamburg Energie* was eventually founded and entrusted with the 'provision of energy for the general public and public institutions', the sale of 'climate friendly electricity (nuclear and coal-free)' and the responsibility to 'plan, erect and run municipal infrastructures' (as recorded in the Commercial Register). The new utility was very successful in both acquiring clients and setting up renewable energy capacities. At the end of 2013 the company served 80,300 customers with electricity and around 11,000 with a gas delivery contract (Hamburg Wasser 2014). It has, as indicated on their website, built wind turbines, photovoltaic installations and various combined heat and power plants. Notably, *Hamburg Energie* was involved in various projects involving citizens, public institutions and local businesses. Additionally, a client advisory board (*Kundenbeirat*) was installed in 2012. Although this body only has a consultative function, a *Hamburg Energie* employee emphasised in an e-mail that the company would grant 'a transparent look into managerial decisions' and claims that 'critical opinions of its members are dealt with in a constructive manner'. The board is composed of 20 members, of which 10 are private clients and 10 represent organised interests and associations from Hamburg, such as the Tenants' Association and the

Chamber of Commerce of the city. Its actual leverage over the business practice of the utility is, however, limited (Interview Consultant).

Hamburg Energie is in two ways different from most of the other newly founded local utilities in Germany. First, it stands out in terms of its clear orientation towards the generation of renewable energy in close cooperation with local citizens and business. Second, installing a participatory body was another novelty – a response to pressure exerted by the referendum campaign.

2.3.2. 'Our Hamburg – Our Network' – a social movement for grid remunicipalisation

As in Berlin, there was a referendum campaign for remunicipalising the energy grid. With *Hamburg Energie* active in the fields of energy generation and sale, the approaching expiry date of the concession with *Vattenfall* signified the advent of a new political conflict. Here, also, a group of social movement activists and representatives of environmental and social organisations gathered as early as 2010 to consider how to remunicipalise the energy networks. Later they formed the campaigning coalition 'Our Hamburg – Our Network' (OHON) highlighting the localisation resulting from possible remunicipalisation. There are four main differences to the developments in Berlin. First, the campaign not only aimed at the remunicipalisation of the electricity grid, but also included district heating and gas networks. Second, the coalition encompassed both grassroots level social movements and larger organisations, such as *BUND* (the German member of Friends of the Earth), the Consumer Advice Centre (*Verbraucherzentrale*) and the charity organisation of the Protestant-Lutheran Church (*Diakonie*). The latter three mainly shouldered the campaign and supported it with their policy networks and organisational capacity (Interviews BUND, Interview Church Interview, OHON Campaigner). Smaller activist groups and NGOs, such as 'Robin Wood' and 'Stop Moorburg Pipelines' (*Moorburgtrasse stoppen*) played a supporting role in the coalition, as did the network 'Enterprises Against Nuclear Power'. Third, the text subject to the referendum only consisted of two sentences, demanding the transition of the city's grids into public ownership and a 'socially just, climate compatible and democratically controlled energy provision from renewable sources' as a 'mandatory target'. Fourth, the referendum was successful with a very narrow majority of 50.9% of the valid votes (Behörde für Inneres und Sport Hamburg 2014). Again in contrast to Berlin, it was only after the referendum that an 'Energy Roundtable' was initiated by grassroots activists to supervise its implementation. Although the Hamburg referendum law was less elaborate than that in Berlin, the OHON campaign in Hamburg showed how a coalition of established actors was able to successfully mobilise and challenge urban energy governance.

2.3.3. Energy Network Hamburg – a cooperative re-orienting its strategy

As another parallel to Berlin, Hamburg has a cooperative that has sought to gain a share of the grid operating utility. As it largely followed the model of Citizen Energy Berlin we need only to address its achievements here. Called Energy Network Hamburg (*Energienetz Hamburg*), it was more successful in terms of gathering capital investment than its Berlin counterpart: according to a press release from September 2013, some 3000 members have accumulated more than 50 million Euro. The cooperative was one of the bidders in the concession awarding process cooperating with the Dutch utility *Alliander*. However, as the successful referendum requires full public ownership of the networks by law, the cooperative *Energienetz Hamburg* is currently looking for other opportunities to invest. It developed a new strategy in May 2015 that targets investments in renewable generation capacities instead of grid ownership. In line with this new investment strategy it completed its first project, a citizen photovoltaic installation on the rooftop of an office building, in the summer of 2015. Further, Energy Network has been active in organising and participating in stakeholder dialogues on energy issues in the city.

2.3.4. Impact and outlook

As in Berlin, the referendum campaign in Hamburg was successful in putting pressure on the local government and generating an intense and polarised public debate. During the first step of gathering signatures, the so-called *Volksbegehren*, the Senate signed a cooperation agreement with *Vattenfall* and E.ON *Hanse* transferring into public ownership 25.1% of the shares of each of the district heating and electricity grid operating branches of *Vattenfall*, and the gas grid operating branch of E.ON *Hanse*. This partial remunicipalisation was accompanied by a catalogue of measures the power utilities agreed to, among them the development of virtual networks and cogeneration capacities for heat and electricity as well as targets for the reduction of CO_2 emissions (Senatskanzlei Freie und Hansestadt Hamburg 2011).

The hope that this step would silence calls for a full remunicipalisation of the grid, however, was confounded by the success of the referendum passing all the required preparatory steps. On the evening of the polling day the Social Democrat Party, hitherto involved in the campaign against the referendum, had to change its strategy and was forced to implement the will of the electorate. While the ownership transaction for the electricity network came into effect in early 2014, the remunicipalisation of the gas and district heating networks was postponed as future options (Meyer-Wellmann 2014). Although there is wide criticism of how the ownership transfer has been conducted and how the principles defined in the second sentence of the referendum text have been implemented, it is argued that the success of the referendum has paved the way for more stakeholder participation in the governance of the city's energy system and beyond (Interview BUND, Interview SPD Environment, Interview Handelskammer).

Taken together, the initiatives in Berlin and Hamburg advocate and advance new models of collective ownership in infrastructures. The cooperatives present a new model of citizen involvement in the running of core urban infrastructures, prioritising direct collective ownership. The forms of public ownership were – with the exception of *Hamburg Energie* – initiated by non-state actors and social movements. These initiatives have not only claimed public ownership as a form of indirect participation (Cumbers 2012), but also sought to inscribe direct measures of participation into the utilities. Even in the case of Berlin, where they were not successful with the referendum, their effective mobilisation to have a say in local energy policy challenged established governance modes and actor constellations. From this vantage point we now explore how the concepts of coproduction and commons can raise our understanding of these initiatives beyond simplistic notions of public vs. private ownership.

3. Coproduction and the commons: understanding citizen participation in urban infrastructure provision

The concepts of coproduction and the commons are gaining increasing attention in the social sciences (on coproduction: Ostrom 1996; Verschuere, Brandsen, and Pestoff 2012; Osborne and Strokosch 2013; on commons: Ostrom 1990; Dietz et al. 2002; Angelis

2003; Bakker 2007; Hardt and Negri 2009). Although the two approaches are connected, they provide different, yet complementary starting points for analysing the transformation of energy provision in Berlin and Hamburg. Each of them develops a perspective on the provision or governance of public services involving more-than-state and more-than-business actors. In this section we introduce coproduction and commons as two theoretical lenses through which to view and understand better the active involvement of citizens in the provision of urban services in general.

3.1. The coproduction of public services

Coproduction is a multi-faceted concept that spans a variety of themes and topics in development studies and public management scholarship, above all (new) models of public service provision especially in the Global South. It originated as a scientific term in the discussion on the complex and interdependent relations of various actors in delivering and maintaining certain public services in public management and administration theory (Osborne and Strokosch 2013, 33). It is strongly influenced by the work of Elinor Ostrom and others (Ostrom, Parks, and Whitaker 1974) from the 1970s onwards, looking at reforms in a number of sectors, such as police, education, housing and water provision (Ostrom and Whitaker 1973; Ostrom 1996; Albrechts 2013, 48). Ostrom also provided the fundamental definition of coproduction as a 'process through which inputs used to produce a good or service are contributed by individuals who are not "in" the same organization' (Ostrom 1996, 1073). At its core, the concept seeks to overcome the traditional dichotomy of centralised public agencies responsible for planning and service provision vs. citizens reduced to passive 'clients'. In contrast, the normative core assumption of coproduction research is that the participation and 'activation' of clients helps to improve the quality and stability of service provision. Clients become 'coproducers of public services' (Alford 1998; Osborne and Strokosch 2013). Clients may usually encompass citizens or 'third-sector' initiatives (Brandsen and Pestoff 2006), although some sources also mention small and medium enterprises as contributors to the coproduction of public services (Ostrom 1996, 1075).

A growing body of literature is devoted to elucidating different arrangements through which coproduction is realised. Bovaird (2007, 849f.), for example, lists different forms such as 'consultation', 'codelivery' and others; all of which are subsumed in the concept of 'coproduction'. Out of these, 'full user-professional coproduction' applies when 'users and professionals fully share the task of planning and designing the service, then delivering it'. An earlier taxonomy developed by Brudney and England (1983, 63) distinguishes different types of coproduction according to the size of the involved group. An advanced form is the idea of 'institutionalised' coproduction introduced by Joshi and Moore, according to which a 'long-term relationship between state agencies and organised groups of citizens' exists and 'substantial resource contributions' from both sides are involved (2004, 31). For the remainder of this article, we will follow a distinction made by Brandsen and Pestoff (2006, 497) between coproduction as 'an arrangement where citizens produce their own services at least in part' on the one hand and co-management and co-governance involving the production, planning and delivery of public services by third-sector parties on the other.

Recently, work on coproduction has expanded the original concept by emphasising its potential to advance social inclusiveness and empowerment. Calabrò (2012) suggests considering coproduction as an alternative to privatisation. The active role that citizens play in coproduction processes, it is argued, can contribute to social inclusiveness and citizenship (Osborne and Strokosch 2013). Most prominently, Mitlin discusses coproduction 'as a grassroots strategy to secure political influence and access to resources and services' (2008, 339). Coproduction, thus conceived, might strengthen both local organisations and provide knowledge about services and processes of social change to those involved (Mitlin et al. 2008, 357). In discussing and addressing needs, processes of infrastructure coproduction are also said to help the 'building of a strong, resilient and mutually supportive community' (Albrechts 2013, 46). This – it is argued – can empower local citizens in a broader political sense, rendering coproduction an enabling factor to challenge 'systems and processes of government in various dimensions' and to prepare citizens for a 'more substantive engagement with the political system' (Mitlin 2008, 353).

Against these recent extensions of the coproduction perspective to emcompass social inclusiveness and empowerment, critics of the concept question its openness and the resulting ambiguity it can induce in institutional, ownership and conceptual terms. McMillan, Spronk and Caswell argue that coproduction as a concept would 'include anything from public-private partnerships between the state and multinational corporations to wells managed by a community and a local non-governmental organization' (McMillan, Spronk, and Caswell 2014, 202). The quest to open up the responsibilities of public agencies to a wider set of actors can be viewed as echoing the onset of neoliberal reforms and thought (Peck 2010). Critics further argue that coproduction was an entry point for privatisation, blurring the responsibilities of the state and thereby reproducing social inequalities in terms of access to basic services (McMillan, Spronk, and Caswell 2014).

Bearing this in mind, we see the value of using coproduction to advance knowledge on issues of citizen participation and involvement, and especially in overcoming the distinction between consumers and producers in public service provision. This way coproduction provides a conceptual angle to transcend simplistic notions of private vs. public infrastructure provision. However, criticism of the concept raises important issues of the need to address contextual factors, questions of ownership and fundamental visions of service provision. We therefore argue that the approach of coproduction alone is not sufficient to capture the breadth of the changes to urban infrastructure governance currently negotiated in our two case study cities. To this end we now introduce the concept of the commons and its different readings.

3.2. Commons, commoning and the right to the city

Research on commons has a long pedigree. To understand the appeal of the commons and the different ways commons have been researched, it is helpful to categorise three schools of thought that have emerged since the 1960s. The idea of the commons first emerged in the 1960s when neo-classical economists developed a theory for classifying goods and services according to the dimensions of excludability and rivalry (Olson 1965; Bromley 1991). Different permutations of these attributes produced the familiar matrix of four categories of goods: common pool resources, club goods, pure public goods and private goods. The purpose behind this exercise was to identify generic problems of providing and protecting collectively used goods in a market economy, such as free-riding through non-payment or externalised negative effects, and using the above categories to help identify suitable modes of provision, use and regulation.

In the 1990s a second strand of commons research arose around the work of Elinor Ostrom (Ostrom 1990; Dietz et al. 2002; Ostrom 2005, 2008). Rather than deducing suitable institutions from theory, she and other institutional economists and political scientists developed eight 'design principles' for the governance of the commons and a framework for institutional analysis and development (IAD) on the basis of a global database of empirical examples of communities managing commons collectively (Ostrom 1990). This strand of commons research focuses primarily on (natural) common pool resources (CPR), such as water or fisheries, and has a clear normative preference for the management of CPRs being entrusted to local communities and polycentric governance structures (Ostrom 2010). Noteworthy, there is some work on energy as a common, an assessment based on both technical and organisational features of decentralised energy systems (Jenny, Fuentes, and Mosler 2007; Vermeylen 2010; Borenstein 2012; Wolsink 2012).

In short, this strand of commons research displays a strong focus on issues of governance in collectively managing a resource. The underlying trust in the benefits of stakeholder cooperation has, however, been criticised for paying inadequate regard to contestation and power relations over resource use (Harvey 2011, 102).

Since the early 2000s, and with recent intensity, a third strand of research on commons has developed alongside goods and institutional economics theory. This body of scholarship goes beyond institutionalist thinking and approaches collective modes of managing the commons not as a complement to market mechanisms and state regulation, but as an alternative. Inspired by neo-Marxist thinking (Harvey 2012) and green activism (Helfrich and Bollier 2012), this literature is interested in the emergent phenomena of post-capitalist forms of collective ownership and production (Angelis 2003; Bakker 2007) or 'participatory economics' (Hahnel 2015). It asserts that commons are more than just commonly governed goods and services, but 'suggest alternative, non-commodified means to fulfil social needs' (Angelis 2003, 1). Commons in this sense constitute a 'common wealth' (Hardt and Negri 2009) of societies which should not be reduced to mere commodities. Likewise, the commons are here seen as both an alternative to, and endangered by, processes of enclosure and accumulation by dispossession (Bakker 2007; Harvey 2012, 148; Jeffrey, McFarlane, and Vasudevan 2012).

Commons from this perspective are not given, but produced through discourse and practices. These activities of 'commoning' (Linebaugh 2008), or commons creation, are based on common interest and sharing. Generally, commoning challenges existing power relations and ownership structures as it is directed against logics of commodification, marketisation and privatisation (Von Winterfeld et al. 2012). In contrast to the openness towards different kinds of ownership in the work of Elinor Ostrom, a number of critical commons thinkers underline the necessity of state or at least collective ownership to ensure the creation of proper commons (Harvey 2012; Cumbers 2015). It follows that attempts to establish commons are often highly contested, as reflected in worldwide oppositional networks aspiring to 'a radical reclaiming of the commons' (Klein 2001, 82).

Recently, the work of David Harvey (2012) and others has been linking the debate on commons to critical urban theory, spawning a growing number of studies that seek to empirically underscore the idea of the commons as an alternative to capitalism in an urban context (Eizenberg 2012; Kip 2015). Nicholas Blomley (2008), for example, has developed the concept of 'urban commons' in this context, using a case study of a social protest movement against the development of a site in Vancouver's Downtown Eastside. Here, the 'urban' in urban commons is not just a denominator of location, but relates to alternative practices in the production of urban space (Eizenberg 2012; Susser and Tonnelat 2013). Examples of urban commons thus cover movements and activities that also display a spatial expression, such as occupy and squatting projects (Radywyl and Biggs 2013; Casa-Cortés, Cobarrubias, and

Pickles 2014, 457f.). Against this, Susser and Tonnelat (2013) take a broader stance, including labour, collective production, arts and also public services in the list of urban commons.

Apart from identifying examples, this critical literature on the urban commons is interested in how the commons get produced through interaction and 'common practices' on different scales (Radywyl and Biggs 2013, 159). Parr (2015) sees urban commoning as an outcome of three different processes that unfold in an interrelated way: a politics that seeks to build coalitions in anti-oppressive struggles on different scales, an alternative process of urbanisation and 'collaborative activities' to push back exclusive, private forms of ownership. They are simultaneously contested by processes of enclosure (Hodkinson 2012) and contesting market-based forms of fulfilling social needs. In this sense, urban commons relate to new political imaginaries based on justice, but also require the ability to 'control and imagine governance in new ways' (Chatterton 2010, 627). Commons, in this debate, are constructed as an alternative to neoliberal urbanism and as a vehicle for transformative urban politics.

3.3. From coproduction to commoning

Coproduction and the commons are important concepts in current debates on urban change towards more sustainable and, perhaps also, more democratic cities. While institutionalist understandings both of coproduction and the commons are connected with the work of Elinor Ostrom, attempts to explicitly combine both approaches are rare. Verschuere, Brandsen, and Pestoff (2012, 1088f.) highlight the condition of excludability in coproduction processes as coproduction is about 'the involvement of users in the delivery of goods that are at the disposal of a group of entitled users'. Accordingly, there has also been some debate on how coproduction can be grasped and regulated in organisational terms. However, here the focus lies on effectiveness and fit of coproduction to inter-organisational processes (Alford 1998) and the types of organisation that enable effective coproduction (Pestoff 2009). Accordingly, in the institutionalist reading of both terms there is some tacit acknowledgement that the two concepts are not mutually exclusive but complementary. In this reading, examples of coproduction could entail features of commons and vice versa.

The value of coproduction approaches lies undoubtedly in their focus on the integration of new actors into the management or provision of public services. We uphold, however, that the conceptual critique directed against the openness of coproduction towards privatisation and a variety of other organisational forms creates the need to include a wider range of contextual factors in the analysis.

We argue that the active notion of commoning addresses these issues and goes beyond a narrow understanding of coproduction, in two ways. First, coproduction is not explicitly concerned with questions of ownership and the character of the service provided (e.g. commodity or common good) on a conceptual level. Second, despite normative claims that coproduction would increase the quality and democratic character of the services coproduced (Verschuere, Brandsen, and Pestoff 2012, 1093f.), more clarity is needed on which visions of urban governance are generally associated with ideas of coproduction. The notion of urban commons, we feel, can help to encapsulate this broader perspective and, at the same time, to build upon the recent critical strand of coproduction research.

4. Discussion: urban energy provision as coproduction, energy utilities as urban commons?

In Section 2 we presented energy initiatives in the cities of Berlin and Hamburg that formulate new models for how urban energy systems should be governed through citizen participation and according to sustainability targets. The initiatives represent different models of collective ownership, spanning cooperatives that are based on direct membership and seek to purchase shares in the grid operating utility, an established green energy provider subsequently complemented with participatory provisions and more wide-ranging proposals for embedding participation in local utilities. Beyond that, both cities experienced a public debate that linked the issue of grid ownership to wider aspirations for renewable energy, social justice and democratic control.

In this section we discuss these developments through the lens of coproduction and the commons. More specifically, we will show how the concept of coproduction helps us to address and identify different forms and models of citizens' involvement in infrastructure governance. We will, however, also demonstrate the need to broaden this perspective with the notion of urban commons in order to account for those aspects of the initiatives inadequately captured by the concept of coproduction. This will, on a more general level, show how the concepts of coproduction and the commons can be applied to analyse alternatives to the privatised provision of energy and other public services.

4.1. Coproduction and energy utilities: going beyond consumers and producers

The origin of research on coproduction is a reassessment of the possible role of consumers in the provision of public services, thereby increasing the quality and accountability of the services provided (Ostrom 1996; Verschuere, Brandsen, and Pestoff 2012). The direct involvement of citizens in service coproduction, it is claimed, alters their relationship towards public or private service providers. While the constellation we have encountered in Berlin and Hamburg is different from the pre-privatisation or developing country contexts in which the concept was developed, we argue here that coproduction can serve as a heuristic to identify different models of how citizens can be involved in energy generation and grid operation on the city level.

While it is clear in each case that there is no strict distinction between consumers and producers in energy provision, it is important to deploy a working definition in order to delineate the contribution of coproduction research. We here refer to a narrow understanding of coproduction as proposed by Brandsen and Pestoff (2006) which sets as a core indicator the involvement of citizens in the production of services and distinguishes proper coproduction from co-management and co-governance. Applied to our examples we can identify three different ways in which coproduction is practised: coproduction on the project scale, coproduction through advisory boards and coproduction through co-ownership.

4.1.1. Coproduction on a project scale

Coproduction can take a number of forms with different levels of durability, resource intensity and institutionalisation (Joshi and Moore 2004). An accessible and relatively straightforward form is the involvement of citizens in projects with a clear aim and limited duration. This mode of coproduction that we term 'coproduction on a project scale' can be identified in a number of collaborative projects that were implemented by

Hamburg Energie. A prime example of this type of coproduction is the '10 MW project'. Here, a great variety of state institutions, private enterprise and citizens were involved in installing a total of 11.3 MW solar power in a short period of time. The State Office for Geoinformation and Topographical Surveying (*Landesbehörde für Geoinformation und Vermessung*) created a 3D model of appropriate areas and rooftops for the installation of solar panels, the so-called 'solar atlas'. Suitable land and rooves were made available by a variety of local enterprises – owning for instance, an aircraft construction site, port areas and warehouses – as well as the famous alternative football club St. Pauli, public authorities and schools. According to a self-released video, the project was cofinanced by citizens, *Hamburg Energie* itself and local bank loans, with an investment volume of €28 million, of which €4 million were direct citizen investments. Significantly, it was the creation of *Hamburg Energie* that provided the organisational platform to implement coproduction projects in the first place. It provides an example of how remunicipalisation can create an institution that enables the involvement of citizens.

4.1.2. Coproduction through advisory boards

The second type of coproduction we could identify in the debates about public utilities is the installation of advisory or supervisory boards that involve citizens and other stakeholders. The installation of a consumer's advisory board in *Hamburg Energie* can be taken as an example of this kind of coproduction. Although it only has a consultative function, it involves both elected client representatives and organised stakeholders, such as the Tenants' Association and the Chamber of Commerce of the city. The numerous mechanisms for democratic control inscribed into the Berlin draft law of the Energy Roundtable illustrate other possible options for ensuring citizen influence in a utility. This type of coproduction is positioned in between the different modes of cooperation Brandsen and Pestoff (2006) have developed. It shows aspects of 'co-governance' as third-sector actors are involved in the planning of service provision, but also 'co-management' in the way that state and third-sector actors cooperate here. The establishment of consumer boards marks a significant difference to previous public enterprises, which in theory were accountable to the voters and public authorities, but in practice were able to act largely independent of public or popular control. In short, public utilities that allow for user participation provide openings for these first two kinds of coproduction to flourish.

4.1.3. Coproduction through co-ownership

The third form of coproduction we can observe in the initiatives in Berlin and Hamburg represents a novel approach to the coproduction of networked infrastructures. It refers to the possible option that a cooperative might gain shares, and thus direct collective co-ownership in a city's energy infrastructure in the future. Enacted by contracts as well as implying a transfer of legal entitlements and duties to the collectively organised citizens, it would signify a highly institutionalised and resource-intensive form of coproduction (Joshi and Moore 2004). Importantly, and in line with the recent, more critical applications of coproduction concepts (Mitlin 2008; Albrechts 2013; McMillan, Spronk, and Caswell 2014), the cooperatives represent a vehicle for citizens to empower themselves to become co-owners and influence the policy and practice of the grid operators. This possible involvement and co-ownership would by virtue of the cooperative's internal decision-making and revenue distribution regulations create a kind of community

(Albrechts 2013); one that is, however, clearly not identical with the group of infrastructure users.

Using coproduction as a heuristic has helped us to identify three types of coproduction. These describe different ways in which citizens are getting involved in the governance of networked infrastructures in the two cities of Berlin and Hamburg. They signify different degrees of institutionalisation, durability and citizen entitlements. The type of cooperative co-ownership promoted in both cities also resonates with recent conceptualisations of coproduction that encompass empowerment. However, this perspective on coproduction has its limitations, as it does not consider the contexts and characteristics of the services provided. Referring to ownership, for example, the cooperatives can be seen as a means to achieve coproduction, yet how these models of collective ownership might actually transform the nature of public services is not made explicit. We therefore now apply the lens of urban commons to see how this perspective can broaden our understanding of the initiatives.

4.2. Beyond coproduction: energy utilities as a form of commoning

Analysing the various initiatives in Berlin and Hamburg from a coproduction perspective reveals different ways of organising citizens' involvement. The aspirations of most of the initiatives, however, extend beyond the simple involvement of citizens: they question the provision of energy by private enterprises and highlight issues of control and social justice. We argue here that these issues are better understood from the perspective of urban commons (Blomley 2008; Harvey 2012; Kip 2015). In applying the urban commons concept to interpret the initiatives in Berlin and Hamburg we will briefly discuss two features of urban commons most prevalent in these cases: first, commons as a means of de-privatisation and de-commodification and, second, new imaginaries of infrastructure and urban governance that challenge conventional policies. These two features help to broaden the coproduction perspective by addressing important context-related arguments articulated by the initiatives.

4.2.1. Urban energy commons: de-privatising energy utilities, de-commodifying energy provision

The creation of urban commons is often discussed in the context of alternative practices that envisage new ways of thinking about and managing a shared resource (Blomley 2008; Linebaugh 2008; Radywyl and Biggs 2013). With our examples from the field of urban energy systems, these practices mainly take the shape of alternative, collective forms of ownership. If implemented, they would push back private ownership (Parr 2015) in some of the most basic infrastructures of urban production and consumption.

The initiatives propose different models of collective ownership of energy networks. Within the cooperative solution, this would consist of the sum of cooperative members, irrespective of their location or the amount of capital they provide. With the participatory public utilities, commoning would have a more indirect character, mediated through public ownership. Here, one could argue that the entire citizenry, defined by the right to vote, would become part of the governance of urban energy. For this to make a difference, however, full use of the various participatory provisions would need to be mobilised. Democratic control and direct participation have played an important role especially in the campaigns for remunicipalisation in Berlin and Hamburg. It, however, is a common characteristic of all the initiatives analysed that they combine visions of democratic control and collective ownership with goals that go beyond profit-seeking. In fact, democratic control is often considered as a condition to foster alternative modes of urban energy provision (Interview Roundtable Professional, Interview OHON Campaigner, Chatterton 2010).

One way to conceptually grasp this non-commercial orientation is the idea of a 'common wealth' which was introduced to describe a sphere that is exterior to capital accumulation (Hardt and Negri 2009), yet endangered by processes of enclosure and capitalisation (Harvey 2012, 74ff.). Therefore, beyond the issues of ownership and the efforts to democratise energy networks, the initiatives proposed a model of a de-commodified energy provision that is concerned less with goals of profit-maximising than with environmental sustainability and social justice. All of the initiatives aim at increasing the generation of renewable energy in their respective cities. The generation of renewable energy, it is argued, helps achieve the cities' climate policy targets and, especially in the face of major fossil power stations planned in Hamburg (and Berlin), produces a cleaner energy system with a lower environmental impact on the city. Social justice issues were also relevant in the referendum campaigns, where energy poverty was addressed as a new political topic in the German context. While the aim of measures against energy poverty was written into the Berlin draft law, the goal of social justice was among the three targets in the Hamburg referendum text. This reinterpretation of the goals of urban energy provision is a step to figuring a non-commodified, common wealth-oriented energy system.

On a more conceptual level, the postulation of taking control over infrastructure services generally questions a market-based and commodified mode of infrastructure provision. Different metaphors of appropriation, as in 'Our Hamburg, Our Network', underscore this line of reasoning. The main argument for both referendum campaigns was that infrastructure for energy provision should be demarcated from market logics. In the view of the initiatives studied, energy provision should be transformed from a service operated by private companies into a common good owned by the people of the city (Interview Roundtable Professional, Interview Roundtable Activist, Interview OHON Campaigner). In the end, the three notions of democratic control and collective ownership, alternative goals and a general reasoning about the future nature of urban infrastructure systems are interlinked and question former forms of energy provision. In doing so, their line of thinking about infrastructure also goes beyond the ideas of coproduction as they challenge the character of private infrastructure provision as such.

4.2.2. Challenging the status quo *of energy provision, articulating new imaginaries for urban governance*

The creation of urban commons is not only connected with new forms of ownership and a fundamental reframing of the provided service. It also entails new imaginaries about urban governance in and beyond the energy sector. As Angelis argues, commons can serve as a platform for envisioning and developing an alternative framework for social relations and social practices (2003; cited in Eizenberg 2012, 766). When articulated, however, they unfold processes of contestation (Chatterton 2010; Parr 2015). Both the referenda and the cooperatives envision future energy provision that is oriented towards democratic governance, ecological sustainability and social justice. All of these break with managerial-style decision-making and purely economic imperatives that dominated past urban governance and energy policy.

Putting these developments in a broader urban context, the energy campaigns in both cities are closely connected with social movements for a 'Right to the City', which address issues of gentrification, rising rents and the preservation of public spaces or resist prestigious projects of urban redevelopment (Beveridge and Naumann 2016). This can be observed, for example, in the involvement of social movements backing these urban causes in the referendum campaigns, namely tenants associations and a number of grass-roots activists. A further example is the way the campaign in Berlin highlighted issues of energy poverty, thus connecting their claims for a remunicipalisation of the electricity grid to wider debates about social polarisation conducted within the city's social movements (Interview Roundtable Activist). In both cities, there was a conscious attempt to include many social movements and civil society players when drafting the resolution to support the referendum (Interview OHON Campaigner, Interview Roundtable Activist). Additionally, the broad discourse on the future of the local energy grids in both cities has raised public interest in energy policy. However, in both cases it was the decision to push for a referendum, with the strategy of conflict escalation it enabled, that stirred intensive public debate, thereby repoliticising this field of urban governance (Beveridge, Hüesker, and Naumann 2014).

The extent of this repoliticisation can be observed in the concerned reactions of the city governments, business associations and also trade unions (for a detailed analysis, see Becker, Beveridge, and Naumann 2015, 82f.). Due to the pressure exerted by the campaigns, the politicisation of energy resulted in the partial creation of public ownership in Hamburg in 2011 and the foundation of *Berlin Energie* but also in ongoing administrative turf battles around the future of the gas networks in Berlin. In Hamburg, the installation of participatory discussion fora can also be attributed to the pressure built up by the referendum. As argued above, commons are 'constantly under threat of being enclosed and become a generative force of capitalist reproduction' (Eizenberg 2012, 779). In that sense the commoning of energy provision in Berlin and Hamburg is still an open process – a process that bears the potential of repercussions beyond the energy sector.

We argue that it is this more far-reaching perspective of commoning, embracing alternative visions and contested futures of collective governance, that fully grasps the significance of the cities' energy initiatives as they strive to deprivatise energy provision. While we acknowledge the way the coproduction concept emphasises citizen involvement, the perspective of urban commons can enrich our understanding of the political and economic contexts that motivate citizens to become active in shaping urban energy futures.

5. Conclusion

This article began with the widely established observation that energy transitions not only decentralise physical infrastructures of generation and distribution, but also bring to the four new kinds of actors – such as citizens, farmers or other small and medium enterprises – that become energy providers: coproducers of energy services. While these findings correspond well with the general understanding of coproduction as the involvement of new actors and their resources (Brandsen and Pestoff 2006), this article has set out to broaden this perspective. Using the cases of Berlin and Hamburg, we looked at how social movements proposed new models for energy utilities that were built around collective or participatory public ownership, thereby challenging the status-quo of urban energy provision.

Our empirical findings in Berlin and Hamburg reaffirm how energy transitions enrol new actors in urban energy provision. Beyond this, however, we have demonstrated how, in both cities, this involvement of citizens and other stakeholders in local energy policies was connected to a debate on new – public or cooperative – forms of ownership of energy utilities. Furthermore, the campaigns for remunicipalisation in Berlin and Hamburg stand as examples of fundamental contestation over urban governance, in that they demanded an ecologically sustainable, socially just and de-commodified urban energy utility, signifying a sharp break with neoliberal understandings of how cities (and their services) should be governed.

Analysing these cases we used the concept of coproduction as a heuristic tool to consider how it helps us to understand these forms of ownership and citizen involvement as well as alternative ideas for governing urban energy utilities. Beyond that, we discussed how the notion of urban commons could extend the perspective on coproduction conceptually. We argue that coproduction is able to grasp a number of phenomena related to the participation and involvement of citizens in the field of energy provision. However, there is a need to consider the broader implications of these ownership changes, such as how they potentially transform the commodity character of infrastructure and energy, and the underlying visions of urban governance. We have argued that these issues are captured better with a critical understanding of commons. On the basis of our findings, we conclude by mapping out promising avenues for future research.

5.1. Social movements and citizen initiatives as coproducers in urban energy provision

We were able to identify different types of coproduction in the energy sector of Berlin and Hamburg. These include a) coproduction on a project scale which is a temporary (or permanent) form of cooperation based on joint investments in renewable energy facilities, b) coproduction through formalised bodies of participation within energy utilities, e.g. advisory boards and c) coproduction through co-owning as prevalent in the plan of the energy cooperatives in both cities. In line with the core meaning of coproduction all of these three types share a new – more active – role of citizens in urban energy provision and challenge the former dichotomy of consumer vs. producer, thereby deserving more scholarly attention.

5.2. Energy utilities as urban commons

The (re)establishment of public utilities as proposed by the referenda in both cities was a way to de-privatise energy provision and transform it from a commodity to a public good accessible for every citizen and amenable to ecological aims rather than a profit-maximising logic. In that sense, urban energy utilities can be understood as urban commons and as an element of urban governance which can be used to develop alternatives to neoliberal urbanism. This highlights the highly contested nature of the production of urban commons and directs future research to investigating attempts at commoning urban energy systems as deeply political processes.

5.3. Beyond coproduction and commons

The approaches of coproduction and urban commons highlight different elements of urban energy movements. With their different, yet complementary, foci, both concepts can raise our understanding of citizen participation in energy provision and beyond. A promising line of enquiry would be to explore which instruments of urban energy or service policy lend themselves to coproduction, which to urban commoning and which to neither of the two. Since coproduction and commons cannot be limited to certain policy sectors, the analysis of citizen participation in urban energy has to be addressed in consideration of broader urban contexts, relying mainly on two points of departure: first, how projects of coproduction and commoning relate to and reshape the institutional ensemble of the local state, thus also might have further repercussions in other sectors; second, how they relate to uneven development and the spatial configuration of infrastructure within and beyond the city level. With the inherent spatiality of networked infrastructures in mind, we have argued here that coproduction and commons could provide a fruitful dual framework to guide research on infrastructure provision from the perspective of critical urban theory.

Disclosure statement

No potential conflict of interest was reported by the authors.

Funding

This article is based on preliminary findings from the project ENERLOG funded by the German Federal Ministry for Education and Research (BMBF) under Grant 01UN1207B and independent scientific work of the corresponding author.

References

Albrechts, L. 2013. "Reframing Strategic Spatial Planning by Using a Coproduction Perspective." *Planning Theory* 12 (1): 46–63. doi:10.1177/1473095212452722.

Alford, J. 1998. "A Public Management Road Less Travelled: Clients as Co-producers of Public Services." *Australian Journal of Public Administration* 57 (4): 128–137. doi:10.1111/j.1467-8500.1998.tb01568.x.

Angelis, M. de. 2003. "Reflections on Alternatives, Commons and Communities." *The Commoner* 6: 1–14. http://www.commoner.org.uk/deangelis06.pdf.

attac Berlin, BürgerBegehren Klimaschutz, and PowerShift. 2011. "Neue Energie für Berlin – Netze in Bürgerhand." http://power-shift.de/wordpress/wp-content/uploads/2011/05/Brosch%C3%Bcre-NeueEnergie-NetzeInB%C3%BcrgerhandBerlin-2Aufl-7-2011.pdf

Bakker, K. 2007. "The "Commons" Versus the "Commodity": Alter-globalization, Anti-privatization and the Human Right to Water in the Global South." *Antipode* 39 (3): 430–455. doi:10.1111/j.1467-8330.2007.00534.x.

Bauer, H. 2012. "Von der Privatisierung zur Rekommunalisierung: Einführende Problemskizze." In *Rekommunalisierung öffentlicher Daseinsvorsorge*, edited by H. Bauer, C. Büchner, and L. Hajasch, 11–33. Potsdam: Universitätsverlag.

Bauriedl, S., and M. Wissen. 2002. "Post-Fordist Transformation, the Sustainability Concept and Social Relations with Nature: A Case Study of the Hamburg Region." *Journal of Environmental Policy & Planning* 4 (2): 107–121. doi:10.1002/jepp.107.

Becker, S., R. Beveridge, and M. Naumann. 2015. "Remunicipalization in German Cities: Contesting Neo-Liberalism and Reimagining Urban Governance?" *Space and Polity* 19 (1): 76–90. doi:10.1080/13562576.2014.991119.

Behörde für Inneres und Sport Hamburg. 2014. "Volksentscheid Energienetze: Endgültiges Ergebnis festgestellt." http://www.hamburg.de/wahlen/4125972/ergebnis-volksentscheid-energienetze/

Berliner Energietisch. 2012. "Neue Energie für Berlin: Eckpunkte des Gesetzentwurfs für eine demokratische, ökologische und soziale Energieversorgung." http://www.berliner-energietisch.net/images/eckpunktepapier%20ge.pdf

Berlo, K., and O. Wagner. 2013. "Stadtwerke-Neugruendungen und Rekommunalisierungen: Energieversorgung in kommunaler Verantwortung." http://wupperinst.org/uploads/tx_wupperinst/Stadtwerke_Sondierungsstudie.pdf

Beveridge, R., F. Hüesker, and M. Naumann. 2014. "From Post-Politics to a Politics of Possibility? Unravelling the Privatization of the Berlin Water Company." *Geoforum* 51: 66–74. doi:10.1016/j.geoforum.2013.09.021.

Beveridge, R., and M. Naumann. 2016. "Another Urban Infrastructure Is Possible: Contesting Energy and Water Networks in Berlin." In *Beyond the Networked City. Infrastructure*

Reconfigurations and Urban Change in the North and South, edited by O. Coutard and J. Rutherford, 138–158. London: Routledge.
Blanchet, T. 2015. "Struggle Over Energy Transition in Berlin: How Do Grassroots Initiatives Affect Local Energy Policy-Making?" *Energy Policy* 78: 246–254. doi:10.1016/j.enpol.2014.11.001.
Blomley, N. 2008. "Enclosure, Common Right and the Property of the Poor." *Social & Legal Studies* 17 (3): 311–331. doi:10.1177/0964663908093966.
Bontrup, H.-J., and R.-M. Marquardt. 2010. *Kritisches Handbuch der deutschen Elektrizitätswirtschaft: Branchenentwicklung, Unternehmensstrategien, Arbeitsbeziehungen.* Berlin: Edition Sigma.
Borenstein, S. 2012. "The Private and Public Economics of Renewable Electricity Generation." *The Journal of Economic Perspectives* 26 (1): 67–92. doi:10.1257/jep.26.1.67.
Bovaird, T. 2007. "Beyond Engagement and Participation: User and Community Coproduction of Public Services." *Public Administration Review* 67 (5): 846–860. doi:10.1111/j.1540-6210.2007.00773.x.
Brandsen, T., and V. Pestoff. 2006. "Co-Production, the Third Sector and the Delivery of Public Services." *Public Management Review* 8 (4): 493–501. doi:10.1080/14719030601022874.
Bromley, D. W. 1991. *Environment and Economy: Property Rights and Public Policy.* Oxford: Blackwell.
Brudney, J. L., and R. E. England. 1983. "Toward a Definition of the Coproduction Concept." *Public Administration Review* 43 (1): 59–65. doi:10.2307/975300.
Bruns, E., and D. Ohlhorst. 2011. "Wind Power Generation in Germany: A Transdisciplinary View on the Innovation Biography." *The Journal of Transdisciplinary Environmental Studies* 10 (1): 45–67.
Bulkeley, H., V. C. Broto, and G. A. Edwards. 2014. *An Urban Politics of Climate Change: Experimentation and the Governing of Socio-Technical Transitions.* Abingdon: Routledge.
Burger, C., and J. Weinmann. 2012. *The Decentralized Energy Revolution: Business Strategies for a New Paradigm.* Basingstoke: Palgrave Macmillan.
Calabrò, A. 2012. "Co-Production: An Alternative to the Partial Privatization Processes in Italy and Norway." In *New Public Governance, the Third Sector and Co-Production*, edited by V. A. Pestoff, T. Brandsen, and B. Verschuere, 317–336. New York: Routledge.
Casa-Cortés, M., S. Cobarrubias, and J. Pickles. 2014. "The Commons." In *A Companion to Urban Anthropology*, edited by D. Nonini, 449–470. Hoboken: Wiley-Blackwell.
Chatterton, P. 2010. "Seeking the Urban Common: Furthering the Debate on Spatial Justice." *City* 14 (6): 625–628. doi:10.1080/13604813.2010.525304.
Couture, T., and Y. Gagnon. 2010. "An Analysis of Feed-In Tariff Remuneration Models: Implications for Renewable Energy Investment." *Energy Policy* 38 (2): 955–965. doi:10.1016/j.enpol.2009.10.047.
Cumbers, A. 2012. *Reclaiming Public Ownership: Making Space for Economic Democracy.* London: Zed Books.
Cumbers, A. 2015. "Constructing a Global Commons In, Against, and Beyond the State." *Space and Polity* 19 (1): 62–75. doi:10.1080/13562576.2014.995465.
Dietz, T., N. Dolšak, E. Ostrom, and P. C. Stern. 2002. "The Drama of the Commons." In *The Drama of the Commons*, edited by E. Ostrom, T. Dietz, N. Dolšak, and P. C. Stern, 3–35. Washington: National Academy Press.
Eizenberg, E. 2012. "Actually Existing Commons: Three Moments of Space of Community Gardens in New York City." *Antipode* 44 (3): 764–782. doi:10.1111/j.1467-8330.2011.00892.x.
Eurostat. 2015. "Share of renewables in energy consumption up to 15% in the EU in 2013." 2015. News release, March 10. http://ec.europa.eu/eurostat/documents/2995521/6734513/8-10032015-AP-EN.pdf/3a8c018d-3d9f-4f1d-95ad-832ed3a20a6b.
Evans, P. 1996. "Introduction: Development Strategies across the Public-Private Divide." *World Development* 24 (6): 1033–1037. doi:10.1016/0305-750X(96)00014-9.
Hahnel, R. 2015. "Participatory Economics and the Commons." *Capitalism Nature Socialism* 26 (3): 31–43. doi:10.1080/10455752.2015.1011069.
Hall, D., E. Lobina, and P. Terhorst. 2013. "Re-Municipalisation in the Early Twenty-First Century: Water in France and Energy in Germany." *International Review of Applied Economics* 27 (2): 193–214. doi:10.1080/02692171.2012.754844.

Hamburg Wasser, and Hamburg Energie. 2014. "Geschäftsbericht." http://www.hamburgwasser.de/formulare-downloads.html?download=1294.

Hardt, M., and A. Negri. 2009. *Commonwealth*. Cambridge: Belknap Press of Harvard University Press.

Harvey, D. 2011. "The Future of the Commons." *Radical History Review* 109: 101–107. doi:10.1215/01636545-2010-017.

Harvey, D. 2012. *Rebel Cities: From the Right to the City to the Urban Revolution*. London: Verso.

Helfrich, S., and D. Bollier. 2012. "Commons Als Transformative Kraft." In *Commons. Für eine neue Politik jenseits von Markt und Staat*, edited by Helfrich and Heinrich-Böll-Stiftung, 15–23. Bielefeld: transcript.

Hess, D. J. 2011. "Electricity Transformed: Neoliberalism and Local Energy in the United States." *Antipode* 43 (4): 1056–1077. doi:10.1111/j.1467-8330.2010.00842.x.

Hisschemöller, M., and I. Sioziou. 2013. "Boundary Organisations for Resource Mobilisation: Enhancing Citizens' Involvement in the Dutch Energy Transition." *Environmental Politics* 22 (5): 792–810. doi:10.1080/09644016.2013.775724.

Hodkinson, S. 2012. "The New Urban Enclosures." *City* 16 (5): 500–518. doi:10.1080/13604813.2012.709403.

Jeffrey, A., C. McFarlane, and A. Vasudevan. 2012. "Rethinking Enclosure: Space, Subjectivity and the Commons." *Antipode* 44 (4): 1247–1267. doi:10.1111/j.1467-8330.2011.00954.x.

Jenny, A., F. H. Fuentes, and H.-J. Mosler. 2007. "Psychological Factors Determining Individual Compliance with Rules for Common Pool Resource Management: The Case of a Cuban Community Sharing a Solar Energy System." *Human Ecology* 35 (2): 239–250. doi:10.1007/s10745-006-9053-x.

Jenssen, T., A. König, and L. Eltrop. 2014. "Bioenergy Villages in Germany: Bringing a Low Carbon Energy Supply for Rural Areas into Practice." *Renewable Energy* 61: 74–80. doi:10.1016/j.renene.2012.08.014.

Joshi, A., and M. Moore. 2004. "Institutionalised Co-production: Unorthodox Public Service Delivery in Challenging Environments." *Journal of Development Studies* 40 (4): 31–49. doi:10.1080/00220380410001673184.

Kip, M. 2015. "Moving Beyond the City: Conceptualizing Urban Commons from a Critical Urban Studies Perspective." In *Urban Commons: Moving Beyond State and Market*, edited by M. Dellenbaugh, M. Kip, M. Bienok, A. K. Müller, and M. Schwegmann, 42–60. Basel: Birkhäuser.

Klein, N. 2001. "Reclaiming the Commons." *New Left Review* 9: 81–89. http://newleftreview.org/II/9/naomi-klein-reclaiming-the-commons.

Krätke, S. 2001. "Berlin: Towards a Global City?" *Urban Studies* 38 (10): 1777–1799. doi:10.1080/00420980120084859.

Kunze, C., and S. Becker. 2015. "Collective Ownership in Renewable Energy and Opportunities for Sustainable Degrowth." *Sustainability Science* 10 (3): 425–437. doi:10.1007/s11625-015-0301-0.

Landeswahlleiterin Berlin. 2013. "Volksentscheid "Neue Energie" am 3. November 2013: Ergebnis des Volksentscheids." https://www.wahlen-berlin.de/Abstimmungen/VE2013_NEnergie/Ergebnisprozent.asp?sel1=6052&sel2=0798

Linebaugh, P. 2008. *The Magna Carta Manifesto: Liberties and Commons for All*. Berkeley: University of California Press.

Matecki, C., and T. Schulten. 2013. "Zwischen Privatisierung und Rekommunalisierung: Zur Entwicklung der öffentlichen Daseinsvorsorge." In *Zurück zur öffentlichen Hand? Chancen und Erfahrungen der Rekommunalisierung*, edited by C. Matecki and T. Schulten, 8–18. Hamburg: VSA-Verlag.

Mayer, M. 2012. "The 'Right to the City' in Urban Social Movements." In *Cities for People, Not for Profit: Critical Urban Theory and the Right to the City*, edited by N. Brenner, P. Marcuse, and M. Mayer, 42–61. London: Routledge.

McDonald, D. A., and G. Ruiters, eds. 2012. *Alternatives to Privatisatization: Public Options for Essential Services in the Global South*. London: Routledge.

McMillan, R., S. Spronk, and C. Caswell. 2014. "Popular Participation, Equity, and Co-Production of Water and Sanitation Services in Caracas, Venezuela." *Water International* 39 (2): 201–215. doi:10.1080/02508060.2014.886844.

Meyer-Wellmann, J. 2014. "Nach Vattenfall-Deal: das passiert jetzt mit dem Netz." *Hamburger Abendblatt*, January 16. http://www.abendblatt.de/hamburg/article123904084/Nach-Vattenfall-Deal-Das-passiert-jetzt-mit-dem-Netz.html.

Mitlin, D. 2008. "With and Beyond the State: Co-Production as a Route to Political Influence, Power and Transformation for Grassroots Organizations." *Environment and Urbanization* 20 (2): 339–360. doi:10.1177/0956247808096117.

Moss, T. 2014. "Socio-technical Change and the Politics of Urban Infrastructure: Managing Energy in Berlin between Dictatorship and Democracy." *Urban Studies* 51 (7): 1432–1448. doi:10.1177/0042098013500086.

Moss, T., S. Becker, and M. Naumann. 2015. "Whose Energy Transition Is It, Anyway? Organisation and Ownership of the Energiewende in Villages, Cities and Regions." *Local Environment* 20 (12): 1547–1563. doi:10.1080/13549839.2014.915799.

Nielsen, S. N., and S. E. Jørgensen. 2015. "Sustainability Analysis of a Society Based on Exergy Studies – A Case Study of the Island of Samsø (Denmark)." *Journal of Cleaner Production* 96 (1): 12–29. doi:10.1016/j.jclepro.2014.08.035.

Norddeutscher Rundfunk. 2014. "Kraftwerk Moorburg: eine Chronologie." http://www.ndr.de/nachrichten/dossiers/kohlekraft/moorburgchronologie100_page-1.html

Olson, M. 1965. *The Logic of Collective Action: Public Goods and The Theory of Groups*. Cambridge: Harvard University Press.

Osborne, S. P., and K. Strokosch. 2013. "It takes Two to Tango? Understanding the Co-production of Public Services by Integrating the Services Management and Public Administration Perspectives." *British Journal of Management* 24 (S1): S31–S47. doi:10.1111/1467-8551.12010.

Ostrom, E. 1972. "Metropolitan Reform: Propositions Derived From Two Traditions." *Social Science Quarterly* 53: 474–493.

Ostrom, E. 1990. *Governing the Commons: The Evolution of Institutions for Collective Action*. Cambridge: Cambridge University Press.

Ostrom, E. 1996. "Crossing the Great Divide: Coproduction, Synergy, and Development." *World Development* 24 (6): 1073–1087. doi:10.1016/0305-750X(96)00023-X.

Ostrom, E. 2005. *Understanding Institutional Diversity*. Princeton: Princeton University Press.

Ostrom, E. 2008. "The Challenge of Common-Pool Resources." *Environment: Science and Policy for Sustainable Development* 50 (4): 8–21. doi:10.3200/ENVT.50.4.8-21.

Ostrom, E. 2010. "Beyond Markets and States: Polycentric Governance of Complex Economic Systems." *American Economic Review* 100 (3): 641–672. doi:10.1257/aer.100.3.641.

Ostrom, E., R. B. Parks, and G. P. Whitaker. 1974. "Defining and Measuring Structural Variations in Interorganizational Arrangements." *Publius* 4 (4): 87–108. doi:10.2307/3329480.

Ostrom, E., and G. Whitaker. 1973. "Does Local Community Control of Police Make a Difference? Some Preliminary Findings." *American Journal of Political Science* 17 (1): 48–76. doi:10.2307/2110474.

Parr, A. 2015. "Urban Debt, Neoliberalism and the Politics of the Commons." *Theory, Culture & Society* 32 (3): 69–91. doi:10.1177/0263276414536234.

Peck, J. 2010. *Constructions of Neoliberal Reason*. Oxford: Oxford University Press.

Pestoff, V. A. 2009. *A Democratic Architecture for the Welfare State*. London: Routledge.

Radywyl, N., and C. Biggs. 2013. "Reclaiming the Commons for Urban Transformation." *Journal of Cleaner Production* 50: 159–170. doi:10.1016/j.jclepro.2012.12.020.

Rügemer, W. 2006. *Privatisierung in Deutschland: Eine Bilanz von der Treuhand zu Public Private Partnership*. Münster: Westfälisches Dampfboot.

Senatskanzlei Freie und Hansestadt Hamburg. 2011. "Hamburg schafft die Energiewende." 2011. News release, November 29. http://www.hamburg.de/pressearchiv-fhh/3168428/2011-11-29-energiewende/

Susser, I., and S. Tonnelat. 2013. "Transformative Cities: The Three Urban Commons." *Focaal. Journal of Global and Historical Anthropology* 66: 105–132. doi:10.3167/fcl.2013.660110.

Trend:Research, and Leuphana University Lüneburg. 2013. "Definition und Marktanalyse von Bürgerenergie in Deutschland." http://100-prozent-erneuerbar.de/wp-content/uploads/2013/10/Definition-und-Marktanalyse-von-B%C3%Bcrgerenergie-in-Deutschland.pdf

Vermeylen, S. 2010. "Resource Rights and the Evolution of Renewable Energy Technologies." *Renewable Energy* 35 (11): 2399–2405. doi:10.1016/j.renene.2010.03.017.

Verschuere, B., T. Brandsen, and V. Pestoff. 2012. "Co-production: The State of the Art in Research and the Future Agenda." *Voluntas* 23 (4): 1083–1101. doi:10.1007/s11266-012-9307-8.

Von Winterfeld, U., A. Biesecker, C. Katz, and B. Best. 2012. *Welche Rolle können Commons in Transformationsprozessen zu Nachhaltigkeit spielen?* Wuppertal: Wuppertal Institut für Klima, Umwelt, Energie.

Wolsink, M. 2012. "The Research Agenda on Social Acceptance of Distributed Generation in Smart Grids: Renewable as Common Pool Resources." *Renewable and Sustainable Energy Reviews* 16 (1): 822–835. doi:10.1016/j.rser.2011.09.006.

Yildiz, Ö., J. Rommel, S. Debor, L. Holstenkamp, F. Mey, J. R. Müller, J. Radtke, and J. Rognli. 2015. "Renewable Energy Cooperatives as Gatekeepers or Facilitators? Recent Developments in Germany and a Multidisciplinary Research Agenda." *Energy Research & Social Science* 6: 59–73. doi:10.1016/j.erss.2014.12.001.

Zawatka-Gerlach, U. 2015. "Senat will sich an Gas- und Stromunternehmen beteiligen: Streit um Energienetze vorerst beigelegt." *Tagesspiegel*, May 5. http://www.tagesspiegel.de/berlin/berlin-streit-um-energienetze-vorerst-beigelegt-senat-will-sich-an-gas-und-stromunternehmen-beteiligen/11733656.html

Zawatka-Gerlach, U., L. V. Törne, and F. Keilani. 2014. "Das ist fürchterlich für die Koalition: Senator Heilmann gegen Senator Nussbaum." *Tagesspiegel*, June 25. http://www.tagesspiegel.de/berlin/senator-heilmann-gegen-senator-nussbaum-das-ist-fuerchterlich-fuer-die-koalition/10095942.html

Appendix. List of interviews referred to in the text

Interview BUND: Interview with a representative of Bund für Umwelt- und Naturschutz Deutschland [Friends of the Earth Germany]. Hamburg, 16 December 2014.

Interview BürgerEnergie: Interview with a spokesperson of BürgerEnergie Berlin. Berlin, 2 September 2013.

Interview Church: Interview with a Hamburg Diakonie representative [charity organisation of the Protestant-Lutheran Church]. Berlin, 20 June 2014.

Interview Consultant: Interview with a consultant who was officially engaged with the formation Hamburg Energie. Hamburg, 20 April 2015.

Interview Handelskammer: Interview with a leading employee of Handelskammer Hamburg [Chamber of Commerce Hamburg]. Hamburg, 17 December 2014.

Interview OHON Campaigner: Interview with a professional campaigner active for the 'Our Hamburg – Our Network' (OHON) campaign. Hamburg, 8 January 2015.

Interview Roundtable Activist: Interview with a left-winged grassroots activist from the Berlin Energy Roundtable. Berlin, 28 August 2013.

Interview Roundtable Professional: Interview with a professional campaigner coordinating the Roundtable's campaign activities. Berlin, 27 August 2013.

Interview SPD Environment: Interview with a high-ranking member of SPD Hamburg specialised in environmental politics. Hamburg, 26 March 2015.

Interview Zukunftsrat: Interview with a leading member of the network Zukunftsrat Hamburg [Future Council Hamburg – Network for Sustainable Development]. Hamburg, 8 April 2015.

‘Co-producing affordability’ to the electricity service: a market-oriented response to addressing inequality of access in Rio de Janeiro’s *favelas*

Francesca Pilo’

User involvement in service organisation is seen as a potential means of improving and resolving service delivery issues. The aim of this article is to review a market-oriented project involving electricity customers in the *favelas* – defined here as an example of ‘co-producing affordability’ to the service – in order to enhance understanding of the diverse collaborative arrangements in service delivery in the South. By examining the part played by the institutional stakeholders involved in the project and the partial dissatisfaction that arose among users, this article will highlight the limitations of this approach for addressing disparities in access to services.

1. Introduction

Inequalities of access to urban services in developing and emerging countries form part of a process of urbanisation characterised by land-use patterns that lie on the margins of formal practices. These habitats, ‘called irregular, precarious, under-integrated, illegal or, depending on the city, *bidonvilles, favelas*, slums, *barriadas*...’ (Clerc 2011, 63) are described, in official definitions, in terms of the inadequacy or absence of urban services. In the quest to integrate these districts into the city and to improve the quality of life of these populations, research emphasises the need to introduce appropriate technical solutions and shows how the provision of urban services is largely dependent on the land ownership and living conditions of the populations (Barbier et al. 2007).

With regard to the *favelas* of Rio de Janeiro, these questions have long been met with partial answers. In these urban areas, present in the city for more than a century, the struggle for access to urban services – particularly intense in the 1980s – has produced results. The electricity and water network’s coverage is today close to universal. However, the first official process of electrification that took place in the 1980s has evolved into illegal individual practices of access to the grid that pose new challenges to electricity supply in these districts: as well as improving the quality of service, which remains highly unreliable, the task today is to regularise access to the grid.

This article focuses on a project in which electricity users from *favelas* are involved in service delivery and which fits into a broader framework of schemes designed to regularize access to the electricity network and transform ‘irregular consumers’ into ‘regular customers’. Under an initiative launched by Rio de Janeiro’s electricity distribution company, Light, a new scheme was implemented in August 2011 to improve environmental sustainability and facilitate the payment of electricity bills by encouraging the direct involvement of customers. Through this scheme, called 'Light Recicla', the company offers customers the opportunity to obtain a discount on their energy bills by collecting their own solid waste.

On the basis of this case study, this article wishes to contribute to an understanding of the diversity of collaborative arrangements to provide service delivery in the Global South. The notion of co-production will provide a useful analytical framework for reflecting on this project, while opening up new questions about the dynamics of user involvement (Section I). The article then goes on to describe the '*Light recicla'* project in terms of its operation and regulation (Section II). Finally, we address some limits of the project's approach from two perspectives: (a) the difficulties of building up a long-lasting response to the question of affordability of the service; and (b) the capacity of this arrangement to regulate conflicts and more generally of responding to the demands of the populations living in irregular districts (Section III).

This article draws on data that I collected from a field survey conducted between August and December 2011 as part of my doctoral research on the regularisation of service access in the Rio de Janeiro *favelas* (Pilo' 2015b). This survey covered Santa Marta, a *favela* located in the southern part of the city and the first to benefit from the "*Light recicla"* scheme. As regards the methodology employed, I chose a qualitative approach based on semi-directive interviews. To this end, I interviewed the institutional actors involved in the scheme (power distribution company and municipality), the people directly concerned (a dozen users), as well as community leaders and the chair of the *favela*'s resident association.

2. Service co-production in the south: engaging citizens or customers?

Efforts to improve service delivery to the poor largely involve a variety of social, organisational and spatial engineering methods. User involvement in service organisation is seen both as increasing investment and management efficiency, and as a potential to improve democracy. Since the 1980s, the 'co-production' concept has been accepted as an appropriate analytical framework for exploring the public service-related interactions between citizens and the state. The approach used by the 'Light Recicla' project, and which is reviewed here, has been defined by other authors as a specific type of co-production, called 'collaborative service': 'a service in which results could be achieved only if people actively participated and were motivated to engage in the service' (Cipolla, Melo, and Manzini 2015, 137). According to these authors, users are seen as co-producers of the service because they play an active role in service delivery, especially in the payment system: they collect the rubbish, wash it, separate it and take it to a recycling collection point, where their recyclable materials are exchanged for energy credits, thus helping reduce their electricity bills (Cipolla, Melo, and Manzini 2015, 132).

Rather than targeting genuine service delivery co-production, the 'Light Recicla' project appears instead to be an arrangement for co-producing affordability to a service undergoing regularisation. Users are encouraged to get actively involved in the service by collecting their rubbish, thereby becoming 'co-working customers'; the aim of this being to improve the sustainability of regularised access to the service, notably by reducing its cost. Thus, in practice, the actual goal is regularised service delivery co-production.

In the available literature, the concept of service co-production has been interpreted and defined in a variety of ways. Thus, whereas some authors consider co-production to involve individual users (as customers, consumers, etc.; see Brandsen and Pestoff 2006), others focus on its collective aspect (communities, associations, etc., see Bovaird 2007). Based on her empirical work, notably on the co-production of urban infrastructures in Brazil (water and sewerage systems) and education in Nigeria, E. Ostrom defines co-production as being "*the process through which inputs used to provide a good or service are contributed by individuals who are not "in" the same organisation'*" (Ostrom 1996, 1073). Under this definition, rather than being passive clients, the recipients of services are citizens who actively contribute to producing public services. According to the author, the complementary relationship between public officials and citizens makes it possible to provide a concrete response to the problem of service provision, improve welfare and, more broadly, build a virtuous circle of stronger reciprocal commitment.

Joshi and Moore redefine this notion as being 'institutionalised co-production', namely '*the provision of public services (broadly defined, to include regulation) through a regular long-term relationship between state agencies and organised groups of citizens, where both make substantial resource contributions*' (Joshi and Moore 2004, 40). The authors stress that in a context where 'Weberian' institutional boundaries are blurred and the state is usually weak, co-production can lead to the ambiguous division of power between the state and groups of citizens; an ambiguity that can have an adverse effect on effectiveness and political responsibility, but which can also have a positive impact on improving access to services (Joshi and Moore 2004). Adopting the same approach, L. Moretto's research on co-production of the water service on the outskirts of Caracas shows that co-production can be effective at improving quality of access to the service (in terms of supply) and integrating low-income residents into the urban development decision-making process (Moretto 2011, 96). However, it also outlines the limitations of this system for building genuine participatory and representative democracy as community-based organisations remain highly dependent on the central public authorities.

However, as D. Mitlin points out, this literature '*does not locate co-production within a broader struggle for choice, self-determination and meso level political relations in which citizens both seek an engagement with the state (to secure redistribution, reduce free riders, etc.) and also are oriented towards selfmanagement and local control over local provision in areas related to basic needs (*i.e. *services with development significance)*' (Mitlin 2008, 347). From this position, D. Mitlin provides several examples of 'bottom-up co-production', understood as a '*self-organized co-production, with grassroots organizations engaging the state while at the same time maintaining a degree of autonomy within the delivery process*' (Mitlin 2008, 352). She invites us to reconsider co-production not only as a system that can help meet the material needs of populations in low-income settlements, but also as a way of constructing a '*consciousness of selfworth among these residents who become aware of their own central contribution to progressive social change*' (Mitlin 2008, 358).

While these 'bottom-up' experiences suggest the potential contribution of citizen driven actions, the annexation of the participatory regime by a managerial approach inspired by New Public Management principles is redrawing the outlines of participation to fit within a managerial framework. In this regard, S. Jaglin wonders whether the political dimension of collective action and its challenges in terms of equity and effectiveness may not be covered up by systems of governance that mitigate power relations (Jaglin 2004). Her view of this question is unequivocal: 'co-production devitalises more conflictual forms of organisation' (Jaglin 2005, 15).

In reality, the literature provides a different view of the potential of co-production to improve services and engage the state. While certain authors see co-production as a way of moving away from a market-centred approach towards a state-/community-centred form (Moretto and Allen 2015), others authors conversely suggest that co-production helps support the user-pays system (Jaglin 2004).

The handful of studies cited here will provide the groundwork for the analysis of the '*Light recicla*' project, in particular on the following dimensions: the relationship between co-producers and the political dimension of user involvement beyond the technical organisation of service delivery.

3. 'Light recicla': a private/individual joint service engagement

3.1. Police and the regularisation of electricity access in the favelas: leveraging the 'light recicla'

The '*Light recicla*' scheme is developed in a security-policy context, which largely determines the actions of the electricity company. In the run-up to the city's hosting of several international events, public safety has become a priority of local political action. Since 2008, the government of the State of Rio de Janeiro has deployed a permanent police presence in certain *favelas* through the introduction of the so-called UPP (Pacifying Police Units). This was a new policing measure introduced with the overall objective of re-establishing the state's territorial control over a limited number of *favelas* marked by the influence of armed groups linked with drug trafficking (38 UPPs have been installed until 2015). The return of the 'armed force' of the state had a direct impact on the way of managing the electricity service in these areas. Taking advantage of a police presence, the distribution company conducted projects to regularise access to the service that was, until then, mostly illegal. Indeed, since the transfer of the electricity distribution service to private companies during the restructuring of the electricity sector in the 1990s, the company has been developing regularization measures. The failure of these measures in the *favelas* was largely attributed to the territorial control of the gangs. The new public safety policy was therefore not just a contextual factor, but the essential condition for the development of new plans for regularising access to the electricity service. In return, the discourse of public authorities underlines the importance of these plans to the fulfilment of the specific public safety objectives: 'to bring an end to the traditional perception of the 'divided city' that characterises the city of Rio de Janeiro'.[1] The importance attributed to the electricity regularisation plans by the authorities is symptomatic of the reinforced idea that the 'integration of the *favelas*' should be promoted through the joint intervention of public and private actors.

These regularisation measures were structured around several elements. As well as technical initiatives such as meter installations and network upgrades, the distribution company also took steps to manage consumption by newly regularised customers, as part of an Energy Efficiency Programme the '*Comunidade Eficiente*' (see Pilo' 2015a), and a commercial policy specifically designed to help regularise commercial relations (see Pilo' 2015b).

Regularising the customer relationship poses a significant challenge as sustainable access to the service needs to be ensured for low-income population groups. This task is complicated by the full cost-recovery pricing system used, which passes on all service costs to the end user. Since privatisation of the electricity sector in the 1990s, the pricing model used is that of the price cap, under which the tariff charged must enable the operator to cover their costs to ensure the economic and financial sustainability of the service.[2] Thus, following privatisation, Light's average tariffs increased by 256% between

1996 and 2008 (Kelman 2010). For instance, in 2015, a kWh of electricity cost 0.61 reais (0.14 euro cents), which is the same as the price per kWh charged by EDF in France. The pricing system also includes a subsidised tariff, known as the "social tariff", which is charged to households identified as poor. However, application of this tariff is not based on type of housing or residential area, but on household income (granted to those with incomes less than or equal to half of the minimum wage per capita). Therefore, this "social tariff' does not specifically target the inhabitants of the *favelas*, who will only receive it if their incomes meet the criteria. Furthermore, in order to be considered for this "social tariff', households also need to be registered on the unique national social assistance programme database (Cadastro Unico). However, as I have shown in earlier research (Pilo' 2015b), although there is a "social tariff" in place for low-income users, the allocation system used to apply this is far from effective in the *favelas*.

Given this situation, the company decided that making people pay the full amount for electricity consumed from the start of the regularisation process could have a negative effect on payment collection rates. To overcome this potential issue, the company set up an incremental payment system intended to prepare users for paying for actual energy consumed. At the end of this incremental payment process, however, the sensitive issue of affordability once again came to the fore. It was because of this major concern that, in September 2011, Light introduced a 'pilot scheme' that involved people recycling solid waste in exchange for a discount on their electricity bills.

3.2. Individual and voluntary participation by customers

The 'Light Recicla' scheme is based on the individual and voluntary participation of customers. In particular, it offers customers who have signed up for the project the opportunity to take their solid waste to a recycling collection point in exchange for receiving a financial discount on their electricity bill in the form of energy credits. The energy credits are financed through a market-based mechanism as clients sell their solid waste to the recycling collection point at the market price for the specific item in question.

Initial assessments of the pilot scheme revealed that the primary beneficiaries were the individual residents of the *favelas* involved the project, as well as certain public and private institutions located in the districts around those *favelas*. Other customers within the distribution company's concession area were also able to benefit, provided that they transferred their energy credits to one of the associations located in Santa Marta (residents' association, NGO, samba school). As described below, this credit-transfer mechanism meant that these associations particularly benefitted from the "Light Recicla" project as their electricity bills significantly decreased. The company presented this transfer mechanism as a way of establishing solidarity between the *favelas* and the surrounding neighbourhoods. It is based on the idea that, in order to "achieve integration", projects need to benefit a whole "urban area" without distinguishing between "rich" and "poor" districts, as the Light employee we spoke to explained:

> 'We didn't want to create a project just for the 'hill' [*favela*]. If we want to put 'integration' into practice, we need to set up projects that link the community[3] with its surroundings. Moreover, for the residents of Botafogo and Humaità, living next door to a community with a regularised service and no bill payment problems is also an advantage. That is why we give them the opportunity contribute to the well-being of the community' (Light social manager, 31 November 2011)

The scheme operated in different stages, set out in Figure 1. First, users were required to sign up individually with the company in order to obtain a card on which the bonuses would be recorded. Subsequently, these customers would be able to reach on foot to certain collection points to hand over and weigh their waste, which they would first have sorted and cleaned: paper, glass, plastic, metal and vegetable oil. The spatial proximity of the collection points was seen as essential in the design of the project. A collection point was therefore built inside the *favela*, following discussions with the chairman of the resident association about its location. The physical layout of the *favela*, located on a hill and with closely packed houses, strongly influenced the choice of position. The eco-point was therefore placed at the main entrance, next to the first cable car stop, a location chosen mainly for logistical reasons, in particular the need for enough space for a truck to collect the recycling material. Other 'eco-points' were installed in the districts where the *favela* is located: Botafogo and Humaità. The photos below show the premises assigned to the 'eco-point' in the construction phase and after (Figures 2, 3 and 4), and the waste sorting (Figures 5 and 6).

At the 'eco-point', Light employed a private company, '3E Engenharia', to manage the interface with customers: it is responsible for sorting and weighing the material and recording the bonuses on the customers's card. Each card has an electronic chip that stores the bonuses and transmits the value directly to Light, which uses the 'customers code' to allocate credits directly to the individual bill. A receipt showing the value of the bonus is given to each customers, so that he or she can check that the reduction is applied to the next month's bill. The selling price of each type of waste varies depending on the product's market value and the prices are displayed at the entrance to the 'eco-point'. Finally, the material is collected,

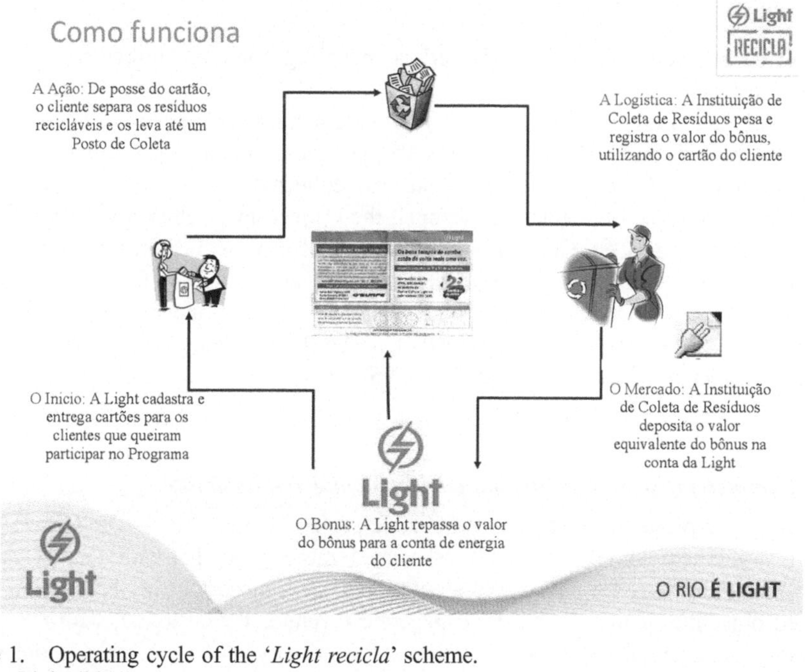

Figure 1. Operating cycle of the '*Light recicla*' scheme.
Source: Light (2011)

Figures 2, 3 and 4. The ‘eco-point’ in Santa Marta before and after.
Image credit: F. Pilo’ (2011).

Figures 5 and 6. Queue in front of the ‘eco-point’ and waste sorting.
Image credit: F. Pilo’ (2011)

transported and recycled by ‘Brasil Pet’, a recycling company linked with an NGO called Ecovida.

In 2011, the ‘Light Recicla’ project was implemented in three *favelas*: Santa Marta, Chapéu Mangueira and Babilonia. Seventy-five per cent of clients signed up to the project and a remarkable 11 tonnes of solid waste was collected (Light 2012). These positive initial results prompted the company to open the project up to other *favelas* with UPPs: Rocinha, Chácara do Céu, Cruzada São Sebastião, Morro dos Cabritos and Ladeira dos Tabajaras. As of April 2014, 9,807 customers had signed up for the scheme and the following volumes of waste had been recycled: 3,098 tonnes of recyclable material and 11,979 litres of vegetable oil (Light 2014). According to the company, these results exceeded expectations by 53% (Light 2014, 96).

3.3. Commercial sustainability and environmental responsibility

This scheme is presented first as a ‘sustainable project’ (Light 2011). The term ‘sustainable’ is used here to refer to goals associated more generally with the ‘sustainable development’ both of the *favelas* concerned and more generally of the city. The first declared objective of the scheme is to generate revenues for customer, with the aim of stabilising commercial relations. In practice, the primary aim is to make a potentially insolvent market sustainable: ‘In order for Light’s commercial results to be sustainable, the pacified communities need to self-develop, amongst other things through revenue generation' (Light's Community Service Manager, 1 September 2011). The bonus of bill discount is therefore presented not only as a tool to help people pay their bills, but as one facet of a wider objective of indirectly generating revenues: 'What they don't spend on their bills is money that stays in their pockets. They can spend it to buy products essential to family well-being' (Light's Community Service Manager, 1 September 2011). This cut in bills should also help to 'minimise clandestine connections and reduce the proportion of unpaid bills' (Light 2011), as well as facilitating the transition to a system of payment based on real electricity consumption (end of the incremental payment policy), thereby increasing individual responsibility, as explained by the Light employee we spoke to:

> 'It is a way to make the end of the incremental payment scheme easier and to get people to pay for their actual electricity use. With a bit of effort by customers, this scheme is an instrument for reducing bill levels. The goal is to create a solution that is sustainable both for the company and for customers' (Light Social Manager, 31 November 2011)

Moreover, the second objective of the scheme, environmental protection and awareness, reinforces and adds a further nuance to the notion of individual responsibility: 'Encouraging a cultural transformation in the population, educating people about the use and reuse of natural resources and raising awareness of the impact of these actions on future generations' (Light 2011). This call for environmental responsibility has a practical scope that is particularly strong in the framework of informal neighbourhoods.

First, it promotes the objective of preserving natural resources and saving energy associated with the treatment of solid waste, based on the idea of the 'good citizen'. As observed by Cipolla *et al.* this mention of citizenship seems particularly attractive to these residents: '*several domestic users understand the environmental benefits brought by the project, beyond the discount in the bill, and this motivation too (*i.e. *to feel good, to be a 'real good citizen') is a meanful driver for their active participation*' (Cipolla, Melo, and Manzini 2015, 11). It is interesting to notice that, the idea of citizenship, for these residents who are widely treated by the authorities as 'second-class citizens', does not build on a deepening relationship between the state and these citizens. Quite the contrary, it is based on a conception of a kind of 'ecological citizenship' which partially intends to respond to the limited role of the State as a provider of waste collection service, but without engaging the state.

In fact, it is a real problem that the *favela* needs to tackle. The constant presence of waste in the streets is a big factor in the persistence of health problems in the *favela*, one that is particularly critical in summer when high temperatures and the seasonal rains tend to increase the risk of disease. The outbreaks of dengue fever are one example. One of the main causes of their development is attributed to the concentration of waste in areas where water tends to stagnate, a situation further exacerbated when household waste mixes with wastewater. The population explains the failure of this service in Santa Marta partly by the municipality's devolution of responsibility, but also by the residents' own rejection of responsibility. In particular, residents complain about the fact that the municipal cleaning services restrict their operations to the *favela*'s main streets, ignoring the many alleyways (Ibase and Eco 2012). The inadequacy of the bins, perceived as too small for the *favela*'s needs, is another factor adduced as encouraging the dumping of waste in the streets and, in this respect, the residents also emphasise the need for greater collective responsibility in maintaining a clean public space (Ibase and Eco 2012).

With regard to '*Light recicla*', Cipolla Melo, and Manzini have in fact observed that '*it is starting to take place in spontaneous, self-organized initiatives. This horizontal collaboration happens when neighbours and family members help each other spontaneously. It may occur without payment or, as in one case we observed, by payment. In this case, a user called Benedito, who owns a bar near the Collection Point, observed that other users were not motivated to separate, clean and take the recyclable materials to the collection points. He started to collect other citizens recyclables in exchange for half the value obtained in the exchange for credits, developing a kind of small business that increased his monthly income while helping others to lower their bills*' (Cipolla, Melo, and Manzini 2015, 13). While E. Ostrom's analyses had identified the emergence of '*horizontal relationships*' around service coproduction systems, understood as a dynamic through which '*local activism through coproduction rapidly spills over to other areas*' (Ostrom 1996, 1083), what Cipolla, Melo and Manzini call '*horizontal collaboration*' seems rather to be primarily a commercialisation of waste. This dynamic shows how the appeal to individual responsibility encourages an extension of commercial principles beyond access to the service, which is far from engaging these customers as citizens.

Finally, this form of user involvement conveys a specific conception of the handling of inequalities based on the delegation to individual responsibility and to market logics of maintaining economic access. It offers a concrete example of what B. Hibou defines as an 'euphemisation of the political nature of inequalities' in the framework of neoliberal poverty reduction policies (Hibou 2012). However, as we see below, this approach is not without critics.

4. Limitations and conflict over a market-oriented approach to addressing inequalities of access

The project I have just described was acclaimed as a 'social innovation of collaborative service in informal settlements' (Cipolla, Melo, et Manzini 2015) and won a FIRJAN award for environmental initiatives in 2014 in the 'public interest' category. The aim here is not to consider it in terms of social innovation or results, but to question both the capacity of the project to build up a long-lasting response in service delivery and the capacity to regulate conflicts and more generally of responding to the urban demands of the populations of irregular districts.

4.1. National regulation focused on the de-territorialised objective of energy efficiency

The scheme described above is not just confined to the city of Rio de Janeiro. 'Light Recicla' was inspired by similar national and international schemes deemed to incorporate 'best practice' for preventing commercial losses (De Mello et al. 2011). In Brazil, M. de Mello et al. have notably identified two schemes that offer customers a discount on energy bills in return for them collecting their solid waste: 'Vale Luz', set up by Coelba, a power distribution company in Bahia State, and 'Ecoelce', set up by Coelce, a distribution company in Céara State (De Mello et al. 2011). As with 'Light Recicla', these are initiatives promoted by electricity companies privatised when the electricity sector was restructured in the 1990s. However, the context in which the three schemes were developed is different. Thus, comparing 'Light Recicla' with these two similar schemes can provide an insight into who produces, regulates and sets the goals for user involvement within these systems.

'Vale Luz', set up by Coelba in 2007, was the first scheme of this type and forms part of a package of corporate social responsibility measures designed to make electricity provision more affordable. It is underpinned by partnerships with the US development agency USAID and other private and civil society structures (De Mello et al. 2011). In this scheme, the material is collected and sold by a waste collection cooperative created by young people in the Novos Alagados community and does not involve the public authorities.

Unlike 'Vale Luz', '*Light recicla*' and 'Ecoelce' are responses to contractual obligations imposed by the federal government. Law 9.991/2000 requires power distribution companies to invest a minimum percentage of their net operating income in R&D (*pesquisa e desenvolvimento* – research and development) projects and in Energy Efficiency Programmes (EEP) (1% in total). Through this law, therefore, the Brazilian government obliges the distribution companies to contribute to the development of research and innovations in the electricity sector and to improve the energy efficiency of the system. The Brazilian Electricity Regulatory Agency (ANEEL – Agência Nacional de Energia Elétrica), is responsible for overseeing and regulating the generation, distribution, transmission and trading of electric power in the country, monitors the fulfilment of these contractual obligations. In this context, 'Vale Luz' is the outcome of a R&D project and is classified as an Energy Efficiency Programme, because of the energy savings that result from less intensive energy use in the production chain. '*Light recicla*' is similarly classified as an Energy Efficiency Programme and is strongly inspired by 'Vale Luz', in particular with regard to individual participation by users living in *favelas* and by surrounding organisations.

In these two schemes, project 'success' is mostly measured by the energy savings made in the production chain. ANEEL agreed to extend the 'Light Recicla' project for a further 3 years (Light 2013, 96) because of the positive results seen in the collection of recyclable materials component. Yet, as far as stakeholder commitment is concerned, the minor role played by the public authorities raises questions over whether it will be possible to extensively scale-up the scheme. Unlike other forms of co-production, 'Light Recicla' relies on partnerships being set up between different public and private stakeholders; however, actual public authority engagement is low.

4.2. A lack of synergy between government levels and sectoral policies

The scheme relies on private–private partnerships, in particular those between Coca-Cola Brasil, Shopping Leblon and Hortifruti, who provide vital support to help install the 'eco-points' (Light 2013), and the different departments within Rio de Janeiro municipality that have stated their 'institutional willingness' to get involved. These departments include the municipal secretariats for the environment and social support, the secretariat for conservation and public services and Comlurb (the municipal urban cleaning company). I call this support 'institutional willingness' because it requires no direct involvement in the scheme on their part. Instead, it consists of a political display of interest prompted by the city's hosting of several international events, in relation to which the municipality is conducting multiple initiatives designed to demonstrate its commitment to constructing a 'sustainable city'.[4] The aim is predominantly to showcase the municipality's commitment to this broader objective, hence why the publicity materials for the 'Light Recicla' scheme always bear the 'Rio 2016' logo, the municipality's official logo for the Olympic Games. Moreover, as outlined previously, the new public safety policy for the *favelas* stresses the importance of establishing greater cooperation between (public and private) stakeholders in order to demonstrate that the state's presence is not restricted solely to its 'armed forces'. For 'Light Recicla', the benefit sharing between stakeholders (citizens, municipality and utility company) is used to highlight the success of both the scheme and the public-private partnership. According to the 2011 Light Sustainability Report, the State and the municipality of Rio de Janeiro 'profit from improvements to their public image and from reduced waste collection and recycling costs' (Light 2011, 10). Although its political profile seems to have risen in the media, the reasons why the main stakeholder – the municipality – has not been more involved in the project still need to be explained.

In Rio de Janeiro, waste collection is a public service run by the municipality via the municipal firm Comlurb. When the project was on the drawing board, Light considered the active participation of Comlurb, but the latter refused to take responsibility for the collection, transport and recycling of the waste:

> 'We proposed a partnership with Comlurb with the idea that the scheme could subsequently become public policy. They liked the idea, but collecting waste carries a fairly high cost, which they did not want to bear. There is a financial return when the quantity of waste is large, but since this was a pilot project, it was not possible to forecast the quantities. As a result, Comlurb remains an institutional partner, because it supports the scheme symbolically, but the company that removes and recycles the waste is Brasil Pet' (Light's Community Service Manager, 1 September 2011)

Comlurb's selective waste collection coordinator confirmed the reasons given by the Light manager for the scheme's limited economic interest. In fact, it creates additional costs: as stated above, the energy credits are financed through the sale of waste, which requires the municipality to buy this waste and pass the corresponding sum on to Light, who in turn transfers this money back to users in the form of energy credits.

In addition, while this scheme undoubtedly offers Comlurb benefits, by reducing the quantity of waste its operators have to collect, it is possible that the initiative could in the future compete with the selective waste collection policy developed by the Municipality in 21 city districts. Indeed, the Municipality is currently reviewing its waste recycling policy. New national and municipal directives, as well as the hosting of several international events, have forced it to commit more strongly to this policy. A large-scale expansion and reorganisation project is set to start in 2015 to install selective waste collection points in every district in the city. While for the moment this policy only applies to 'formal' districts, debate is still underway on the possibility of extending it to the *favelas*, particularly those with UPPs.

Finally, Comlurb's unwillingness to get involved is also explained by the fact that it would be difficult to replicate the scheme in all the *favelas*:

> 'The central issue that led Comlurb to reject Light's proposal is to do with the fact that Light was proposing a 'pilot scheme'. We cannot think in terms of 'pilot schemes', especially as we have felt from the start that this could not be extended to all the *favelas*. Can you imagine setting up eco-points in all Rio's 700 *favelas*? We need to be devised a broader selective waste collection policy for the *favelas*. What is missing in this scheme is a global vision for the handling of recyclable waste in the *favelas*. Of course, that is not for Light to do, it's our job. It is a good project when you think that it was set up by an electricity company. It's a win-win. But it is essentially a scheme to help customers pay their bills. Our role is to devise a broader policy, not a one-off scheme' (Comlurb Selective Collection Coordinator, 29 November 2011)

At present, '*Light recicla*' would appear to be more of a one-off, experimental and temporary arrangement, nothing like a structure in which the distribution company, the municipality and the *favelas* concerned cooperate within a framework of 'institutionalised coproduction', characterised by '*the provision of public services (broadly defined, to include regulation) through regular, long-term relationships between state agencies and organised groups of citizens, where both make substantial resource contributions*' (Joshi and Moore 2004, 40).

4.3. A commercial response to a socio-political demand

I share the opinion advanced by S. Jaglin, who argues that 'the appropriation of participatory principles by the managerial approach dominant in service reform is nonetheless not entirely unproblematic. In particular, it induces shifts in meaning and simplifications that are the source of multiple confusions and, more generally, leads to a de-politicisation of the debate about the place and role of users' (Jaglin 2005, 83). Without using the vocabulary of participation, the electricity company – through its demand for customer involvement – is endeavouring to provide a commercial response to problems of affordability and disparities in access to electricity services. However, this also appears to have highlighted the socio-political aspect of disparities in access to electricity services, as well as certain limitations of the scheme that has been put in place.

Firstly, there are a number of limitations that could be resolved by the company paying more attention to the needs of the populations concerned. Based on the interviews I conducted with customers, the opening times of the "eco-point" (three days a week, from 8am to 4pm) are inadequate and unsuited to working hours. The inconvenient opening hours are further exacerbated by the time it takes to use the service. Whereas, on the one hand, the long queues outside the "eco-points" demonstrate the *favelas* inhabitants' strong adherence to and interest in the scheme, and on the other hand, these queues also indicate that the service needs to be adapted to ensure households do not find the task too cumbersome and become discouraged. In addition, most people do not have enough suitable space at home to sort their waste, meaning they either have to go to the "eco-point" several times a week or only partially sort their waste, as one woman we spoke to at the entrance to the eco-point explained:

> 'I don't sort everything. It's impossible. There are five of us in the house, we generate a lot of waste, but we don't have the space to keep all that waste for long and I don't have the time to come here too often. So sometimes I throw it straight in the bin.' (Woman, Santa Marta, 15 December 2011)

On top of these practical limitations, a further identified factor of discouragement is often the fact that the effort required outweighs the limited economic gain (Cipolla, Melo, and Manzini 2015; Ninives Gonçalves and Valadão 2012). Yet, calculating the average savings for households is not a straightforward task. In 2011, the average savings for each customer were 22 reais per month (around €9) and rose to 40 reais per month in 2012 (Light 2013, 79). However, these figures include not only the savings made by households, but also those made by businesses and associations, which appear to be the main beneficiaries of the 'Light Recicla' scheme.

As stated above, customers living outside the *favelas* directly involved in the scheme can take part in the project, as can associations located in the districts around Santa Marta, namely Botafogo and Humaitá. However, their participation is subject to the condition that the bonuses obtained are transferred to one of the associations within the *favela*. Santa Marta's

Table 1. Reduction in association electricity bills – Santa Marta.

	August 2011			September 2011		
Benefiting Santa Marta Association	Bill amount (reais)	Reduction amount (reais)	Amount of bill without reduction (reais)	Bill amount (reais)	Reduction amount (reais)	Amount of bill without reduction (reais)
Resident Association	−5	46	41	−23	64	41
NGO Attitude social	−34	62	28	−4	34	30
Samba School	352	56	408	225	136	361

Source: Compiled by the author from (Light 2011).

local associations have indeed been particular beneficiaries of the bonus transfer mechanism. Table 1 shows the discount acquired by the *favela*'s three main associations in August and September 2011. The residents association's electricity bill fell by 111% in August 2011 and by 155% in September of the same year. Similarly, the electricity bill of the NGO *Atitude sociale* was reduced by 222% in August and by 114% in September. As a result, their bills are negative, allowing them to allocate credits to their future bills. As regards the samba school, the discount was significantly smaller, though still substantial: 14% in August and 38% in September (Light 2011).

This approach appears to have fostered a gradual alliance between the company and local associations, possibly contributing to the wider goal of 'reinforcing links with the community' (Light 2011). Far from being a secondary priority, this objective is much stressed in the company's institutional discourse.

> 'In these communities, waste is a real problem. This scheme can improve their situation. In addition, it is an energy company that is developing the scheme. All these improvements are therefore linked with Light's image. The company's image in the community will improve and this is very important for other measures to be accepted by the community. Always for the purpose of helping customers pay their bills. This is energy efficiency and financial efficiency for the company' (Light social manager, 31 November 2011)

The preferential treatment local associations have received seems to have contributed to their strong commitment to the scheme, as explained by the chair of the resident association:

> 'We are managing to combine shared objectives: the residents need to save money and keep the community clean. People used to dump waste anywhere. Today, everyone brings their waste to the eco-point here in the community, in an accessible location' (Chairman of the Santa Marta resident association, 15 December 2011)

This alignment in positions between Light and the local associations that benefit from the scheme is not without its critics, starting with certain community leaders, who see the preferential treatment of local associations as a strategy to get political backing in the *favela*. In fact, some community leaders expressed their objections to the ideas promoted by '*Light recicla*', in particularly at the institutional presentation of the scheme to the inhabitants of the *favela*:

> 'When the scheme presentation meeting took place, several local associations were present, but the ECO association was the only one to raise objections. First, the problem of waste is a communal problem which should have an organised and collectively developed response. Selective sorting should not be implemented on an individual – and above all commercial – basis. Second, this type of project prioritises the idea of individual responsibility, which implies the idea of blame for those who do not carry out selective sorting, when in fact the protection of people who have problems paying their bills should be a collective responsibility. This scheme devolves responsibility exclusively to the individual inhabitant, to his capacity to adapt to the system, to the rules. We therefore proposed setting up collective sorting and organising a communal fund in order to bring real benefits to those who need protection. But they didn't even consider the idea' (Member of the Eco NGO, Santa Marta, 15 December 2011)

The challenge to commercial approaches to the resolution of problems considered as political and communal in nature goes no further, in this context, than the view expressed by a few community leaders. However, recent protests by the inhabitants of Santa Maria against electricity cost recovery reflect the emergence of a conflict which could not be resolved in advance by this system of involving the residents in maintaining access to the service.

In March 2014, 250 people took to the streets and blocked the main street of the Botafogo district, in order to demand affordable prices for the electricity system and to object to bill collection practices by Light considered as abusive (Favela 247 2014). Beyond the bill levels, '*Light recicla*' was attacked as a way of maintaining access to the service, as explained by one of the community leaders: 'you have to pick through waste (*catar lixo*) to get a small reduction on a bill in the amount of 500 reais (around 165 euros). You have to accumulate waste inside your house, because the eco-point is not open every day' (Favela 247 2014).

Although these demonstrations did not target the 'Light Recicla' project specifically, they nonetheless indirectly challenge the ability of this scheme to provide an effective response to high service prices for low-income users and thus to make electricity more affordable. Finally, these protests suggest that there is a need to rethink the solidarity system to ensure it is able to overcome the effects of commodification of the electricity service. Where there is no public authority involvement and thus no political response to the long-standing inequalities affecting these irregular settlements, the commercial approach can only provide a partial and individual response to the service affordability issue, whereas what is needed is a collective response.

5. Conclusion

In areas where there are widespread socio-economic and spatial inequalities, implementing the full cost-recovery system has to be balanced against the need to ensure access to the service remains economically sustainable for the inhabitants of irregular districts. More broadly, it challenges the role of the electricity service as a political instrument capable of improving the lives of these inhabitants and of reducing inequalities. The 'Light Recicla' project aims to provide a pragmatic response to service affordability issues and stabilise a potentially insolvent market through the individual involvement of customers. We have interpreted this approach as an attempt to co-produce service affordability in order to ultimately co-produce a sustainable regularised service delivery system. Service affordability in low-income areas of towns in the global South is a major issue; thus, the aim of this project review has been to provide an insight into the type of collaborative arrangements used to improve the sustainability of service delivery in these areas.

However, this market-oriented approach has a number of limitations. Primarily, there is a lack of institutional commitment to the scheme at multiple levels – for instance, municipal involvement is too low to ensure the waste collection and service access policies are properly linked, and the customers' participation is voluntary – tending to suggest this is a one-off approach. Moreover, the fact that the municipality does not adhere to any rules seems to be a failure of governance; one which has an impact on urban cohesion. This is because there is no systematic approach, but rather an assumption that the project cannot be extended to all *favelas*, which seems plausible given that, up to 2015, "Light Recicla" had only been implemented in 15 *favelas*. As a consequence of this, the selection of certain *favelas* as beneficiaries can create territorial differentiation.

Finally, this scheme raises questions over the nature of user involvement. Unlike other service co-production systems, where the terms 'participation' and 'empowerment' are repeatedly employed and which lead to a better service to the poor and the construction of a new democratic space, this scheme is overtly based on market principles and individual responsibility. In the light of the – admittedly limited – protests by the inhabitants of Santa Marta, a less fictively politicised deployment of user participation in service delivery might prompt discussions about the socio-political nature of electricity access. In other words, it may lead to politicisation in response to an overtly depoliticised approach. The recent widespread protests in Brazilian society, in which the inhabitants of the *favelas* were involved, reflect a new awareness about public services. However, it remains to be seen whether energy users as citizens will look beyond the client relationship and extensively challenge the political dimension of the electricity service.

Disclosure statement

No potential conflict of interest was reported by the author.

Notes

1. UPP website: www.upprj.com last access February 2015.
2. Ensure high-quality energy supply, provide service operators with sufficient income to cover operational costs and finance service expansion.
3. The urban services providers (electricity, water) use the term 'community' as an operational category to refer to the *favelas*.
4. http://www.ciclusambiental.com.br/rio_sustentavel.php accessed 7th July 2014

References

Barbier, C., P.-N. Giraud, J. Ruet, and M.-H. Zérah. 2007. "L'accès aux services essentiels dans les pays en développement au cœur des politiques urbaines." *IDDRI* 4: 18.

Bovaird, T. 2007. "Beyond Engagement and Participation: User and Community Coproduction of Public Services." *Public Administration Review* 67 (5): 846–860. doi:10.1111/puar.2007.67.issue-5.

Brandsen, T., and V. Pestoff. 2006. "Co-Production, the Third Sector and the Delivery of Public Services." *Public Management Review* 8 (4): 493–501. doi:10.1080/14719030601022874.

Cipolla, C., P. Melo, and E. Manzini. 2015. "Collaborative Services in Informal Settlements: Social Innovation in a Pacified Favela in Rio De Janeiro." In *New Frontiers in Social Innovation Research*, edited by A. Nicholls, J. Simon, and M. Gabriel, 128–142. Basingstoke: Palgrave Macmillan.

Clerc, V. 2011. "Du formel à l'informel dans la fabrique de la ville. Politiques foncières et marchés immobiliers à Phnom Penh." *Espaces et sociétés* 143 (3): 63–79. doi:10.3917/esp.143.0063.

De Mello, M., M. Frota, C. Rufin, and C. Smyser. 2011. "Combate a Perdas Não-Técnicas nas Comunidades de Baixa Renda Ocupadas por Unidades de Polícia Pacificadora." In *Anais do VI Congresso de Inovação Tecnológica em Energia Elétrica (VI CITENEL)*. Fortaleza, Brazil.

Favela 247. 2014. Santa Marta Protesta Contra Contas Da Light. *Jornal Brasil 247*. Accessed 28 March 2014. http://www.brasil247.com/pt/247/favela247/134579/Santa-Marta-protesta-contra-contas-da-Light.htm

Hibou, B. 2012. *La bureaucratisation du monde à l'ère néolibérale*. Paris: La Découverte.

Ibase and Eco. 2012. *Projeto cidade, mudança climatica e ação jovem. Relatório de pesquisa-diagnóstico socio-ambiental do Santa Marta*. Rio de Janeiro: Ibase, Grupo Eco Santa Marta.

Jaglin. 2005. "La participation au service du néolibéralisme ? Les usagers dans les services d'eau en Afrique subsaharienne." In *Gestion de proximité et démocratie participative : une perspective comparative*, edited by M.-H. Bacqué, H. Rey, and Y. Sintomer, 271–91. Paris: La Découverte.

Jaglin, S. 2004. "Consumérisme, co-production et territorialisation dans les services d'eau en Afrique subsaharienne." In *Démocratie et management local. 1ères rencontres internationales*, edited by R. Le Duff and J.-J. Rigal, 325–351. Paris: Dalloz.

Joshi, A., and M. Moore. 2004. "Institutionalised Co-Production: Unorthodox Public Service Delivery in Challenging Environments." *Journal of Development Studies* 40 (4): 31–49. doi:10.1080/00220380410001673184.

Kelman, J. 2010. "O outro lado do balcão da concessão de serviço público." *Revista Custo Brasil* 5 (26): 6–11.

Light. 2011. *Light recicla. Projeto de troca de resíduos recicláveis por bônus na conta de energia*. Rio de Janeiro: Slideshow corporate presentation.

Light. 2012. *Relatório de Sustentabilidade 2011*. Rio de Janeiro: Light.

Light. 2013. *Relatório de Sustentabilidade 2012*. Rio de Janeiro: Light.

Light. 2014. *Relatório de Sustentabilidade 2013*. Rio de Janeiro: Light.

Mitlin, D. 2008. "With and beyond the State—Co-Production as a Route to Political Influence, Power and Transformation for Grassroots Organizations." *Environment and Urbanization* 20 (2): 339–360. doi:10.1177/0956247808096117.

Moretto, L. 2011. "Coproduction du service d'eau et recomposition de l'espace intra-urbain dans la périphérie sud de Caracas." *Espaces et sociétés* 3: 81–99. doi:10.3917/esp.143.0081.

Moretto, L., and A. Allen. 2015. "Co-Producing Water Services in Peri-Urban Caracas: Political Democratisation without Administrative Decentralisation?" In *Territoires périurbains: développement, enjeux et perspectives dans les pays du sud*, edited by J. Bogaert and J.-M. Halleux, 231–245. Gembloux: Presses Agronomiques de Gembloux.

Ninives Gonçalves, M. D., and R. Valadão. 2012. "Análise das Questões dos Resíduos Sólidos e Seus Impactos nas Práticas Cotidianas das *Favelas* Santa Marta e Cantagalo/ Pavão- Pavãozinho no Contexto das Recentes Intervenções Urbanísticas e das UPPs." *Chão Urbano* 6: 21.

Ostrom, E. 1996. "Crossing the Great Divide: Coproduction, Synergy, and Development." *World Development* 24 (6): 1073–1087. doi:10.1016/0305-750X(96)00023-X.

Pilo', F. 2015a. "La régularisation du service d'électricité dans une *favela* « pacifiée » de Rio de Janeiro: outil de construction du "consommateur responsable?" In *Sociologie de l'énergie. Gouvernance et pratiques sociales*, edited by M.-C. Zélem and C. Beslay, 97-103. Paris: CNRS Editions.

Pilo', F. 2015b. "La régularisation des *favelas* par l'électricité. Un service entre Etat, marché et citoyenneté." PhD diss., Université Paris-Est and Universidade Federal Fluminense.

The co-production of a constant water supply in Mumbai's middle-class apartments

Cat Button

The lush gardens and gleaming cars that surround Mumbai's middle-class apartment buildings hint at plentiful water supplies. However, piped mains water is only supplied for a few hours per day. This research explores the pragmatic choreography of water sources to co-produce a constant supply. Middle-class households respond to the limited municipal water supply through the use of mains water storage tanks, wells, water trucks, packaged water and rainwater harvesting. This portfolio of water supplies involves various actors and is an important instance of domestic service co-production. This article suggests that introducing rainwater harvesting creates opportunities for more water use in these households and allows a reconsideration of water provision and governance citywide.

1. Introduction

Water infrastructure is the focus of several key debates centred on cities in the Global South (see Bakker et al. 2008; Gandy 2004; Smith and Ruiters 2006), and there has been a great deal of research conducted in Mumbai, particularly focussing on housing and water infrastructure of the urban poor majority (see, e.g., Gandy 2008; Mcfarlane 2008b). The infrastructure deficits of both these systems shape the everyday experience for the 60% of Mumbai's residents who live in informal settlements, but are also felt to some extent by the middle classes. Studies of urban India have therefore rightly focussed on the urban poor majority, sometimes using the elites as a counterpoint to demonstrate inequalities, but there is limited academic research on the Indian middle classes and their access to infrastructure (Lemanski and Lama-Rewal 2013; Mawdsley 2004). However, as Harvey (1996) points out, it is resources that are needed by all society, including the wealthy middle classes, that gain the attention of politicians and businesses, and thus, water provision is a focus of action in Mumbai. This highlights justice debates around the focus of responses by political elites that promote solutions that benefit the middle classes, whilst research focusses on the urban poor. This article therefore aims to understand how the middle classes achieve constant domestic water supplies through co-production with the municipality and the creation of decentralised water supply routes. Two key questions are addressed: How do Mumbai's middle classes achieve constant domestic water supplies through co-production with the municipality and the creation of decentralised water supply routes? And, what implications might these decentralised approaches to water provision have on Mumbai's water supply? This focus on decentralised water provision by the middle classes leads to the implications this might have for the provision and governance of water supplies in Mumbai.

This article firstly discusses co-production as a conceptual framework for this research into domestic water supplies. Secondly, I introduce Mumbai's middle classes and their housing. Thirdly, I explain the careful choreography of supply routes of water in these apartments. Mains water storage tanks, bottled water, wells and water trucks are all part of this co-produced water service. This research also explores how rainwater harvesting is being installed in buildings to increase the water quantities and to replace some of the other (expensive) supply routes. This takes the co-production of the water supply beyond the management of supply by the residents and servants to also create the domestic building as site of service provision. Finally, this enquiry into middle-class service provision reveals how the co-production of a constant water supply is part of being middle class in Mumbai and suggests some of the positive and negative justice implications that could arise from promoting co-production as a response to water shortage.

2. Co-production of a domestic water supply from many sources

Co-production is a process of service delivery that involves multiple actors from different organisations (or no organisation), and in many instances, citizens are involved in the production of services that they consume (Alford 2014; Ostrom 1996). This participation of citizens in service production can increase their power and improve trust between partners (Fledderus, Brandsen, and Honingh 2014). Thus, the concept of co-production has been looked to for the provision of public services for the urban poor; however, it is also a useful framing for understanding the ways in which the middle classes and elites gain access to services in many parts of the world. If we take the example of an urban water supply, it may be that several organisations are involved in the production of service provision from one supply. A domestic water supply may be delivered from several sources, and each of these might be provided by a different set of actors. Brandsen and Pestoff (2006) have identified three levels of co-production – co-governance, co-management and co-production, although it should be noted that the levels can also work together and be present in the same arrangement. If we use this tighter definition of co-production, then co-production only truly takes place when multiple actors are also producing at least part of a service (Brandsen and Pestoff 2006). This is the case for domestic water supply in Mumbai, where a seamless water supply can be created by a portfolio of water sources from public and private organisations, and sometimes the residents themselves.

Disconnection from the mains water supply occurs on a daily basis in Mumbai. 'Disconnection produces learning, adaptation and improvisation. All infrastructural systems are prone to error and neglect and breakage and failure, whether as a result of erosion or decay or vandalism or even sabotage' (Graham and Thrift 2007, p. 5). However, this shortage and disconnection of water is not just through accident or sabotage but also by design to distribute water from a mains system that was never envisaged for universal supply. Decentralised supplies of water and electricity are considered by residents of many cities across the world to be only secondary systems to supplement centralised mains supplies, even as decentralised sources become more popular. As Bakker (2010, p. 4) says, 'The network is assumed to be the norm, and the continued existence within urban areas of nonnetworked technologies of water supply provision controlled by communities is often portrayed as problematic'. Several water systems are part of each building's assemblage in Mumbai to increase resilience, and new ways are being found to increase the water supplies to keep up with demand. When water was stretched further by light monsoons, many residents took action to secure their own supplies by retrofitting rainwater harvesting systems to fill the gap in provision and reduce flood risk. This decentralised infrastructure through harvesting rainwater creates a new role of housing as a place of service provision. This gives control of resource supply to the residents and builds the middle classes as a resilient group towards environmental stresses, particularly water shortage.

Joshi and Moore (2004, p. 31) point out, 'There is much agreement that monopolistic provision entirely through state agencies is unfeasible, undesirable, or simply rather old fashioned'. And so, these decentralised systems are being promoted by the municipality through information campaigns to co-produce the water supply and build resilience to water shortage. This is not the co-production of one source but the supply of various sources by different actors, which can be drawn together to co-produce one constant water supply. Having a constant, sufficient supply of good quality water is a signifier of middle class or elite status (Bakker 2010; Kaika and Swyngedouw 2000), but for many residents, this is becoming increasingly difficult to maintain when per capita water provision is reduced by the municipality because of Mumbai's rapidly growing population, coupled with a changing climate and extreme weather events (Mall et al. 20016). The official population of the Mumbai metropolitan area calculated in the 2011 census was 18,394,912, making it the most populous urban area in India (Census Population Data 2015). This is a significant increase from 16,360,000 reported from the previous census in 2001 and stretching the city's infrastructure (Risbud 2003). Mumbai's water supplies have been under particular strain due to poor monsoons in recent years, and the municipality have responded to preserve water levels by cutting the water supply by 20% to domestic properties and up to 50% decrease in water supplied to businesses (H.T. Correspondent 2016; Venkatraman 2015).Therefore, many middle-class residents are looking for other sources to maintain constant water supplies. This article qualitatively explores how Mumbai's middle classes react to these regular disconnections with a variety of ingenious adaptations and improvisations to supplement the centralised water service and thus co-produce a plentiful supply to their homes.

The ways in which various water sources are drawn together to create a seamless water supply begins our understanding of the co-management of this water supply. Zérah has previously written about some strategies as ways of coping with water shortage in Delhi in the 1990s. Zérah (2000) surveyed a variety of households at different income levels in Delhi with in-house piped water connections to discover the proportion of households used strategies and equipment to cope with water shortage. A decade later in Mumbai, I found that the collection and storage of rainwater has been added as an important new strategy that makes housing a site of water supply co-production. This research explores how several methods are used on a daily basis to produce an adequate water supply and begins to consider the wider implication of some residents of Mumbai co-producing adequate water supplies when there is a shortage citywide. This will further develop understandings of co-production by highlighting how the domestic scale as a site of analysis requires also paying attention to the co-management of networks that extend far beyond the confines of a home.

In this article, I present research carried out in Mumbai between November 2009 and February 2011. Water provision and everyday use were examined using empirical data drawn from site visits including ethnographic observations and interviews with cooperative (in both senses) housing secretaries and presidents, other residents and servants at 22 residential properties in Northern Mumbai, particularly in the areas of Bandra, Andheri and Powai. The apartments and buildings used in this study range from the modest apartments in five-storey buildings to large apartments in high-rise developments and townships. This range is demonstrative of the different buildings that the middle classes reside in, but the general commonality of apartment living has been used to define the middle classes within this research. The majority of middle-class buildings are run as co-operatives with elected presidents and secretaries. This has implications for the individual home in terms of governance, resource provision and boundaries. Some decisions can be made by the representatives alone, or with a majority support, whilst others need all parties to be in agreement particularly when funds must be collected to provide the capital to install new infrastructure. Co-operative societies are also involved in employing servants to carry out tasks relating to the whole building, such as security and waste management. It is these co-operative buildings and the apartments inside them that are the site and scale for this investigation into everyday water practices. The biggest challenge of researching middle classes in their homes was access, which is an issue that Smith (2006) also encountered. It was very difficult to get residents to engage with me even in buildings where the society secretary or building manager (who could be considered a 'gatekeeper') was enthusiastic. Thus, research with the middle classes and professional respondents for this study was limited to traditional methods of interviews, ethnographic observations and site visits, supported by taking photographs and videos. I combined these research methods with auto-ethnography of my time residing in middle-class apartments in Mumbai to reflect my own experiences and enrich the study.

3. Mumbai's middle classes

India's middle classes are growing rapidly, and nowhere is their presence more evident than in Mumbai. In 2006, the journal *Critical Asian Studies* ran a special issue on class in South Asia that decries the decline of class analysis in the subcontinent (Chibber 2006; Herring and Agarwal 2006) and points to a renewed focus on India's middle classes (Fernandes and Heller 2006; Harris 2006). There are notable difficulties in defining India's large and heterogeneous middle classes (Fernandes 2011; Mazzarella 2011); however, the global, crosscutting nature of the Indian middle classes places them as a significant population to study (Brosius 2010; Fernandes 2000; Varma 2007). Estimates of the number of middle classes in India vary between 50 million and upwards of 400 million people (Fernandes 2006; Mawdsley 2004; Varma 2007). Lemanski and Lama-Rewal (2013) report that the figure has been put at anywhere between 6% and 54% of the entire Indian population. This uncertainty arises from the difficulties in forming a general definition of the Indian middle class(es) because of their multifaceted, heterogeneous and ever-changing nature (see, for example, Fernandes 2006, 2011; Qayum and Ray 2011; Varma 2007). The task of defining the middle classes is complicated by employment, education, spending patterns, caste, language and regional variation within India, leading India's middle classes to be one of the most diverse in the world and especially difficult to define (Beteille 2001; Dickey 2012). Nijman (2006) points out that incomes and costs in Mumbai are higher than elsewhere in India, and so, a direct comparison between middle classes across the country is unfair because Mumbai is an extreme outlier.[1] For the purposes of this research and to sidestep the difficulty of finding an overarching definition of India's middle class (Brosius 2010; Mazzarella 2011; Nijman 2006), housing is used in this article to frame Mumbai's middle classes as living in apartment buildings where the residents employ servants. This research has identified three necessary attributes for the middle-class apartment: firstly, it must be solidly constructed with occupancy permits in place (in Mumbai, middle-class housing is usually legal); secondly, the building management and the individual families within will employ servants to keep their apartments safe, clean and comfortable and, finally, the building must be connected to services and the residents will aim for a convenient 24/7 water supply.

The land and property prices are extremely high in Mumbai and so bungalows, or detached villas, set within their own grounds are the preserve of some elites. The middle classes reside in apartments of varying size, position, age and quality. I have determined two main subgroups: the small established suburban apartment block and the new multi-storey luxury towers in South Mumbai. The small suburban apartment block is between 4- and 20-storeys tall and is generally occupied by what would be termed the traditional middle class, but also attracts young white-collar migrant workers taken in as paying guests (or lodgers). These apartment buildings are sometimes extended vertically to increase the number of floors, and other buildings are demolished and rebuilt into much taller buildings, with the original residents making a profit from the sales. Such a building is represented in the novel *Last Man in Tower* in which a developer wants to demolish the building for redevelopment, a timely illustration of the shift in trend from old established buildings to new buildings that display wealth (Adiga 2011). The book is a parable of the changing norms of middle-class aspirations that have also been observed by Varma (2007), Qayum and Ray (2011) and Mazumdar (2007). The new apartment buildings particularly attract residents who would fit into the 'new' middle class: the young globalised group who value conspicuous consumption (Fernandes 2006). These buildings usually have extensive grounds and will often have their own gymkhana with swimming pool for the exclusive use of residents. It is the smaller co-operative buildings and the apartments inside them that are the site and scale for this investigation.

The extent of servant employment in India is high and hiring servants can provide the convenience and lifestyle desired (Dickey 2000; Qayum and Ray 2011; Varma 2007). The employment of servants is central to the creation of both middle-class status and lifestyle (Varma 2007), and all the middle-class apartment buildings visited for this research employed watchmen in the grounds as guards and handy men. Each apartment employs a maid for at least an hour every day but apartments in the same block may or may not share the same maid as relationships of trust between maid and employer are often more important (Qayum and Ray 2011). The water supplies are managed by the servants in a middle-class home and so they are a key part of the co-production of water supplies. Zérah (2000) points out that storing water or accessing alternative supplies can be time consuming; however, I found that the middle classes in Mumbai both install technology to help with this and employ servants to make water access convenient. This careful choreography of water also allows many more practices to be undertaken that reinforce the middle-class status of the residents.

> The labour is so cheap you get used to all this, you know, it's so comfortable. We have a couple of people working at home and everything is just set the way you want it and you don't have to do anything. (Developer; Interviewed in Mumbai, 16/12/2009)

It is these dual aspects of affordability and convenience that makes the employment of others within the home an almost universal practice for the Mumbai middle classes and convenience is experienced through the use of labour, rather than labour-saving devices. It is cheaper and easier to hire a person than to purchase several machines to aid the same practices: a dishwasher or washing machine for example (Shove 2003). The employment of domestic servants to perform everyday practices distances the resident from some of the material and maintenance aspects of the home, and this can have an effect on the uptake of technologies as the resident would not directly interact with them and there would be no direct benefit of convenience to the resident.

4. Portfolio of middle-class household water supply

> The landlord had a tap turned to stop the water of a dripping pipe in my flat but unfortunately this also stopped the supply to the water filter that gave us drinking water. My landlord explained that there are three separate supplies to my flat in Mumbai, but he's not sure which supplies what. The first is the direct mains connection, the second comes from roof/attic tanks (filled by BMC [mains] water) and the third source is a bore-well (this water is mainly used for flushing toilets). This differentiated system works well to help the residents cope with the unreliability of the water supply. (Excerpt from author's research diary; Mumbai, 08/01/2010)

Drawing on my own experiences of living in Mumbai, I learnt about the differentiated nature of the water supply to middle-class homes and how it can impact on lives when it is misunderstood. The preceding excerpt from my research diary demonstrates the complexity of the water supply routes at the building level and how residents may not be aware of them. The schematic diagram (later) was developed to explain water infrastructure in Mumbai by showing that middle-class apartments are the nexus and point of use of many water supplies and allowing each part of the co-produced supply to be considered from this starting point. It should be noted that not every apartment has access to all these water supplies and the residents will use a variety of coping strategies (Zérah 2000) that are available and most suitable to deal with water shortage. The water supplies to a middle-class home are differentiated on entering the building compound. The main split is between potable and non-potable water, which correlate with specific taps and other outlets in the building, as shown in the schematic diagram in Figure 1. The alternative sources include bore wells (used to access groundwater and aquifers) and underground storage tanks filled with water delivered by water tankers, which can be ordered in times of water shortage. This leads to water being controlled by an enmeshed network of public and private actors (Anand 2011; Gandy 2008). The municipality are just one of the actors in a system of supply and governance (Graham, Desai, and Mcfarlane 2013; Zérah 2008). Beyond the centralised supply, several other institutions and individuals are involved in the water provision portfolio to co-produce a system of water supply, such as the provision of tankers by private enterprises (Nallathiga 2006). The Municipal Corporation of Greater Mumbai (MCGM, also known as BMC) acknowledges that there is a shortfall in this supply and this has led the municipality to implement water-saving tactics and to shift responsibility on to the consumer in ways already enacted in middle-class residences, in what Roy (2009) terms 'calculated informality'.

For poorer households, mains water connections are often from standpipes in the street, shared between several households, and water must be collected in buckets whenever the taps spring to life (Anand 2011; Graham, Desai, and Mcfarlane 2013). Many other informal residents have no mains connection at all, leading to a reliance on expensive water tankers run for profit by middle men or the creation of illegal connections to mains water pipes (Graham, Desai, and Mcfarlane 2013). These connections may not always appear illegal to the residents, who may have even paid money to government officials, only to later discover that corruption was involved and their water supplies are illegal and they are removed. Co-production of water supplies by the middle classes has the potential to free-up mains water supplies for poorer residents but could also have the opposite effect and actually decrease water availability through changes in governance or extended practices of water use.

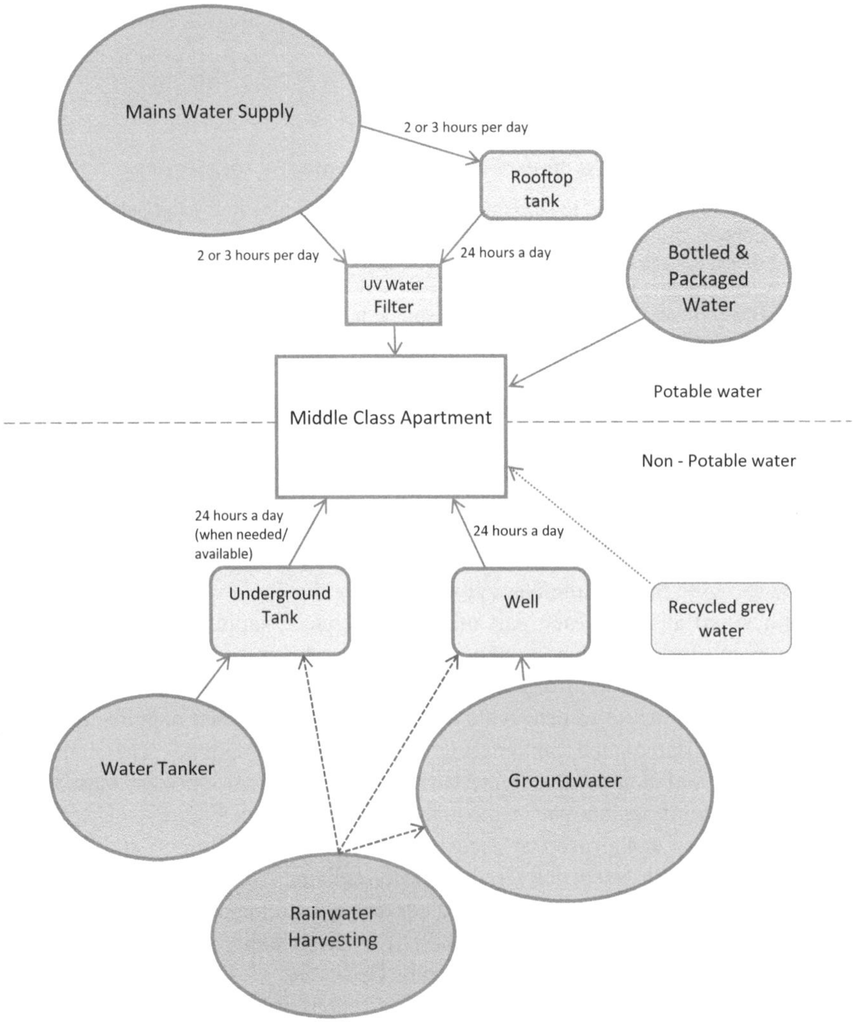

Figure 1. Schematic diagram of water supplies to middle-class housing in Mumbai.
Source: Author.

In this section, I use the portfolio of water supplies to the middle-class home by investigating the main water sources in turn (as depicted by ovals in Figure 1). This tracing of the water supply begins with a discussion of the largest water supply into Mumbai's middle-class homes, the municipal-supplied mains system. I then briefly discuss the use of bottled water to supply further potable water. The use of water trucks is explained from both the point of view of the middle-class domestic building and the supply to informal settlements, to consider some of the justice issues around water supply in Mumbai. Groundwater drawn from wells is then considered as the fourth major source of water. Finally, rainwater harvesting is discussed in relation to the other sources.

4.1. Mumbai's direct mains water supply

Mumbai is a mega city on the west coast of India and one of the cities most vulnerable to climate change exacerbated droughts and floods due to its position, the density of its population and the high levels of urban poverty (Nicholls et al. 2008; Timmerman and White 1997). These issues are putting additional strain on Mumbai's water infrastructure, as indicated by the current temporary cuts after 2015's poor monsoon. This is in sharp contrast to the devastating flooding caused by heavy monsoon rains in 2005, and demonstrates the unpredictability of the monsoons and vulnerability of local water supplies in a changing climate (Mall et al. 20016; Revi 2008). The mains water infrastructure in Mumbai has roots in the colonial planning of the city. The water department was created in 1860 to supply water from lakes through a centralised infrastructure system, provided and controlled by the government, because the existing wells and tanks became insufficient due to drought and urbanisation (Gandy 2008; Zérah 2008; Anand 2011). The colonial government did not have aspirations that mains water would be universally provided and only supplied water to wealthy households (Anand 2011; Gandy 2008). The water system was popular with wealthy residents, and an increase in the number of connections combined with droughts led to the extension of the original Vehar system and creation of the Tulsi scheme by 1879 (both of which still serve South Mumbai), followed by the ambitious Tansa scheme completed in 1948 (Gandy 2008). Even with these expansions, there were still insufficient and uneven water supplies into the city at the time of India's independence. Post-independence, there have been several more schemes bringing water from distant lakes. The most recent of which is the Bhatsai scheme completed in several phases from 1983 until the present day and there are preparations under way for several more schemes to increase water supplies (Bambale 2012). Thus, the legacy of this centralised system is a reliance on a mains water supply network that falls short of the technical ideal, does not supply all residents and is only updated, and new water sources tapped, when water shortages are felt by wealthy residents.

Mains drinking water now comes from these reservoirs or lakes outside the city (Brihanmumbai Municipal Corporation 2003; Sule no date), but water is only supplied to buildings that the municipality consider legal, which means that water is not supplied to informal settlements constructed after 1 January 2000 (previously 1995) (Bambale 2012). The residents of newer informal settlements will not be granted individual connections, and this can lead to expensive alternative water sources (Graham, Desai, and Mcfarlane 2013). Although the network of supply pipes has been extended, it has not kept up with urban growth and a shortage of water supply has been created. Water connections are given by the municipality in a stratified manner that takes into consideration whether the property is in a formal area and the purpose of the connection (Anand 2011). For a connection in a formal area, this can include connections for construction work and drinking water for labourers (Municipal Corporation of Greater Mumbai 2016b). To apply for a water connection to a property in a slum (as per the MCGM's wording), the applicant must prove that the structure was standing before the beginning of 2000, and also proof of residency before then (Municipal Corporation of Greater Mumbai 2016c). By 2003, the municipality had acknowledged the water shortage and that the problem had accelerated faster than expected (Brihanmumbai Municipal Corporation 2003). The MCGM states that current water supply levels to Mumbai are 180 litres per person per day, which is higher than supplies in London (Bambale 2012). However, due to not all residencies being supplied, the poorly maintained and inefficient network, leakages and thefts, the actual per capita water supply is much lower than that and the dream of a 24/7 supply for all residents is a long way off (Graham, Desai, and Mcfarlane 2013; Mckenzie and Ray 2009).

The MCGM technically still bears the sole responsibility for water supply in the city, unlike the privatised electricity supplies (Brihanmumbai Municipal Corporation 2003; Zérah 2008). Ruet, Saravanan, and Zérah (2002) explain that the water supply is still public because of the economic benefits as the returns far outweigh the expenditure, making water a lucrative source of revenue for the MCGM. Although this in some ways limits the commodification of water resources, the lack of an autonomous water agency reduces the efficient management of the system (Bakker 2010). Ruet, Saravanan, and Zérah (2002) also point out that the number of divisions within the MCGM with responsibilities for part of the water infrastructure, and the large number of other institutions involved at the state level in provision of water, has created a very complicated system that has led to failures, and corruption is also a serious problem across all parts of the water supply system (see also Asthana 2008). The mains water is not enough to ensure an adequate supply for residents; therefore, those who have the means co-produce a plentiful domestic water supply by adding other sources to this principal centralised supply.

4.2. Mains supplies and roof top tanks

Mains water remains the major source of water for Mumbai's middle classes but, even to middle-class domestic buildings, the centralised mains supply provided by the municipality is not constant and is supplied only for approximately 2–3 hours per day. The hours that the supply flows depends on the area in which the building is situated and the supply rolls out across the city from the treatment plant at Bandup (or one of the three smaller plants) (Gandy 2007). To cope with this intermittent supply from the municipality, storage tanks are installed by residents in the roof spaces of apartments or on the roof terrace of buildings and filled daily during the few hours of mains supply for later usage. Zérah (2000) found this strategy is also popular in Delhi and she highlights that only the wealthy residents have this kind of equipment, whilst other residents collect the water in buckets. In middle-class housing, an illusion of constant mains supply is created through the storage of mains water in these tanks to be used throughout the day, and supplemented by other decentralised water sources for non-potable purposes, such as tankers and borewells.

The watchman in an apartment building usually carries out the process of managing the water storage, with instructions from the co-operative society members, to ensure a constant supply to point of use in the building. This is achieved by monitoring when the municipal supply is flowing and turning taps to ensure that the roof tank is filled and that it can then be accessed a few hours later when the municipal supply has stopped again. The municipal water is used for indoor practices, such as bathing, and this is also the drinking water in most middle-class homes. The MCGM are proud of the quality of their water supplies, saying 'We ensure that the quality of water supplied to our Connection Holder each day is in compliance with Indian Standard ISI 10500:2012' (Municipal Corporation of Greater Mumbai 2016a). However, it should be noted that in middle-class homes, mains water will be passed through an ultraviolet filter in the kitchen before it is considered potable and, in some households, mineral water is bought for drinking and cooking (as discussed later). However, the MCGM says that its water supply is potable and the majority of the population (who have little choice) do not filter it (Bambale 2012;

Ruet, Saravanan, and Zérah 2002). A major issue of water quality is the way in which the water is delivered to the residents and how it is stored, with the materials and cleanliness of pipes and tanks necessitating the (re)treatment of water in many homes (Gandy 2007).

4.3. Bottled and packaged water

Bottled water is another supply of potable water for the middle classes and elites. Some elite and middle-class citizens of Mumbai do not drink the water from the taps, even after filtering, believing that this packaged water is of higher quality. Therefore, in a minority of apartments, the drinking water is differentiated even further and separated from the city's system of pipes entirely with mineral water delivered in refillable 20-litre bottles each with a tap at the bottom for ease of use and delivered from a local supplier on a hand cart. The Bisleri water-bottling plant at Andheri in Northern Mumbai is a controversial moment in the metabolism of water flowing through the city as it draws in groundwater to filter, add minerals and package (Bisleri 2013). This could reduce residential supplies to the rest of the city and means that the packaged water industry could benefit from the many domestic rainwater harvesting systems (described in Section 4.6) that are being installed to recharge groundwater.

The main benefit of this system to a resident is the lower capital costs and maintenance requirements of bottled drinking water compared to installing a water filter that then needs maintenance. The use of bottled water also creates a whole new water source outside of municipal control, but is an expensive way of accessing drinking water. Thus, the rich are creating an alternative water pathway that excludes many Mumbaikars whilst using the city's groundwater. This is the one part of the portfolio of supply that cannot be hidden to create part of the seamless illusion of water provision but is perhaps seen as a prestigious and safe source of drinking water.

4.4. Water tankers and underground tanks

Water tankers are a main source of water supply to many informal settlements, especially those not recognised by the municipality as being legal. Water tankers are used to deliver water to properties and individuals without a water connection but also used by the middle classes to top up their supply by filling large underground tanks with water for non-potable use (in contrast to the small roof tanks used for storing potable water). The tankers are often filled with water from the municipal mains supply by municipal workers or private water vendors, either legally, illegally or as a result of bribing officials (Gandy 2007; Mckenzie and Ray 2009). The water is thus technically potable water, although by the time it has been in the tanker and then sat in an underground tank the quality has been impaired by particulate matter and microorganisms, and no longer potable. Corruption and racketeering are endemic in the provision of water tankers, leading to this loosely connected group of people involved in water vending as being described as the 'water mafia' (Gandy 2007; Graham, Desai, and Mcfarlane 2013). In fact, sometimes tankers full of drinking water are even diverted to building sites or to Bollywood sets (Graham, Desai, and Mcfarlane 2013). In times of political wrangling, such as elections, water tankers are sometimes publicly delivered to informal settlements in a move to secure votes from the residents.

Mumbai's infrastructure of water provision is visible, differentiated and therefore adaptable. The water tanker sums up these three interlocking properties of supply by being highly visible, used only for certain practices and capable of being called to any area at times of shortage to substitute for another water source. This is possible partly through the differentiation of the supply to middle-class housing, meaning that the private water tanker can be used to fill the tank and that water will only be used for certain practices, critically it will not be sent to kitchen taps and so not used as potable water. This differentiation is key to unlocking possibilities for co-producing water supplies as different water sources can be supplied to different parts of the building. The underground tank is filled and used when necessary – the accessibility and differentiated nature of the water supply to housing allows for different sources to be supplied for different practices around the building. These tankers are another expensive way to secure a water supply, and some middle-class residents are now turning to rainwater harvesting as a cheaper option to fill their underground tanks that also gives them more control.

4.5. Wells

Middle-class domestic buildings have water pipes snaking up their facades with red painted pipes denoting borewell or tubewell water. They must be painted red as borewell water is prohibited from being used for bathing, cooking or drinking due to high bacteria and particulate content as well as discolouration and often an unpleasant smell. The many visible pipes on the facade demonstrate the differentiated nature of the water supply, allowing different water sources to be more easily incorporated into the supply portfolio.

Wells have been used for supplying water in India for hundreds of years. The use of dug-up wells (groundwater) and bore wells (aquifer) in urban areas has been growing in recent years. The groundwater table is dropping, and aquifers are being emptied, so new wells must be dug deeper and old wells are drying up. This also leads to the encroachment of saline water into the groundwater supply, which becomes unusable in Mumbai (Bapat and Agarwal 2003). In reaction to this, there are now strict regulations on the digging of new wells in an attempt to regulate the amount of water drawn from the ground. Rainwater harvesting is one way of replenishing the groundwater and could help to push back the seawater encroachment.

4.6. Rainwater harvesting creates new water supplies

Rainwater harvesting was identified as the leading response to water shortage in Mumbai during my preliminary fieldwork. This is unsurprising due to the insufficient centralised water infrastructure and increasing pressures from urbanisation and climate change. In simple terms, rainwater harvesting is the collection of precipitation but there are many different ways to configure a rainwater harvesting system depending on the specific circumstances and thus the process itself. Rainwater can be substituted into the domestic water supplies to fill a tank or to replenish a well. Rainwater harvesting can be used as an adaptation to water shortages by collecting and using the rainwater which in turn reduces consumption of treated mains water often drawn from outlying areas. It also reduces localised flooding by collecting the water, thus helping the citizens to adapt to extremes of weather.

Rainwater harvesting has been discussed as a solution to water shortages in the Global South, both in rural (Kahinda, Taigbenu, and Boroto 2007) and urban (Handia, Tembo, and Mwiindwa 2003) contexts. Pandey, Gupta, and Anderson (2003) use historical data to suggest that some communities in India may have developed rainwater harvesting to adapt to changing climates in the past, rather than migrating to other areas. The emergence of rainwater harvesting in Indian cities, and the uptake into legislation as mandatory for new constructions, is a reaction to this unreliability and the difficulty in securing the water supply for a rapidly increasing population. The catastrophic Mumbai flood of 2005 was followed by poor monsoons in subsequent years, exacerbating water shortages, demonstrating the disruptive agency of water (Revi 2008). This led many residents to secure their own water supply by retrofitting rainwater harvesting, which also reduces localised flood-risk. Middle-class residents are installing rainwater harvesting systems to maintain their constant water supplies as groundwater supplies are being depleted and water tankers are expensive. This is encouraged by the municipality who are trying to reduce demand on the mains water in an attempt to keep up with rapid urbanisation (Gandy 2006). The municipality provide information on their website and in leaflets distributed by the dedicated rainwater harvesting officer. Rainwater harvesting was observed during fieldwork mainly as retrofits, primarily instigated by residents. Small established suburban middle-class apartment buildings are where rainwater harvesting retrofits are taking place to secure water supplies, reduce local flooding and address environmental concerns. Thus, rainwater harvesting is being retrofitted in buildings to increase the water quantities and to replace some of the other (expensive) supply routes. This creates not only new water supply but also new suppliers of water, as the residents become both the users and the utility suppliers. In these new build projects, the rainwater harvesting systems were generally used to percolate the water into the ground, which replenishes the groundwater and can reduce localised flooding in the grounds of the building, as suggested by Sunil Prabhu, Mayor of Mumbai (quoted in Municipal Corporation of Greater Mumbai 2013), but does not directly augment the water supply of the building and are often there only to meet the targets for occupancy certificates. This kind of rainwater harvesting can create new pathways for water through the city and be used by other urban residents.

5. The significance of a plentiful and seamless domestic water supply

The lush gardens and gleaming cars that surround Mumbai's middle-class apartment buildings hint at a plentiful water supply and affluent lifestyle. Residents (individually or as housing co-operatives) and the municipality are co-managing water sources and provision, leading to an adequate supply in many homes as a strategy of calculated informality (Roy 2009). This co-production, as Brandsen and Pestoff (2006) have termed it, when rainwater harvesting is added to the portfolio and residents begin to create their own water supplies. The installation of decentralised water infrastructure to create this is part of being middle class in Mumbai. Kaika and Swyngedouw (2000) consider infrastructure networks as not merely fulfilling a function but as a status symbol and Bakker (2010) argues that access to a mains water supply is a 'material emblem of citizenship'. The middle classes in Mumbai may use their access to sufficient water supplies as proof of status. The provision of a constant supply of water from several sources in the middle-class home so that it appears to be seamlessly provided from one source is an illusion choreographed by cooperative society leaders or building managers and carried out by their employees, as discussed earlier. Fledderus, Brandsen, and Honingh (2014) suggest that co-production increases trust by building up relationships between partners. However, in the situation presented here, co-production seems to be a way of side stepping the lack of trust to increase reliability of water supply. This is because co-production here is seen as different organisations and individuals providing a range of water sources to co-produce one water service, thereby increasing individual control over water supplies. This constant provision of water allows practices to be performed that indicate middle-class status, such as frequently washing cars and maintaining gardens. Thus, if having access to mains water is an emblem of citizenship (Bakker 2010), then having a plentiful supply in your building, which allows you to water plants, shower twice a day and have your car kept gleaming, is an emblem of middle-class status.

Watering gardens with collected rainwater can increase water consumption as there is no longer a need to water sparingly with scarce and expensive municipal or tanker-delivered water, and in this way, the middle-class lifestyle is secured. This has led to lush green gardens surrounding many buildings with rainwater harvesting, which is good for well-being and for the microclimate but is an example of an environmental technology being used to facilitate increased usage rather than conserve resources. Changing expectations of provision from new sources and increased quantities of water supply can increase consumption and be at odds with environmental strategies (Shove et al. 2008). Bakker et al. (2008) point out that the fragmented infrastructure of cities in the Global South is often designed into the system and the highly differentiated modes of urbanisation that have taken place since the colonial era have led to uneven distribution of services that prioritises wealthy areas and residents (Kooy and Bakker 2008; Mcfarlane 2008a). Roy (2009) also points out that this calculated informality is not just used by the poor and can be instigated from above. The urban poor also draw together a portfolio of water sources to secure their water supplies; however, they are limited by costs and especially by space constraints. Collecting and storing water takes up a large volume, and rainwater harvesting needs an even larger area of land or roofscape, meaning that systems within informal settlements are rare. The poorest residents of Mumbai struggle to access sufficient and good quality water, and pay the highest prices for water from vendors (Gandy 2008; Graham, Desai, and Mcfarlane 2013). This differentiation of water supplies does two things: firstly, it increases the number of actors with a role supplying water, and secondly, it means that the service provided to different citizens is inconsistent. Those middle-class residents with a mains connection are also those with the means to be involved in co-producing their water supplies by installing additional sources. It is frustrating that those with the most to gain are unable to participate in this way, and hope that the co-production by the middle classes might make more water available to others.

The municipality draw attention to the water that is pilfered by the residents of informal settlements who have no legitimate access to the mains supply, and the media promote this narrative by often showing the pumps removed in the newspapers (Graham, Desai, and Mcfarlane 2013), which reflects wider global trends such as the vilification of 'benefit scroungers' in the United Kingdom. However, the losses from leaks of the ailing system and illegal selling of water for tankers play a more substantial role in the reduction in water supply. The media depiction of the poor as the ones at fault for their desperate actions to get water is highly problematic and feeds the well-rehearsed narratives of wealthier residents to clear informal settlements (see Baviskar 2002; Fernandes 2006; Mawdsley 2004). This concentration on blaming the poor for theft and encouraging the middle classes to save water through education campaigns (including the promotion of rainwater harvesting by the Mumbai municipality) could divert attention from investment in the current mains supply to remove leakages. It has been noted before that the middle classes have disproportionate political influence (see Baviskar 2002; Mawdsley 2004). We can take this further by applying Mitlin's (2008) ideas about co-production as a way of increasing political influence. Co-production can be seen as a mechanism for the neighbourhood organisations described by Zérah (2007), and seen widely in Mumbai, to gain power. Co-operative housing associations join together into neighbourhood groups that work in conjunction with local government to improve their neighbourhoods. The ability to coproduce a constant water supply with input from the municipality shows power and status. Anand (2011) points out that the ways in which water is accessed in Mumbai are inherently political and tend to be more successful when a community comes together. The middle classes gain the benefits of collective actions as they co-produce their water supplies. These residents, or representatives of their neighbourhood groups, develop working relationships with officers in the municipality, and this can aid future interventions in a neighbourhood (Zérah 2007). The inadequacies of centralised services have not escaped developers, who offer increasingly more private services in their new luxury apartment buildings (water, electricity, fire services, etc.). The desire to create the illusion, and preferably reality, of a plentiful water supply is a reflection of being part of the global middle class.

The co-produced water supply in middle-class Mumbai homes could be a golden opportunity to relieve stress on the mains supply and allow for more water to be supplied to the poorer residents of the city. However, although this would be the ideal scenario, it looks unlikely for two reasons. Firstly, the creation of a plentiful water supply unlocks the potential to consume more water for new or extended practices. Working and hidden infrastructure causes separation from particular ideas about nature and thus has been shown to cause increased consumption by reducing awareness of the provision mechanisms and increasing convenience (Kaika 2005; Shove 2003). Thus, it could be argued that supplementing the supply with other sources to give the illusion of plentiful resources might increase consumption and negate any social and environmental benefits. Secondly, it shows the municipality that (at least some of) Mumbai's residents can supply and secure extra water resources and co-produce an adequate supply with the municipality. Co-production can increase political capital through greater control over resource provision, which can have beneficial consequences for those involved (Mitlin 2008). This could therefore set a precedent by which the municipality expects the citizens to co-produce their water services, allowing the state to roll-back aims for universal provision. In this way, co-production may not increase overall resilience to water shortage and does little to address current inequalities.

6. Conclusions: co-producing the illusion

The MCGM is unable to provide the desired 24/7 plentiful piped water supply that many people take for granted, and so, the middle classes of Mumbai co-produce their supply, in particular using rainwater harvesting to become truly producers of water supplies. In Bakker's (2010) terms, this is a small-scale community service provision and a system that goes beyond privatisation. An ingenious portfolio of water supplies is choreographed to maintain constant water provision and aim to create the appearance of one seamless source in middle-class and elite apartments in Mumbai. A constant, sufficient supply of good quality water is becoming increasingly difficult to maintain. Therefore, many middle-class residents are looking for other sources. In this article, I have explained how the middle classes draw together several sources in their homes to co-produce the illusion of one plentiful water supply with the municipality's support. The provision of a constant supply of water from several sources in the middle-class home so that it appears to be seamlessly provided is an illusion encouraged by the municipality and choreographed by cooperative society leaders or building managers and carried out by their employees.

Plentiful water supplies in middle-class homes, from certain viewpoints, could furthermore create the illusion that the city has enough water and the residents are coping with the limited mains supply. The concern presented in this article is that the seeming abundance of water displayed by the middle classes and elites of Mumbai will be interpreted as an overall abundance and used as justification for the rolling back of centralised supplies. This could have wide reaching unintended consequences for the urban poor, who are unable to build up the levels of resilience to water shortage demonstrated here by the middle classes. Thus, whilst applauding the encouragement of decentralised solutions to water shortage and environmental change to co-produce an adequate water supply, I urge caution when providing solutions to Mumbai's endemic water crisis.

Acknowledgements

This article was first presented at the RGS-IBG Annual International Conference 2014 in a session entitled Geographies of Networked Service Co-Production. I am indebted to the organisers and to all those who provided questions and advice. I also presented this article at the School of Planning and Architecture in New Delhi and comments from faculty helped to refine some points. I am grateful to my supervisors, Harriet Bulkeley, Jonathan Rigg, Colin McFarlane and Diane Deacon, and to my examiners Emma Mawdsley and Simon Marvin, whose suggestions inspired the genesis of this article. Thanks to those who kindly gave me valuable comments on drafts of this article, especially Rose Gilroy, Louise Medland and Nick Rush-Cooper. My final thanks go to the anonymous reviewers and the editors, whose comments were instructive in refining the final article.

Disclosure statement

No potential conflict of interest was reported by the author.

Funding

This research was conducted whilst author was an affiliate of Durham University Department of Geography, as part of an ESRC CASE funded PhD with the Building and Social Housing Foundation.

Note

1. Mumbai's role as economic capital of India mean that it attracts young ambitious people from all over India, and indeed the world, particularly for employment in the financial sector.

References

Adiga, A. 2011. *Last Man in Tower.* London: Atlantic Books.

Alford, J. 2014. "The Multiple Facets of Co-Production: Building on the work of Elinor Ostrom." *Public Management Review* 16 (3): 299–316. doi:10.1080/14719037.2013.806578.

Anand, N. 2011. "Pressure: The Politechnics of Water Supply in Mumbai." *Cultural Anthropology* 26 (4): 542–564. doi:10.1111/j.1548-1360.2011.01111.x.

Asthana, A. N. 2008. "Decentralisation and Corruption: Evidence from Drinking Water Sector." *Public Administration and Development* 28: 181–189. doi:10.1002/pad.496.

Bakker, K. 2010. *Privatizing Water: Governance Failure and the World's Urban Water Crisis*. New York: Cornell University Press.

Bakker, K., M. Kooy, N. E. Shofiani, and E.-J. Martijn. 2008. "Governance Failure: Rethinking the Institutional Dimensions of Urban Water Supply to Poor Households." *World Development* 36 (10): 1891–1915. doi:10.1016/j.worlddev.2007.09.015.

Bambale, R. B. 2012. *Water Reforms - Mumbai.* Maharashtra, Mumbai: Municipal Corporation of Greater Mumbai.

Bapat, M., and I. Agarwal. 2003. "Our Needs, Our Priorities; Women and Men from the Slums in Mumbai and Pune Talk about Their Needs for Water and Sanitation." *Environment and Urbanization* 15 (2): 71–86. doi:10.1177/095624780301500221.

Baviskar, A. 2002. "Between Violence and Desire: Space, Power, and Identity in the Making of Metropolitan Delhi." International Social Science Journal 55 (175): 89–98.

Beteille, A. 2001. "The Indian Middle Class." *The Hindu* February 5 2001.

Bisleri. 2013. "Purification Process." Accessed January 17, 2014 http://www.bisleri.com/#/Water_And_More/Product/Purification.

Brandsen, T., and V. Pestoff. 2006. "Co-Production, the Third Sector and the Delivery of Public Services." *Public Management Review* 8 (4): 493–501. doi:10.1080/14719030601022874.

Brihanmumbai Municipal Corporation. 2003. *Water Conservation & Rainwater Harvesting for Brihanmumbai*. Mumbai: BMC.

Brosius, C. 2010. *India's Middle Class: New Forms of Urban Leisure, Consumption and Prosperity Cities and the Urban Imperative*. New Delhi: Routledge.

Census Population Data. 2015. "Mumbai (Greater Mumbai) Metropolitan." Accessed April 16, 2016. http://www.census2011.co.in/census/metropolitan/305-mumbai.html

Chibber, V. 2006. "On the Decline of Class Analysis in South Asian Studies." *Critical Asian Studies* 38 (4): 357–387. doi:10.1080/14672710601072970.

Correspondent, H. T. 2016. "B.M.C. Takes Stock of City's Water Supply." *Hindustan Times*, March 7 2016.

Dickey, S. 2000. "Permeable Homes: Domestic Service, Household Space, and the Vulnerability of Class Boundaries in Urban India." *American Ethnologist* 27 (2): 462–489. doi:10.1525/ae.2000.27.2.462.

Dickey, S. 2012. "The Pleasures and Anxieties of Being in the Middle: Emerging Middle-Class Identities in Urban South India." *Modern Asian Studies* 46 (3): 559–599. doi:10.1017/S0026749X11000333.

Fernandes, L. 2000. "Nationalizing 'The Global': Media Images, Cultural Politics and the Middle Class in India." *Media, Culture & Society* 22: 611–628. doi:10.1177/016344300022005005.

Fernandes, L. 2006. *India's New Middle Class: Democratic Politics in an Era of Economic Reform*. Minneapolis: University of Minnesota Press.

Fernandes, L. 2011. "Hegemony and Inequality: Theoretical Reflections on India's 'New' Middle Class." In *Elite and Everyman: The Cultural Politica of the Indian Middle Classes*, edited by A. Baviskar and R. Ray, 58–82. New Delhi: Routledge.

Fernandes, L., and P. Heller. 2006. "Hegemonic Aspirations: New Middle Class Politics and India's Democracy in Comparative Perspective." *Critical Asian Studies* 38 (4): 495–522. doi:10.1080/14672710601073028.

Fledderus, J., T. Brandsen, and M. Honingh. 2014. "Restoring Trust through the Co-Production of Public Services: A Theoretical Elaboration." *Public Management Review* 16 (3): 424–443. doi:10.1080/14719037.2013.848920.

Gandy, M. 2004. "Rethinking Urban Metabolism: Water, Space and the Modern City." *City* 8 (3): 363–379. doi:10.1080/1360481042000313509.

Gandy, M. 2006. *Water, Sanitation and the Modern City: Colonial and Post-Colonial Experiences in Lagos and Mumbai* (No. HDOCPA-2006-06). New York: Human Development Report Office (HDRO), United Nations Development Programme (UNDP).

Gandy, M. 2008. "Landscapes of Disaster: Water, Modernity, and Urban Fragmentation in Mumbai." *Environment and Planning A* 40: 108–130. doi:10.1068/a3994.

Gandy, M., dir. 2007. *Liquid City*. DVD. London: UCL Urban Laboratory.

Graham, S., R. Desai, and C. Mcfarlane. 2013. "Water Wars in Mumbai." *Public Culture* 25 (1 69): 115–141. doi:10.1215/08992363-1890486.

Graham, S., and N. Thrift. 2007. "Out of Order: Understanding Repair and Maintenance." *Theory, Culture & Society* 24 (3): 1–25. doi:10.1177/0263276407075954.

Handia, L., J. M. Tembo, and C. Mwiindwa. 2003. "Potential of Rainwater Harvesting in Urban Zambia." *Physics and Chemistry of the Earth, Parts A/B/C* 28: 893–896. doi:10.1016/j.pce.2003.08.016.

Harris, J. 2006. "Middle-Class Activism and the Politics of the Informal Working Class: A Perspective on Class Relations and Civil Society in Indian Cities." *Critical Asian Studies* 38 (4): 445–465. doi:10.1080/14672710601073002.

Harvey, D. 1996. "The Environment of Justice." In *The Urbanization of Injustice*, edited by A. Merrifield and E. Swynedouw, 65–99. London: Lawrence & Wishart Limited.

Herring, R. J., and R. Agarwal. 2006. "Restoring Agency to Class: Puzzles from the Subcontinent." *Critical Asian Studies* 38 (4): 323–356. doi:10.1080/14672710601072954.

Joshi, A., and M. Moore. 2004. "Institutionalised Co-Production: Unorthodox Public Service Delivery in Challenging Environments." *The Journal of Development Studies* 40 (4): 31–49. doi:10.1080/00220380410001673184.

Kahinda, J.-M.-M., A. E. Taigbenu, and J. R. Boroto. 2007. "Domestic Rainwater Harvesting to Improve Water Supply in Rural South Africa." *Physics and Chemistry of the Earth, Parts A/B/C* 32: 1050–1057. doi:10.1016/j.pce.2007.07.007.

Kaika, M. 2005. *City of Flows: Modernity, Nature, and the City*. Oxon: Routledge.

Kaika, M., and E. Swyngedouw. 2000. "Fetishising the Modern City: The Phantasmogoria of Urban Technological Network." *International Journal of Urban and Regional Research* 29 (1): 26–49.

Kooy, M., and K. Bakker. 2008. "Technologies of Government: Constituting Subjectivities, Spaces, and Infrastructures in Colonial and Contemporary Jakarta." *International Journal of Urban and Regional Research* 32 (2): 375–391. doi:10.1111/ijur.2008.32.issue-2.

Lemanski, C., and S. T. Lama-Rewal. 2013. "The 'Missing Middle': Class and Urban Governance in Delhi's Unauthorised Colonies." *Transactions of the Institute of British Geographers* 38 (1): 91–105. doi:10.1111/tran.2012.38.issue-1.

Mall, R. K., A. Gupta, R. Singh, R. S. Singh, and L. S. Rathore. 20016. "Water Resources and Climate Change: An Indian Perspective." *Current Science* 90 (12): 1610–1626.

Mawdsley, E. 2004. "India's Middle Classes and the Environment." *Development and Change* 35 (1): 79–103. doi:10.1111/dech.2004.35.issue-1.

Mazumdar, R. 2007. *Bombay Cinema, an Archive of the City*. Minneapolis: University of Minnesota Press.

Mazzarella, W. 2011. *Middle Class*. London: School of Oriental and African Studies, University of London, Centre of South Asian Studies.

Mcfarlane, C. 2008a. "Governing the Contaminated City: Infrastructure and Sanitation in Colonial and Postcolonial Bombay." *International Journal of Urban and Regional Research* 32 (2): 415–435. doi:10.1111/ijur.2008.32.issue-2.

Mcfarlane, C. 2008b. "Sanitation in Mumbai's Informal Settlements: State, 'Slum', and Infrastructure." *Environment and Planning A* 40: 88–107. doi:10.1068/a39221.

Mckenzie, D., and I. Ray. 2009. "Urban Water Supply in India: Status, Reform Options and Possible Lessons." *Water Policy* 11: 442–460. doi:10.2166/wp.2009.056.

Mitlin, D. 2008. "With and beyond the State – Co-Production as a Route to Political Influence, Power and Transformation for Grassroots Organizations." *Environment and Urbanization* 20 (2): 339–360. doi:10.1177/0956247808096117.

Municipal Corporation of Greater Mumbai. 2013. *Flood Preparedness Guidelines 2013*. Mumbai: MCGM.

Municipal Corporation of Greater Mumbai. 2016a. "About Us. Welcome to MCGM Water Department." Accessed April 22, 2016. https://aquaptax.mcgm.gov.in/aqua/citizenportal/uboutUs

Municipal Corporation of Greater Mumbai. 2016b. "List of Required Documents for New Water Connection (Non-Slum)." Accessed April 22, 2016. https://aquaptax.mcgm.gov.in/aqua/citizenportal/openNewWaterNonSlumDISCLAIMERpage

Municipal Corporation of Greater Mumbai. 2016c. "List of Required Documents for New Water Connection (Slum)." Accessed April 22, 2016. https://aquaptax.mcgm.gov.in/aqua/citizenportal/openNewWaterSlumDISCLAIMERpage

Nallathiga, R. 2006. "Reforming Water Sector Governance and Institutions for Improving Efficiency: The Case of Mumbai." *International Journal of Regulation and Governance* 6 (1): 43–77.

Nicholls, R. J., S. Hanson, C. Herweijer, N. Patmore, S. Hallegatte, J. Corfee-Morlot, J. Château, and R. Muir-Wood. 2008. "Ranking Port Cities with High Exposure and Vulnerability to Climate Extremes: Exposure Estimates." In *OECD Environment Working Papers*. Paris: OECD Publishing.

Nijman, J. 2006. "Mumbai's Mysterious Middle Class." *International Journal of Urban and Regional Research* 30 (4): 758–775. doi:10.1111/ijur.2006.30.issue-4.

Ostrom, E. 1996. "Crossing the Great Divide: Coproduction, Synergy, and Development." *World Development* 24 (6): 1073–1087. doi:10.1016/0305-750X(96)00023-X.

Pandey, D. N., A. K. Gupta, and D. M. Anderson. 2003. "Rainwater Harvesting as an Adaptation to Climate Change." *Current Science* 85 (1): 46–59.

Qayum, S., and R. Ray. 2011. "The Middle Classes at Home." In *Elite and Everyman: The Cultural Politics of the Indian Middle Class*, eds A. Baviskar and R. Ray, 246–270. New Delhi: Routledge.

Revi, A. 2008. "Climate Change Risk: An Adaptation and Mitigation Agenda for Indian Cities." *Environment and Urbanization* 20: 207–229. doi:10.1177/0956247808089157.

Risbud, N. 2003. "Urban Slums Reports: The Case of Mumbai, India." *UNDERSTANDING SLUMS: Case Studies for the Global Report on Human Settlements 2003.*

Roy, A. 2009. "Why India Cannot Plan Its Cities: Informality, Insurgence and the Idiom of Urbanization." *Planning Theory and Practice* 8 (1): 76–87. doi:10.1177/1473095208099299.

Ruet, J., V. S. Saravanan, and M.-H. Zérah. 2002. *The Water & Sanitation in Indian Metropolitan Cities: Resources and Management in Delhi, Calcutta, Chennai, Mumbai.* CSH Occasional Paper No. 6. New Delhi: Centre for Social Sciences and Humanities.

Shove, E. 2003. *Comfort, Cleanliness and Convenience. The Social Organization of Normality.* Oxford: Berg.

Shove, E., H. Chappells, L. Lutzenhiser, and B. Hackett. 2008. "Comfort in a Lower Carbon Society." *Building Research & Information* 36 (4): 307–311. doi:10.1080/09613210802079322.

Smith, K. E. 2006. "Problematising Power Relations in 'Elite' Interviews." *Geoforum* 37: 643–653. doi:10.1016/j.geoforum.2005.11.002.

Smith, L., and G. Ruiters. 2006. "The Public/Private Conundrum of Urban Water: A View from South Africa." In *In the Nature of Cities: Urban Political Ecology and the Politics of Urban Metabolism*, edited by N. Heynen, M. Kaika, and E. Swyngedouw, 190–207. Oxon: Routledge.

Sule, S. no date. "Mumbai's Water Supply." In *Understanding Our Civic Issues*, edited by N. Mukherjee. Mumbai: Bombay Community Public Trust.

Timmerman, P., and R. White. 1997. "Megahydropolis: Coastal Cities in the Context of Global Environmental Change." *Global Environmental Change* 7 (3): 205–234. doi:10.1016/S0959-3780(97)00009-5.

Varma, P. K. 2007. *The Great Indian Middle Class*. 2nd ed. New Delhi: Penguin Books.

Venkatraman, T. 2015. "Mumbai: Water Cuts to Continue till 2016 Due to Poor Monsoon." *The Indian Express*, October 2 2015.

Zérah, M.-H. 2000. "Household Strategies for Coping with Unreliable Water Supplies: The Case of Delhi." *Habitat International* 24 (3): 295–307. doi:10.1016/S0197-3975(99)00045-4.

Zérah, M.-H. 2007. "Middle Class Neighbourhood Associations as Political Players in Mumbai." *Economic & Political Weekly* 42 (47): 61–68.

Zérah, M.-H. 2008. "Splintering Urbanism in Mumbai: Contrasting Trends in a Multilayered Society." *Geoforum* 39: 1922–1932. doi:10.1016/j.geoforum.2008.02.001.

Index

Note: Page numbers in *italic* type refer to figures
Page numbers in **bold** type refer to tables
Page numbers followed by 'n' refer to notes